Monographs in Computer Science

Editors

David Gries
Fred B. Schneider

Springer
New York
Berlin
Heidelberg
Barcelona
Hong Kong
London
Milan
Paris
Singapore
Tokyo

Ernst L. Leiss
Department of Computer Science
University of Houston
Houston, TX 77204-3475
USA
coscel@cs.uh.edu

Series Editors:
David Gries   Fred B. Schneider
Department of Computer Science   Department of Computer Science
Cornell University   Cornell University
Upson Hall   Upson Hall
Ithaca, NY 14853-7501   Ithaca, NY 14853-7501
USA   USA

Library of Congress Cataloging-in-Publication Data
Leiss, Ernst L., 1952–
    Language equations/Ernst L. Leiss.
      p.   cm. — (Monographs in computer science)
    Includes bibliographical references.
    ISBN-13:978-1-4612-7436-0   e-ISBN-13:978-1-4612-2156-2
    DOI: 10.1007/978-1-4612-2156-2

    1. Natural language processing.   2. Computational linguistics.
    I. Title.   II. Series.
    QA76.9.N38L445   1998
    006.3'5—dc21   98-31040

Printed on acid-free paper.

© 1999 Springer-Verlag New York, Inc.
Softcover reprint of the hardcover 1st edition 1999

Production managed by Francine McNeill; manufacturing supervised by Joe Quatela.
Photocomposed copy prepared from the author's WordPerfect files using Springer's
svsing6.sty macro.

9 8 7 6 5 4 3 2 1

ISBN-13:978-1-4612-7436-0 Springer-Verlag New York Berlin Heidelberg   SPIN 10692736

*This book is dedicated to my wife, Benigna
and my son, Ernst*

Preface

My first excursion into what eventually became the theory of language equations was joint work with John Brzozowski in the late seventies that related formal descriptions for regular languages, finite automata, and sequential networks. The central notation turned out to be that of equations. Because negation plays a significant role in sequential networks, I became interested in the nonmonotonicity of complementation of formal languages, an operation with a reputation for being "difficult" in language theory. This had been most glaringly demonstrated by the fact that certain decision problems for regular expressions become nonelementary if complementation is present. Also, for the study of language equations, a serious defect of complementation is that the substitution property does not hold for this operation, even though it holds for many other language operations. Nevertheless, it turned out that one can solve equations in which the complementation operator was permitted, although no parametric representations of solutions are possible. This problem was solved in a series of papers revolving around the notion of boolean automata [Brzoz/Leiss 80; Leiss 81a; Leiss 81b; Leiss 85a; Leiss 85b; Leiss 86].

Both the classical equations and these equations involving complementation employed the standard operations, used to define (extended) regular expressions: union, concatenation, star, and complement. After working on these problems for several years, an idea crystallized: Instead of defining, and attempting to solve, separate and independent classes of equations, it should be far more fruitful if one were to define a general theory of equations between languages; consequently, one could treat these different problems as specializations of the more general one, namely, how to solve language equations. In a way, a 1981 conference paper [Leiss 81d] already indicated embryonically the path I intended to pursue, although the final goal was then still very vague, primarily because I had very few results to support my intentions.

This has changed somewhat, almost two decades later. At least, I am now clear about my *goal* in the study of language equations in general, and in this book in particular (even if the path to that goal is still not as obvious as I would like it to be); it is to

> establish a comprehensive framework for a theory for solving systems of equations and relations between languages, where the operators are the standard "regular" ones—union, concatenation, star, and complementation—plus possibly nonstandard ones.

The equations and relations may be implicit or explicit, or a combination of both. I hope to establish this theory as independent of, but equally important as, the two standard techniques for defining and studying formal languages, namely, grammars and automata. In fact, I contend that the results obtained by way of language equations tend to be more interesting since they allow one to capture not just one "solution" as in the case of grammars and automata—for example, the language $L(G)$ generated by a grammar G is in some sense a minimal solution of the corresponding system of language equations that, in general, may admit many more solutions than $L(G)$. Furthermore, since additional operations can be naturally introduced within the framework of equations, they permit the study of questions on languages that tend to lie outside the realm of grammars and automata (e.g., perfect shuffle, reversal). In fact, even the standard operations are not necessarily naturally dealt within the context of grammars or automata (e.g., complementation, for any grammars as well as for nondeterministic finite automata or pushdown automata).

There are, of course, several major problems in attaining this admittedly quite lofty goal. I mention the two major ones, namely, the number of results required to establish a general theory and the problems with general approaches to solving diverse types of equations.

1. *How many results are needed to establish a general theory?* In addressing my claim that the study of language equations should be considered on an equal footing with that of grammars and automata, it is only fair to raise the question of whether there are "enough" results. Undoubtedly, both of these well-established branches of formal language theory offer many more results than the relative newcomer, language equations. Nevertheless, to date, there are several interesting results extant, and it stands to reason that more will follow, as the field is still very young. More importantly, it is clear that some questions are unsuitable or very cumbersome for the other formalisms (again, complementation, for grammars and, to some extent, for automata; union, unrestricted concatenation, star, and comple-

mentation for languages over a one-letter alphabet, for both grammars and automata).

Until now, there are at least five noteworthy results that may be considered to form the foundation of a theory of language equations and relations:

- The complete solution of classical equations; these are explicit language equations where union and left-concatenation operate on arbitrary languages and where each variable has exactly one equation.
- The comprehensive coverage of complementation in explicit language equations where the other operators are union and left-concatenation [Brzoz/Leiss 80; Leiss 81a; Leiss 81b; Leiss 85b; Leiss 86].
- The complete solution of explicit language equations over a one-letter alphabet where the operators are union, (unrestricted) concatenation, and star [Leiss 94a].
- The proof that certain explicit equations over a one-letter alphabet with concatenation and complementation have only noncontext-free solutions even if the constants are single letters [Leiss 94b].
- The complete characterization of implicit language equations and relations where the operators are union and left-concatenation. For the equations, this is a direct analogue to classical (i.e., explicit) language equations; interestingly, for explicit relations, the general problem is still open.

Still, in order to have better assurances that my overarching goal is attainable, more results are needed. In particular, even though the solution of implicit equations with union and left-concatenation has been completely resolved [Leiss 95], the question of complementation in implicit equations is wide open. This is even true if the alphabet contains only one letter—something that usually greatly simplifies the situation; in fact, the technique used in [Leiss 97c] does not work in the presence of complementation (even though I conjecture that such equations have regular solutions if they have any, assuming all constants are regular). I present additional results in this book that I hope will flesh out the skeleton suggested by the above solutions. I also sincerely hope that this book will tempt others to try their hand on some of the many open problems in language equations and relations.

2. *Lack of generality of solution techniques.* Whereas the first problem is essentially an external one, the second is predominantly internal. So far, I have not been able to devise a single general technique that would allow one to address substantially different problems within the same conceptual framework. The problems themselves form a very elegant part of a general theory of equations and relations, but the solution techniques vary widely from one problem to the next. For explicit equations with union, left-concatenation, and complementation, we used boolean automata

[Brzoz/Leiss 80; Leiss 81a; Leiss 81b; Leiss 85a; Leiss 85b; Leiss 86]. For explicit equations over a one-letter alphabet with union, concatenation, and star, two key theorems essentially provided a parameterized regular expression representing the solution [Leiss 94a]. For implicit language equations, a rather complicated construction of a vector of languages provided a test that determined whether a solution exists or not [Leiss 95]. Although it is true that the technique for implicit equations outlined in [Leiss 95] is the basis for the method for implicit relations in [Leiss 97b], very few similar situations exist. Much more representative is the situation of the two papers [Leiss 94a; Leiss 97c] that treat the very same problem, except that in the first it is for explicit and in the second for implicit equations. Even the results are similar: [Leiss 94a] shows that there is always a regular solution; [Leiss 97c] shows that if there is a solution there must also be a regular one. Yet, the techniques in which these answers are obtained are totally different. One gives a parameterized regular expression, whereas the other shows that if there is a word w in a solution that is "long enough", there exists another solution that contains $w(a^s)^*$; this implies that a newly constructed solution must be regular.

It is, of course, not required that subproblems of a theory have solution techniques that are subtechniques of a general solution framework, but it would be more aesthetically pleasing if this were the case. I admit that I do not have high hopes for such a general synthesis of solution approaches to appear any time soon. This book certainly will not make any strides toward this goal. Nevertheless, collecting all the approaches in one place may enable someone to synthesize them—perhaps!

Structure of the Book

The book is organized as follows. In Chapter 1, I give an informal introduction that draws close parallels between systems of arithmetic equations and systems of language equations. This chapter also stresses the fundamental difference between language operators and arithmetic operators, namely, the latter are typically invertible while the former are not. Chapter 2 provides the basic definitions required for the subsequent chapters. It ends with six examples that can be understood before beginning the book; they are intended to provide the reader with a taste of language relations and an impressionistic view of the issues involved in solving them. Chapter 3 gives a sketch of the classical language equations and discusses the importance of the substitution property for this approach. The importance of this property is illustrated by the results of equations over a one-letter alphabet described in Chapter 7. Chapter 3 is also where context-free grammars and the resulting equations are mentioned. Chapter 4 is devoted to boolean language equations; these are explicit language equations where the operators are union, left-concatenation, and unrestricted complementation. The approach uses boolean automata and yields a comprehensive theory of solving such equations. It is quite possible that this rather powerful approach will be helpful in studying the analogue for the implicit version of these equations. However, so far it is not clear how this can be done. The most general approach to solving (explicit) language equations is provided by generalized derivatives. These are introduced and discussed in Chapter 5. Star equations are studied in Chapter 6; this is a short chapter included only for the sake of completeness. I do not feel that this approach is likely to provide significant ideas or insight for solving additional problems in the area of language equations.

Chapter 7 is devoted to language equations over a one-letter alphabet. It is well known that such languages have special properties, such as commutativity, that can be profitably exploited. Specifically, I give a completely general solution approach for equations with union, (general) concatenation, and star, which yields a parameterized representation of all solutions (possible since the substitution property holds for precisely these operators!). Then, I show that language equations can define languages that lie far outside the class of languages from which the operands are drawn. Specifically, an equation is exhibited whose operands are single letters, the operators are concatenation and complementation, and the (unique) solution is not context-free.

All chapters up to and including Chapter 7 deal with explicit equations whereby one equates a variable to an expression involving variables and constant languages, operated upon by language operators. Chapter 8 commences the treatment of implicit equations; in this type of equations, it is a constant language that is equated to an expression. Specifically, this chapter poses the exact analogue of the classical (explicit) equations for implicit ones. The solution approach is altogether different, and so are the results. In particular, in contrast to the explicit equations, implicit ones need not have any solution. However, it is possible to give a complete characterization of existence and uniqueness of solutions of systems of such equations. Chapter 9 deals with the analogue of the equations in Chapter 7, but for implicit ones. It is interesting to note that parameterized solution representations are known only for explicit equations, but not for their implicit analogues. It is not clear why this should be so.

Chapter 10 generalizes the explicit equations of Chapter 3 (classical equations) to explicit relations, and Chapter 11 deals with the same question, but for implicit relations; in both cases, the operators are union and left-concatenation. Chapter 12 discusses two-sided language equations, the most general paradigms of equality between expressions we study in this book. Unfortunately, even the most simple two-sided language equations are very difficult to solve. Chapter 13 defines mixed systems of equations (implicit and explicit) and establishes a number of interesting results. Finally, Chapter 14 formulates numerous open problems related to the various types of language equations mentioned in the previous chapters.

The diagram at the end of Chapter 1 gives a graphical overview of the various chapters and how they relate to each other.

Acknowledgments

The results reported in this book have accumulated over a long period, almost two decades. The references reflect this. Thus, any synthesis requires a good deal of work. During the last few years, Professor Maurice Nivat had encouraged me strongly to produce a synthesis of my work on language equations. Several stays abroad were crucial for producing the monograph that is the outcome of synthesizing this work, without the usual odious counterproductive interruptions. Most important were a 2-month stay at the Universitat de les Illes Balears in Palma de Mallorca, arranged by Professor Ramon Puigjaner, in 1996, and a 1-month stay at the Université de Montpellier, arranged by Professor Jean Ferrié and facilitated by Professor Michel Habib, in 1997. I am indebted to these individuals at the two institutions who contributed more than they know to the timely completion of this book. I used a preliminary version of this book as class notes in summer 1997 for a doctoral course on language equations at the University of Houston; this "test drive" allowed me to iron out several kinks in the presentation. I appreciate the willingness of the students in this course to serve as "guinea pigs". Last, but not least, I acknowledge Springer-Verlag, through its editor Dr. William R. Sanders, for its willingness to publish this book on a topic that (at least at present) is not considered a central subject in computer science—and therefore most likely will not be a bestseller. Thanks to all of you!

Ernst L. Leiss
Ipanema, RJ
June 1998

Contents

1
An Informal Introduction to Language Equations

About This Chapter: We give a very informal overview of language equations; this is done by drawing on analogies between them and well-known, ordinary arithmetic equations, such as linear equations. The purpose of this chapter is to provide motivation for our study of language equations; more exact definitions are provided in the next chapter.

This book is about equations, one of the most fundamental notions in mathematics. Everybody knows about equations. More specifically, this book is about language equations. In most people's minds, these two concepts, equations and languages, are not closely related. True, languages are about as fundamental a notion in computer science as equations are in mathematics, but to marry these two basic notions is a stretch for many computer scientists.

In the following chapters of this book, we will show that there is an extensive theory about language equations. Moreover, in many cases, there are elegant techniques that allow one to determine either one or even all solutions of a given system of equations. In other cases, there are surprising results related to the "generative power" of various operations.

In the following, we will delineate our program by drawing an extended analogy with the linear equations. In mathematics, linear equations are considered "nice" because they have a (more or less) complete theory of existence and uniqueness of solutions. Throughout this book, we will employ an underlying correspondence between (arithmetic) addition and (language-theoretic) union, and between multiplication and concatenation. This allows us to relate the rather unfamiliar language equations to the extremely familiar linear (arithmetic) equations. In fact, the vast majority of our language equations will turn out to be analogues of linear equations (even though the ultimate results about solutions turn out to be very different).

1.1   Arithmetic Equations

Arithmetic equations are defined with a certain set N of numbers in mind (these may be the integers, or the reals, or the complex numbers), with the understanding that the only acceptable solutions are those whose values lie in N and satisfy the given equation. By this we mean that an equation in n variables $x_1, \ldots, x_n$ has a solution $(\alpha_1, \ldots, \alpha_n)$ with all α_i in N, if substituting the number α_i for every occurrence of the variable x_i yields an identity between members of N. For example, the equation $2x + 3y = 10$ in the variables (x, y) has the solution $(-10, 10)$ over the integers; this is one of infinitely many solutions (given by $\{(34 + 2, 2 - 2k) \mid k \text{ integer}\}$). If N is the set of positive integers, this equation has exactly one solution, namely $(2, 2)$. As another equation over the integers, consider the equation $x \cdot y = 36$. Here, there are exactly 18 solutions:

$$x: \quad 1 \quad -1 \quad 2 \quad -2 \quad 3 \quad -3 \quad 4 \quad -4 \quad 6 \quad -6 \quad 9 \quad -9 \quad 12 \quad -12 \quad 18 \quad -18 \quad 36 \quad -36$$
$$y: \quad 36 \quad -36 \quad 18 \quad -18 \quad 12 \quad -12 \quad 9 \quad -9 \quad 6 \quad -6 \quad 4 \quad -4 \quad 3 \quad -3 \quad 2 \quad -2 \quad 1 \quad -1$$

In the following, we will view $2x + 3y$ and $x^* y$ as arithmetic expressions; in this way, an (arithmetic) equation is then an (arithmetic) expression that is set equal to a number. The operations involved in these two example expressions are addition and multiplication; for ordinary equations, this is usually sufficient. The operands involved in these operations are constants and variables. Separating the operands into these two classes allows us to differentiate linear and nonlinear equations in a purely syntactic way. (This way of viewing equations will be particularly useful when defining language equations where there are more than two operations.) We first define a normal form for our arithmetic expressions, which follows in the obvious way using the fact that addition and multiplication are commutative and associative. Assume that all variables occurring in the expression are in some (total) order, say $x_1, x_2, \ldots$. Furthermore, assume that all elements of N are in some total order. An arithmetic expression involving addition and multiplication of constants and variables is in normal form if it is written as a sum of terms, each of which is a product of constants and variables and each term is organized so that all constants occur on the left of the term and all variables on the right; furthermore, in each term, the constants and the variables are ordered ascendingly. For example, if we have the variables x and y (x comes before y) and a N as the integers (with the customary ordering), then a normal form representation of the arithmetic expression $(2xyx + 3yx)(4y - 3yx)$ is $8xxyy - 6xxxyy + 12xyy - 9xxyy$ (the order among the terms is immaterial here, but could be prescribed additionally). Note that we assume that multiplications involving two constants are carried out (the result being another constant). Then we can state: An equation is a linear equation if every binary multiplication occurring in the expression involves at most one variable. Thus, since the expression in the preceding example fails this test, it can never give rise to a linear equation.

[This syntactic approach has a fundamental problem, illustrated by the following example. Consider the expression $(x+y)(x-y) - (x+y)^2 + 2y(x+y)$; using the fact that like terms with opposite sign cancel each other, its normal form is determined to be 0. Thus, even though the original equation has various multiplications of two variables, after simplification everything cancels. Therefore, it is possible that under certain simplifications, the basic character of a problem changes. On the other hand, if these simplifications had not been applied, the question would be very different.]

1.2   Language Equations

To define language equations, we start with an alphabet A. Then, we determine which operations will be admitted. For arithmetic expressions, this was usually easy, since we had mainly addition and multiplication. For languages, there are quite a few more operations. Throughout this book, we will consider the following five basic types:

Union
Intersection
Complementation
Concatenation (and a restriction, left-concatenation)
Star

[It is true that union and complementation allow one to express all set operations; however, because sometimes we may want to consider only union and intersection but not complementation, we must still retain intersection.]

Left-concatenation (or more completely, concatenation from the left by a constant) is exactly the analogue of the restriction on multiplication that gave rise to linear equations. In other words, we restrict concatenation so that in any concatenation, the left operand must be a constant language while the right operand may be arbitrary (a constant, or a variable, or an expression involving constants and variables). This restriction turns out be very important in a many language equations.

Having chosen the alphabet A and the set of operations, we must also choose a set CONST of constant languages (which will take the place of the set of numbers N in our arithmetic equations). Here, we can consider regular languages, context-free languages, context sensitive languages, recursive languages, or recursively enumerable languages, or any other class of languages that is of interest.

Using the class CONST of constant languages and a finite set of variables $\{X_1, \ldots, X_n\}$, we can now combine them into expressions by applying the selected operators to them; this yields the set $\text{EX}_A(\text{CONST}; X_1, \ldots, X_n)$ of expressions in the constant languages and the variables. A language equation is now obtained by taking an element α from the set $\text{EX}_A(\text{CONST}; X_1, \ldots, X_n)$ and setting it equal to either a variable X_i or a constant language L. In the first case, we obtain conventional language equations (we will call them explicit; see below); in the second case, we obtain a new type of language equations which will be called implicit.

1.3 An Example

As an example, consider the explicit language equation

$$X = \{a^n b^n \mid n \geq 1\} X \{b^n a^n \mid n \geq 1\} \cup \{\lambda\},$$

where X is the variable, the class CONST is the set of all context-free languages (λ denotes the empty word), and the operations considered are (unrestricted) concatenation and union. It is rather easy to see that this equation has a unique solution (in CONST) in X, namely the language $L(G)$, where G is a context-free grammar:

$$G = (\{S, A, B\}, \{a, b\}, \{S \to ASB \mid \lambda, A \to aAb \mid ab, B \to bBa \mid ba\}, S).$$

This follows by substituting $L(G)$ for X on both sides of the equation and verifying that the resulting equation is indeed an identity between languages; the uniqueness follows by a separate argument.[1]

Note however that a seemingly minor change can result in rather significant differences; to wit, consider the equation

$$X = \{a^n b^n \mid n \geq 0\} X \{b^n a^n \mid n \geq 0\} \cup \{\lambda\}$$

whose only difference with the one above is that n starts from 0, not from 1. In this case, there are infinitely many solutions (of CONST) in X; to see this, define for any language L in CONST a context-free grammar G': Let $G_L = (N_L, T_L, P_L, S_L)$ be a context-free grammar for L. Then, G' is given by

$$(\{S, A', B'\} \cup N_L, \{a, b\} \cup T_L,$$
$$\{S \to A'SB' \mid S_L \mid \lambda, \ A' \to aA'b \mid \lambda, \ B' \to bB'a \mid \lambda\} \cup P_L, S).$$

---

[1] Assume there is another solution. Let w be a shortest word that is in one but not in the other solution. Since $w \neq \lambda$, $w = uw'v$, where $|w'| < |w|$. But then w must be in both solutions: Contradiction!

It follows that $L(G')$ is a solution for any L; since there are infinitely many different $L(G')$, there are also infinitely many solutions of this equation. The important point to note is that solutions of language equations are not restricted to be minimal, as the language generated by a (context-free) grammar is; instead, any language whose substitution for the variable converts the equation into an identity between languages is a solution.

Another important point to make is that the definition of the class CONST matters. To see this, consider the equation

$$X = aXb \cup \lambda.$$

Here, one might argue that CONST should be the class of all regular languages, since $\{a\}$, $\{b\}$, and $\{\lambda\}$ are clearly regular. (We frequently omit the set braces if this is feasible.) However, if we do that, this equation does not have any solution: Recall that we insist that any solution must be in CONST, and the only language that satisfies this equation is $\{a^n b^n \mid n \geq 0\}$, which obviously is not regular.

1.4 Nonlinear Equations

We are quite comfortable with linear arithmetic equations, primarily because we know exactly how to determine whether they have a solution, and if they do, how many. Furthermore, not only do we know how to determine one solution, but we can, in fact, give a parametric representation of all solutions even if there are infinitely many. As we will see, this largely carries over to "linear" language equations. Nonlinear equations tend to be much more complicated. For example, one might consider the following two equations in the integer variables x and y:

$$2x^2 + 3xy^2 + y^3 - 35 = 0,$$
$$x^4 y^2 + x^3 y^3 + x^2 y^4 - 252 = 0.$$

It turns out that these two equations have a solution $(x, y) = (2, -3)$, but is it the only one?[2] In terms of our analogy between multiplication and concatenation, nonlinearity in language equations is also much more difficult to handle, even though we do have a well known mechanism for dealing with it in certain circumstances, namely context free grammars.

---

[2] Yes: The second equation can be rewritten as $x^2 y^2 (x^2 + xy + y^2) = 252$. Since $252 = 2 \cdot 2 \cdot 3 \cdot 3 \cdot 7$ and x and y must be integers and because of the symmetry in x and y in this equation, we have to consider exactly the following 20 possibilities: $(x, y) = (\pm 1, \pm 1), (\pm 1, \pm 2), (\pm 1, \pm 3), (\pm 1, \pm 6), (\pm 2, \pm 3)$. None of these yields a solution different from $(2, -3)$.

1.5   Invertibility of Operations

There is an additional complication related to language equations; it has to do ultimately with the properties of the underlying language operators, or rather lack thereof. We are referring to the fact that addition and multiplication (with one exception, by 0) are invertible, but neither union nor concatenation are. In fact, all the standard language operators are not invertible in general.

The fact that addition and multiplication are invertible obscures the differences among the following three linear arithmetic equations:

$$2x + 3y = 10, \quad 3x + 3y - 10 = x, \quad \text{and} \quad 3x + 3y = 10 + x.$$

Clearly, they are equivalent because we can transform one into the other since addition has an inverse operation in subtraction; not so for language equations. Since neither union nor concatenation are invertible, the equation

$$LX \cup MY = N$$

in the variables X and Y and the constant languages L, M, and N is quite different from the equations

$$(L - \{\lambda\})X \cup MY \cup N' = X \quad \text{and} \quad (L - \{\lambda\})X \cup MY = X \cup N$$

for any language N'. To see this very directly, assume that M is empty and $L = \{\lambda\}$; thus, the three equations become

$$X = N, \quad N' = X, \quad \text{and} \quad \emptyset = X \cup N.$$

If these three equations were equivalent, it would follow from the first two equations that $N = N'$, while the third equation obviously requires that both N and X be empty. However, jointly, these conclusions are untenable; therefore, the three equations cannot be equivalent.

1.6   Implicit and Explicit Equations

We have seen that for language equations we must differentiate between those equations where the right-hand side is a constant and those where the right-hand side is a variable. The first class of language equations will be called implicit; the variables are not expressed by the equations but must instead be determined within the context of the equation. The second class of language equations will be called explicit since a variable is explicitly equated with an expression. Explicit language equations have a much longer history than implicit ones. In fact, until recently, the only language equations that people studied were the classical, explicit ones. In this book we will look at both classes.

1.7 Overview of the Book

In the next chapter (Chapter 2), we give a more detailed technical introduction to language equations, including formal definitions. Chapter 3 gives a brief review of classical language equations; in our terminology, these are explicit (linear) language equations with arbitrary constant languages and the operators union and left-concatenation. In Chapter 4, we give a complete solution of equations in which, in addition to the operators of the classical equations, the complementation operator occurs as well. Chapter 5 discusses generalized derivatives and shows that under very mild and easily tested for conditions, there always exists a unique solution. In Chapter 6, we study the type of equations one obtains from the classical equations by adding the star operator (without adding arbitrary concatenation, even though the star is iterated concatenation). Chapter 7 deals with nonlinear language equations. Specifically, in most of Chapter 7, the operators are union, unrestricted concatenation, and star, whereas in Section 7.7, we add complementation to this set of operations. However, while all previous equations assumed an arbitrary alphabet, in this chapter we restrict the alphabet to one letter. The fact that such languages are commutative turns out to be useful in our effort of solving equations over such alphabets.

All equations up to this point were explicit. Chapter 8 begins our treatment of implicit language equations by assuming the exact same setting as for the classical equations, but for implicit ones. In Chapter 9, we study implicit equations with union, unrestricted concatenation, and star, assuming the languages are over a one-letter alphabet. This is the implicit analogue of the explicit equations studied in the first part of Chapter 7.

In Chapter 10, we deal with explicit relations using the classical operations (union and left-concatenation). Language relations are just like equations except that the identity operator is replaced by inclusion and containment (and possibly other relations, such as inequality $\neq$). Solving explicit language relations with the operators left-concatenation and union turns out to be surprisingly difficult. Chapter 11 uses these same operations for implicit relations. Interestingly, the solution is easier for implicit relations than for explicit ones. Two-sided language equations are discussed in Chapter 12; Chapter 13 studies various combinations of equations and relations, both implicit and explicit. In the final chapter, we raise a number of open problems and relate them to the problems solved in the preceding chapters of this book.

We can summarize the various kinds of equations and relations studied in these chapters in the following diagram:

Chapter	Kind		Type		Alphabet		Operations				
	Equations	Relations	Explicit	Implicit	Arbitrary	One Letter	Union	Concatenation Left	Concatenation Arbitrary	Star	Complement
3	x		x		x		x	x			
4	x		x		x		x	x			x
6	x		x		x		x	x			
7	x		x			x	x		x	x	
7	x		x			x	x		x	x	x
8	x			x	x		x	x			
9	x			x		x	x		x	x	
10		x	x		x		x	x	x	x	
11		x		x	x		x	x			
12	x	x	x	x	x	x	x	x	x	x	x
13	x		x	x	x		x	x	x		
13	x		x	x		x	x		x	x	

1.8 Assumed Background of the Reader

We assume that the reader is reasonably conversant with formal language theory (in particular, regular languages, finite automata, regular expressions, and context-free languages and grammars). However, even though this book is written as a research monograph, no advanced knowledge of these topics is required in order to understand the presentation of language equations given in the following pages. Our aim throughout is to work with elementary concepts to keep the results accessible even to undergraduate students with a course in automata theory.

2
Basic Definitions

About This Chapter: Formal definitions of the central concepts of our study are given, along with comments on their influence on, and relevance to, language equations. We first discuss alphabets, constant languages, operations, variables, and expressions; then, we give formal definitions of equations and relations and what constitutes a solution of a given system. The chapter concludes with numerous examples of systems of equations and relations which outline and delineate the research to be discussed in subsequent chapters.

2.1 The Alphabet

Any definition involving languages must start with an alphabet. Throughout this book, the underlying alphabet will be denoted by A. Often, the choice of the alphabet A has significant implications; while the individual letters in an alphabet are not important, the cardinality of the alphabet is very much so. For example, if A consists of one letter, all resulting languages L (subsets of A^*) are commutative, i.e., for all words $v, w \in L$, $v \cdot w = w \cdot v$. (This property will be important in Chapters 7 and 9.) As is customary, we will use a centered dot ($\cdot$) to denote concatenation of words and of languages, but we suppress it most of the time.

2.2   The Constant Languages

Once the alphabet A is fixed, we can define the class CONST of constant languages. In principle, any subset of the set of all languages over A is a possible choice for CONST. In practice, however, one tends to restrict one's attention to well-known and well-studied classes of languages; in this book, we will consider almost exclusively the following classes of languages:

The regular languages (REG)
The context-free languages (CFL)
The context-sensitive languages
The recursive languages
The recursively enumerable (r.e.) languages (RE)

We do this not out of capriciousness; rather, our choice is based on the closure properties of these languages. For example, the regular and the recursive languages are closed under all the operations that will be considered in this book. (In addition to the operations listed below, taking the quotient of a language will also be of concern, primarily in Chapter 8.) Similarly, all but the r.e. languages have effective tests for membership. It should be noted that the choice of alphabet here may have some consequences already; for example, if the alphabet A contains exactly one letter, the classes of regular and of context-free languages are identical. One of the questions that we will address is whether a certain class CONST of languages is closed under the "operation" of forming certain types of equations using languages from CONST such that all (or perhaps all minimal or all maximal) solutions of these equations are from that class CONST.

2.3   The Language Operations

The basic language operations considered in the book are the following well-known five:

Union ($\cup$)
Intersection ($\cap$)
Complementation ($-$)
Concatenation ($\cdot$)
Star ($\star$)

The first three are set operations; they come from the fact that every language over A is a subset of A^*. It is of course true that one can express any set operation using only union and complementation, and therefore listing intersection may appear redundant. However, there are instances where we want to consider only the set operations union and intersection, but not complementation; it is for this reason that intersection is listed. To understand why one may want to exclude complementation, recall that in regular expressions (which, of course, will always denote regular languages), permitting only union and intersection as set operations (in addition to concatenation and star) will give elementary complexity for the resulting expressions (the complexity of an expression α being the number of states of the reduced or minimal deterministic finite automaton accepting the language denoted by α), whereas permitting complementation will result in nonelementary complexity.

Of the five operations listed, concatenation is the most interesting and, easily, also the most complex. (In view of the comments in the last paragraph about complementation, this assessment may surprise the reader—but read on!) For example, of the three operations that are binary, it is the only one that is not generally commutative. More importantly for our purposes, while complementation is usually blamed for the nonelementary complexity of unrestricted regular expressions, it is, in fact, the interplay between complementation and concatenation that is the real culprit. (For the following, we exclude the star operator because it is essentially iterated concatenation.) In recognition of the complexity of unrestricted concatenation, we define a restriction of general concatenation, concatenation from the left by a constant, or left-concatenation for short, which is defined as follows: Whenever the concatenation operator $\cdot$ occurs within an expression, the left operand must be a constant language (or an expression consisting exclusively of constant languages) while the right operand may be arbitrary. This restriction of concatenation has two important implications.

The first implication stems from the observation that a regular expression α of length n in which the operations are union, left-concatenation, and complementation has a complexity of no more than 2^{2^n}. Note that except for the restriction on concatenation, this is exactly the setting for general unrestricted regular expression (which of course have nonelementary complexity). Thus, this seemingly minor restriction on concatenation has a very significant influence on the complexity of the resulting regular expressions.

The second implication is a crucial one for this book; it centers around our assertion that for most equations, left-concatenation gives rise to effective methods of finding solutions, whereas unrestricted concatenation creates major problems, except if the constant languages are severely restricted (specifically, if they are over a one-letter alphabet). Indeed, all classical language equations effectively restrict their concatenations to be left-concatenations. Also, as we pointed out in the previous chapter, what are generally known in mathematics as linear equations in effect use a form of "left-multiplication" whose analogue for language equations is exactly left-concatenation. (We excluded context-free grammars from this discussion since they only use union and concatenation, but see Section 3.5.)

Different classes of equations will use different subsets of these operations. In the following, we will use OP to denote the class of operations that have been selected in a specific instance. We will assume that OP may contain either concatenation or left-concatenation, but never both.

These language operators have certain elementary properties; specifically, the following:

Union is commutative:

$$L \cup M = M \cup L \quad \text{for all languages } L \text{ and } M.$$

Concatenation (both types) distributes over union:

$$L \cdot (M \cup N) = L \cdot M \cup L \cdot N$$

and

$$(L \cup M) \cdot N = L \cdot N \cup M \cdot N \quad \text{for all languages } L, M, \text{ and } N.$$

Other properties will be derived when they are needed. This applies in particular to operations when the argument languages are commutative (see Chapters 6 and 7).

2.4 The Variables

All nontrivial equations contain variables. For our purposes, these variables will take on constant languages from CONST as values. Throughout this book, we will use $X, Y,$ and Z as variables, with or without subscripts. The interpretation of variables is that any constant language can be substituted for a variable, provided that the same variable is always replaced by the same language. Since the operations considered here may be applied to all languages, this is valid; note, however, that the resulting language need not be a member of the class CONST. To see this, define CONST as the class of all languages consisting of words of odd length and consider the expression (see below) $a \cdot X$, where $a \in A$ and X is a variable; clearly, substituting any language consisting of words of odd length will yield a language whose words are of even length and which is therefore not a member of CONST. While this example is quite contrived, the situation changes when one considers equations (see below). For example, if CONST is the class of regular languages, it is well known that the equation $X = aXb \cup \lambda$ has the unique solution $X = \{a^n b^n \mid n \geq 0\}$, which of course is not an element of CONST even though the constant languages in the equation are.

2.5 The Expressions

An expression will always be defined over a given alphabet, using constant languages taken from CONST and applying operations from a given set

OP to constant languages and to variables. The fact that variables occur in our expressions obviously differentiates them from ordinary regular expressions. However, the reader should also note that the constant languages from CONST need not be regular; thus, it is even less appropriate to think of our expressions as analogues of regular expressions, even though all operations are those of regular expressions. Specifically, we define the class of all expressions over the alphabet A in the variables $X_1, \ldots, X_n$ for given set CONST and OP:

$$\text{EX}_A(\text{CONST}; \text{OP}; X_1, \ldots, X_n),$$

where we may suppress A, CONST, OP, and even the variables, if this is clear from the context. The elements of $\text{EX}_A(\text{CONST}; \text{OP}; X_1, \ldots, X_n)$ are precisely those expressions that can be formed using as operands variables $X_1, \ldots, X_n$ and elements of CONST and applying operations taken from OP to them. Specifically, $\text{EX}_A(\text{CONST}; \text{OP}; X_1, \ldots, X_n)$, or EX_A for short, is defined as follows:

1. Any language L in CONST is in EX_A; L is called a constant. The variable X_i is in EX_A, for $i = 1, \ldots, n$.
2. Let $\circ$ be any binary operator in OP. If α and β are expressions in EX_A satisfying restrictions imposed by the operator $\circ$, then $\alpha \circ \beta$ is also an expression in EX_A.
3. Let $''$ be any unary operator in OP. If α is an expression in EX_A, then α'' is also an expression in EX_A.

Let us illustrate this with a few examples. Assume $A = \{a, b\}$, CONST is the class of regular languages, and OP contains precisely union and left-concatenation. The expression

$$(ab^* \cup ba^*)X \cup a^*Y \cup b^*Z$$

is contained in $\text{EX}_A(\text{CONST}; \text{OP}; X, Y, Z)$ since all the constant languages (here ab^*, ba^*, a^*, and b^*) are in CONST and only union and left-concatenation are used. On the other hand, the following three expressions are not in $\text{EX}_A(\text{CONST}; \text{OP}; X, Y, Z)$:

$$aX \cup Yb$$
$$(aX)^*$$
$$\{a^n b^n \mid n \geq 1\}X$$

the first because Yb cannot be written using left-concatenation, the second because the star operator is not in OP, and the third because the constant language $\{a^n b^n \mid n \geq 1\}$ is not contained in CONST. However, the expression

$$\{a^n a a^n \mid n \geq 1\}X$$

is in $\text{EX}_A(\text{CONST}; \text{OP}; X, Y, Z)$ since the constant language $\{a^n a a^n \mid n \geq 1\}$ is regular in spite of its appearance. This is related to the fact that languages over a one-letter alphabet are commutative and will become obvious in Chapter 6. Note, however, that the situation becomes much more complicated if OP contains the complementation operation! This will lead to a rather surprising result which we derive in Chapter 7.

We note that for various choices of A, CONST, and OP, one can determine a normal form for all expressions in $\mathrm{EX}_A(\mathrm{CONST}; \mathrm{OP}; X_1, \ldots, X_n)$. Such normal forms are often quite important when one solves a given system of equations, as we will see in subsequent chapters.

With every expression $\alpha \in \mathrm{EX}_A(\mathrm{CONST}; \mathrm{OP}; X_1, \ldots, X_n)$ we can associate a function $F_\alpha(X_1, \ldots, X_n)$ in the following way: For every choice of n languages $(L_1, \ldots, L_n)$, we determine the language $F_\alpha(L_1, \ldots, L_n)$ by substituting L_i for every occurrence of X_i. Given two expressions $\alpha, \beta \in \mathrm{EX}_A(\mathrm{CONST}; \mathrm{OP}; X_1, \ldots, X_n)$, we say that α and β are equivalent $(\alpha \equiv \beta)$ if and only the functions defined by the two expressions are identical,

$$F_\alpha = F_\beta.$$

(Two functions are identical if they yield the same language for every choice of languages for the n arguments $X_1, \ldots, X_n$.) For example, consider the following two regular expressions α and β:

$$\alpha = (ab^*)^* X \cup a(aa)^* Y \cup aa(aaa)^* Y,$$

$$\beta = (a(a \cup b)^* \cup \lambda) X \cup (aaaaaa)^* (a \cup aa \cup aaa \cup aaaaaa) Y.$$

One can verify that $(ab^*)^* = a(a \cup b)^* \cup \lambda$ and $a(aa)^* \cup aa(aaa)^* = (aaaaaa)^* (a \cup aa \cup aaa \cup aaaaa)$; thus, $F_\alpha = F_\beta$, and therefore the two expressions are equivalent. Note that equivalence of expressions may depend on the underlying alphabet A. For example, if $A = \{a, b\}$, the two expressions α and β below are not equivalent, but if $A = \{a\}$, then α and β are equivalent:

$$\alpha = aX \cup Ya,$$

$$\beta = Xa \cup aY.$$

This is because the variables X and Y can assume any values (languages) in CONST.

2.6 The Equations

We now have the necessary formal machinery to define equations. The most general type of equations are the two-sided equations. All equations studied in this book are special cases of them; however, since there is no known method for dealing with general two-sided equations (even for the simplest choices of CONST and OP), they are ultimately not of great practical interest. In spite of this, they allow us to give a unified presentation of all language equations.

2.6.1 Two-Sided Equations

Let the alphabet A, the class of constant languages CONST, and the set of operations OP be given. Let $\alpha_1, \ldots, \alpha_m$ and $\beta_1, \ldots, \beta_m$ be expressions in $EX_A(CONST; OP; X_1, \ldots, X_n)$. Then

$$\alpha_1 = \beta_1$$
$$\vdots$$
$$\alpha_m = \beta_m$$

is a *system of two-sided language equations* in the variables $X_1, \ldots, X_n$. This system has a solution in $X_1, \ldots, X_n$ if and only if there exist languages $L_1, \ldots, L_n$ in CONST such that substituting L_i for every occurrence of X_i, for all $i = 1, \ldots, n$, in all expressions, simultaneously converts the m equations into m identities between languages.

2.6.2 Explicit and Implicit Equations

Explicit and implicit equations can now be defined by specifying the form of the expressions β_i. A system of language equations is called *explicit* if and only if

$$\text{for all } i = 1, \ldots, m, \quad X_j = \beta_i \quad \text{for some } j \in \{1, \ldots, n\}.$$

Note that this definition does not require that $m = n$; in particular, it is possible that one variable may have several equations. Having the same variable occur with several equations can make sense and, in fact, raises a very interesting and rather tricky problem which will be discussed in Chapter 10. It is true that the equations that are derived from finite automata, which will be called classical in this book, do stipulate that $m = n$ and that each variable have exactly one defining equation; they will be reviewed in Chapter 3.

A system of language equations is called *implicit* if and only if

$$\text{for all } i = 1, \ldots, m, \quad L_i = \beta_i \quad \text{for some language } L_i \in CONST.$$

Thus, each expression α_i is equated with a constant language. Whereas in explicit equations, variables are explicitly expressed, implicit equations require us to determine solutions for the variables from the context within which they occur—in other words, implicitly.

2.7   The Relations

Finally, we come to relations. In a system of two-sided language equations, two expressions are equated: $\alpha_i = \beta_i$ for $i = 1, \ldots, m$. Instead of equating the two expressions, we may replace the equality sign ($=$) by the inclusion sign ($\subseteq$) or the containment sign ($\supseteq$); this gives rise to *systems of two-sided relations*. *Systems of explicit and implicit relations* can then be obtained in analogy with explicit and implicit equations. Relations can occur together with equations. In this sense, relations are more general than equations since they contain them. Solving language relations is completely analogous to solving equations; a system of relations in the variables $X_1, \ldots, X_n$ has a solution if there exist constant languages $L_1, \ldots, L_n$ such that substituting the language L_i for every occurrence of the variable X_i for $i = 1, \ldots, n$ simultaneously converts the system of relations into valid relations between constant languages. Various types of relations (explicit and implicit) will be studied in Chapters 10 and 11.

2.8   Examples

1. Let $A = \{a, b\}$, CONST be the regular languages REG, and OP consist of union, left-concatenation, and star. Consider the following system of two-sided language equations in the variables X and Y:

$$(aX \cup b^*Y)^* \cup bX = bY \cup aX \cup \lambda,$$
$$(a^* \cup b^*)(X \cup aY) = aX \cup Y.$$

It is easily *verified* that there are at least two solutions in (X, Y), namely

$$(X, Y) = (\emptyset, \emptyset) \quad \text{and} \quad (X, Y) = (A^*, A^*).$$

However, it is not at all clear how one might *determine* all solutions of this system, or even how one might *determine* one solution. In fact, no method is known that allows us to even determine whether there exists a solution of general two-sided equations of this type. Consequently, the question of existence of solutions and the determination of any solutions must be resolved through ad hoc approaches.

[In this example, it is easy to verify whether two languages in fact constitute a solution of the system; this is because in the case of regular languages, we have effective methods available that allow us to construct the union, the concatenation, and the star of regular languages, and to test whether two regular languages are identical. Note that for other (larger) classes of languages, some or all of these constructions and tests may not be effective; for example, already for context-free languages, it is undecidable in general whether two languages are identical, a test of central importance for our verification process. Since we have no methods at this point that allow us to *determine* solutions, we can only *verify* that given languages are solutions; this explains our preference for regular languages in the examples.]

2. Let $A = \{a\}$, CONST be the regular languages, and OP consist of union, left-concatenation, and complementation. Consider the following system of implicit language equations in the variables X and Y:

$$a\bar{X} \cup aY \cup \lambda = (aaa)^*,$$
$$a^*(aX \cup aaaY) = aa^*.$$

One can verify that there exist solutions, for example,

$$(X, Y) = ((\lambda \cup a)(aaa)^*, \emptyset);$$

in fact, one can verify (by direct substitution) that there are infinitely many solutions in CONST:

$$(X, Y) = ((\lambda \cup a)(aaa)^*, T),$$

where T is any (regular) subset of the language $aa(aaa)^*$.

3. Implicit equations need not always have solutions. For example, let $A = \{a\}$, CONST be the regular languages, and OP consist of union and concatenation. Consider the following system of implicit language equations in the variables X and Y:

$$aaX \cup aY = aaa^*,$$
$$aaX \cup aaaY = aaa(aa)^*.$$

[Note that in this case, we could have written $aXa \cup Ya$ instead of $aaX \cup aY$, or $aXa \cup aYaa$ instead of $aaX \cup aaaY$, because the languages are commutative.] It follows from the first equation that

$$aX \cup Y = aa^*,$$

and from the second equation, we derive that

$$X \cup aY = a(aa)^*.$$

Now consider the word aaa. Clearly, aaa is contained in aa^*; therefore, by the first equation, either aaa must be contained in Y or aa in X. However, if aa is in X, then by the second equation, aa must also be contained in $a(aa)^*$, which is obviously not true; if on the other hand, aaa is in Y, then by the second equation, $aaaa$ must be contained in $a(aa)^*$, which is also clearly wrong. Thus, no solution exists!

That this rather trivial system (which, moreover, is over a one-letter alphabet) has no solution may be surprising, since, for the classical language equations, there always exists a solution. However, throughout this book we will encounter many situations where the existence of a solution is not guaranteed. This is not only the case whenever complementation occurs but also for most implicit equations. To see how complementation can ensure that no solution exists even for explicit equations, consider the following example.

4. Let $A = \{a\}$, CONST be the regular languages, and OP consist of union, left-concatenation, and (arbitrary) complementation. Consider the following system of explicit language equations in the variables X and Y:

$$a^*\overline{X} = X.$$

It is clear that λ is contained in a^*, therefore, $\overline{X}$ must be contained in X. The only way in which this is possible is if $X = a^*$. However, this implies that $\overline{X}$ is the empty language $\emptyset$, which, in turn, implies that the left-hand side of the equation is $\emptyset$ and the right-hand side is a^*. This is impossible; therefore, no solution can exist.

5. Let $A = \{a, b\}$, CONST be the regular languages, and OP consist of union and left-concatenation. Consider the following system of explicit language relations in the variables X and Y:

$$abX \cup baY \subseteq X,$$
$$bb^*X \cup aa^*Y \subseteq X,$$
$$aaX \cup bbaY \cup a^* \supseteq X,$$
$$(aaa)^*X \cup ab^*Y = X,$$
$$ba^*X \cup (bb)^*Y = Y,$$
$$(bb)^*X \cup aY = X.$$

It can be easily verified that $(X, Y) = (\emptyset, \emptyset)$ is a solution, but it is not at all obvious that there are no other solutions. However, in Chapter 9 we will describe a general technique for obtaining solutions of such systems of relations if any exist. That there need not be any solution is shown in the next example.

6. Let $A = \{a, b\}$, CONST be the regular languages, and OP consist of union and left-concatenation. Consider the following system of explicit language relations in the variables X and Y:

$$abX \cup (a \cup b)^* \subseteq X,$$
$$aaX \cup a^* \supseteq X.$$

From the first relation, it follows necessarily that $X = A^*$. However, this does not satisfy the second relation. Therefore, no solution exists.

2.9   Bibliographical Notes

The result that unrestricted regular expressions (with unrestricted complementation and unrestricted concatenation) have nonelementary complexity (i.e., the number of states of a deterministic finite automaton accepting the language denoted by an expression of length n is a nonelementary function of n) is contained in [Meyer/Stock 73]. That this depends significantly on the unrestrictedness of concatenation was shown in [Leiss 85a], where it was derived that an expression of length n in which unrestricted complementation is combined with left-concatenation has complexity at most 2^{2^n}. For classical language equations (explicit equations with union and left-concatenation), we refer to [Salom 69].

3
Classical Language Equations and the Substitution Property

About This Chapter: We define classical language equations and relate them to nondeterministic finite automata. Then, we give two quite different solution approaches, both constructive. One is based on syntactic properties of the equations and essentially yields regular expressions as solutions. The other is by construction of nondeterministic finite automata. Advantages and disadvantages of both approaches are discussed; the second method (construction of a nondeterministic finite automaton) prepares us for the construction of a different kind of finite automaton (namely boolean) in the next chapter. The first method (construction of a regular expression) motivates a discussion of the substitution property, a property that holds for our solutions if OP does not contain the complementation or the intersection operator. We conclude this chapter by commenting on context-free grammars and the equations they engender.

3.1 Introduction

Consider a nondeterministic finite automaton (nfa) $\mathbb{N} = (A, Q, \tau, q_0, F)$, where A is (as always) the underlying alphabet, Q is the finite, nonempty set of states, q_0 is the (single) initial state ($q_0 \in Q$), F, a subset of Q, is the set of final states, and τ is the transition function

$$\tau \colon Q \times A \to 2^Q.$$

We can associate a system of explicit language equations with $\mathbb{N}$ in the following way: Let CONST be a class of languages (we stipulate that it contain at least the regular languages, for reasons that will become clear soon), let OP consist of the operations union and left-concatenation, and let the set of variables be $\{X_q \mid q \in Q\}$. Then, the system of explicit language equations associated with the nfa N is given by

$$X_q = \bigcup_{a \in A} \bigcup_{p \in \tau(q,a)} a \cdot X_p \cup \delta(q) \quad \text{for all } q \in Q,$$

where $\delta(q) = \{\lambda\}$ if $q \in F$ and $\delta(q) = \emptyset$ if $q \notin F$. For example, let N be given by the following transition table (with 1 being the initial state indicated by $\to$, and the last column having a 1 for state i if and only if state i is accepting):

	a	b	c	
$\to 1$	1, 2	2, 4	/	0
2	/	1, 2, 3	3	1
3	4	4	4	0
4	/	/	1, 2, 3	1

The corresponding system of explicit equations is then:

$$\begin{aligned}
X_1 &= aX_1 \cup aX_2 \cup bX_2 \cup bX_4, \\
X_2 &= bX_1 \cup bX_2 \cup bX_3 \cup cX_3 \cup \lambda, \\
X_3 &= aX_4 \cup bX_4 \cup cX_4, \\
X_4 &= cX_1 \cup cX_2 \cup cX_3 \cup \lambda.
\end{aligned}$$

This system has the property that its solution (which is always unique) for the variable corresponding to the initial state is equal to $L(\mathsf{N})$. This can be easily seen by considering that the set of all words accepted when starting in state 1 (for example) is equal to the set of all words where the letter a is followed by all words accepted when starting in states 1 or 2, plus the set of all words when the letter b is followed by all words accepted when starting in states 2 or 4, plus λ if the state were accepting (1, of course, is not). It is quite obvious that such a system of equations can always be transformed into one where each variable occurs at most once in each equation:

$$\begin{aligned}
X_1 &= aX_1 \cup (a \cup b)X_2 \cup bX_4, \\
X_2 &= bX_1 \cup bX_2 \cup (b \cup c)X_3 \cup \lambda, \\
X_3 &= (a \cup b \cup c)X_4, \\
X_4 &= cX_1 \cup cX_2 \cup cX_3 \cup \lambda.
\end{aligned}$$

Note that, in this way, a variable is concatenated from the left by a constant language. This observation leads us to the most general form of these equations:

$$X_i = \bigcup_{j=1}^{n} L_{i,j} \cdot X_j \cup L_{i,0}, \quad i = 1, \ldots, n, \tag{3.1}$$

where the $L_{i,j}$, for all $i = 1, \ldots, n$ and all $j = 0, 1, \ldots, n$ are constant languages from CONST. It is clear that only union and left-concatenation occur in these equations. Furthermore, there is exactly one equation for each variable. Note that in this formulation, the constant languages need not be regular; CONST can, in fact, be completely arbitrary, which moves us definitely away from our original starting point—the nfa which defines, of course, a regular language. However, this is an important consideration to which we will return later.

It is an easy exercise to show by induction on the structure of α that any expression $\alpha \in \text{EX}_A(\text{CONST}; \text{OP}; X_1, \ldots, X_n)$ with A and CONST arbitrary and OP consisting of union and left-concatenation can be transformed, using elementary properties of union and left-concatenation (namely the commutativity of union and the distributivity of concatenation over union), into an equivalent expression of the form

$$\bigcup_{j=1}^{n} L_j \cdot X_j \cup L_0. \tag{3.2}$$

Any equation in the normal form (3.2) will from now on be called *classical*.

We now have to address the problem of how one can solve a system (3.1) of classical language equations. In the following, we will consider two very different approaches. The first is based on syntactic properties of the equations; it is the more general of the two. The second is applicable only if all the constant languages involved in the equations are regular. The first approach constructs an expression that could be considered a regular expression, but strictly speaking it is not, because it contains the constant languages as atoms and these languages need not be regular. The second approach constructs a nondeterministic finite automaton for each variable; this construction as we formulate it is valid only if none of the languages $L_{i,j}$ in (3.1) contains the empty word (although this condition could be somewhat relaxed—see the discussion at the beginning of Section 3.4).

3.2 The Syntactic Solution Approach

This approach takes as its starting point the following proposition:

Proposition 3.1. *Consider the equation $X = L \cdot X \cup M$ over the alphabet A in the variable X with arbitrary constant languages L and M. The following statements hold:*

a. *The language $L^* \cdot M$ is a solution of the equation.*
b. *If $\lambda \notin L$, then $L^* \cdot M$ is the unique solution.*
c. *If $\lambda \in L$ then all solutions are given by $L^* \cdot (M \cup T)$ for T ranging over all languages over A.*

PROOF.   (a) It is trivial to verify that $L^* \cdot M$ is indeed a solution. On the left-hand side of the (supposed) equation, we have $L^* \cdot M$, on the right-hand side we get by substitution $L \cdot L^* \cdot M \cup M$ which is obviously equal to $L^* \cdot M$.

(b) Let S' be a solution different from $S = L^* \cdot M$. Therefore, there must exist a shortest word w in the symmetric difference of S and S'. First, we observe that w cannot be in M (as w is in one solution but not the other). Now assume that $w \in S - S'$; since $w \in S$ and hence $w \in L \cdot S$, $w = u \cdot v$ with $u \in L$ and $v \in S$, and v is strictly shorter than w as $\lambda \in L$. Since w was shortest, v must also be in S'. But now $w = u \cdot v \in L \cdot S'$, and since S' contains $L \cdot S'$, $w \in S'$ in contradiction to the assumption that $w \in S'$. If $w \in S' - S$, the argument is analogous (with S and S' interchanged). Therefore, no S' with $S' \neq S$ can exist; S is unique.

(c) First we show that $L^* \cdot (M \cup T)$ is a solution for any choice of T. Then, we show that any solution can be represented in this form. The first claim follows again by substitution into the supposed equation: The left-hand side is $L^* \cdot (M \cup T)$, and the right-hand side yields $L \cdot L^* \cdot (M \cup T) \cup M$. Since $\lambda \in L$, $L \cdot L^* = L^*$ and $L \cdot L^* \cdot (M \cup T)$ contains M; therefore, $L \cdot L^* \cdot (M \cup T) \cup M = L^* \cdot (M \cup T)$. The second claim is derived as follows: Let S be any solution; by definition $S = L \cdot S \cup M$, therefore $M \cup S = S$. We show that $L^* \cdot S = S$. That S is contained in $L^* \cdot S$ is trivial. Therefore, assume $w \in L^* \cdot S$; we must show $w \in S$. Clearly, $w = u \cdot v$ with $u \in L^*$ and $v \in S$. By definition of the star operator, $u = u_1 \cdot \cdots \cdot u_s$ with $s \geq 0$. If $s = 0$, $u = \lambda$, and $w = v \in S$. If $s \geq 1$, we obtain from $S = L \cdot S \cup M$ by substituting $L \cdot S \cup M$ for S on the right $s - 1$ times successively that

$$S = L^s \cdot S \cup L^{s-1} \cdot M \cup L^{s-2} \cdot M \cup \cdots \cup L^1 \cdot M \cup M$$

and, therefore, $w \in S$. Therefore, we conclude that $S = L^* \cdot (M \cup T)$ for $T = S$. This implies that any solution S can be written in the parametrized form

$$L^* \cdot (M \cup T) \quad \text{for some language } T. \qquad \square$$

We remark that the constant languages L and M (and also T if $\lambda \in L$) can be completely arbitrary; in particular, they need not be regular, even though the solution is represented as a regular expression *in terms of the constant languages*. [Strictly speaking, the expression $L^* \cdot (M \cup T)$ is not a regular expression if L, M, and T are not regular.]

Using Proposition 3.1, we can now formulate the theorem for arbitrary systems of classical language equations.

Theorem 3.2. *Let a system (3.1) of n classical language equations in n variables X_i be given, where the constant languages $L_{i,j}$ for $i = 1, \ldots, n$ and $j = 0, 1, \ldots, n$ are arbitrary. Then, for each variable X_i, there exists a regular expression α_i in terms of the constant languages such that $\alpha = (\alpha_1, \ldots, \alpha_n)$ is a solution.*

PROOF. We carry the proof out by induction on n, the number of variables (as well as equations).

Basis, $n = 1$: If there is one variable in one equation, Proposition 3.1 applies; the result is an expression in constant languages only, since the only variable was eliminated.

Induction step: We assume we can solve any system of $n - 1$ equations in $n - 1$ variables such that the solution is $(\beta_1, \ldots, \beta_n)$ and β_i is a regular expression in terms of the constant languages of these $n - 1$ equations; we show that under this assumption, we can solve any system of n equations in n variables so that $(\alpha_1, \ldots, \alpha_n)$ is the solution and each α_i is a regular expression in terms of the constant languages of the system with n equations. Consider the equation for X_i, $i \in \{1, \ldots, n\}$. (It is important to see that we can choose any variable that is present at this point in the construction; the argument below holds for any such choice.) Without loss of generality, we may assume that the system of equations is in the form (3.1). We distinguish two cases, $L_{i,i} = \emptyset$ and $L_{i,i} \neq \emptyset$. In the second case, we first apply Proposition 3.1 to the equation for X_i whereby $L = L_{i,i}$ and M is equal to all other terms of the equation. This yields an expression for X_i in terms of the constant language $L_{i,i}$ and the non-X_i terms of the equation. If $L_{i,i} = \emptyset$, we skip this step. In both cases, we now substitute the expression for X_i into the expression for X_j, where j ranges over all values $\{1, \ldots, n\} - \{i\}$. It follows that in the resulting equations, there is no occurrence of X_i and the number of equations is reduced by one, from n to $n - 1$. Furthermore, all resulting equations are of the form (3.2). Consequently, we have reduced the problem for n equations in n variables to a simpler problem for $n - 1$ equations in $n - 1$ variables. Finally, if we have expressions for the solution of this system of $n - 1$ equations in $n - 1$ variables, in terms of that system's constant languages only, we can substitute these expressions into the equation for X_i in the original system with n equations and obtain an expression in terms of the constant languages only for that variable as well. Therefore, the proof is complete. $\square$

The question of uniqueness is somewhat more complicated, because the condition $\lambda \notin L_{i,i}$ in the equation for X_i is not sufficient. To see this, consider the following equations:

$$X = aX \cup b^*Y \cup \lambda,$$
$$Y = a^*X \cup bY \cup \lambda.$$

Clearly, for $i = 1, 2$, $\lambda \notin L_{i,i}$, solving the equation for Y, we get

$$Y = b^*(a^*X \cup \lambda)$$

and substituting this into the equation for X yields

$$X = aX \cup b^*b^*(a^*X \cup \lambda) \cup \lambda$$
$$= (a \cup b^*b^*a^*)X \cup (b^*b^*a^* \cup \lambda)$$

and this implies by Proposition 3.1 that there are multiple solutions for X (and, consequently, also for Y). It follows that uniqueness is guaranteed if the following condition holds:

> For all $i = 1, \ldots, n$, there does not exist a sequence of indices $m_{i,0}$, $m_{i,1}, \ldots, m_{i,r}$ with $1 \leq r \leq n$, $m_{i,0} = m_{i,r} = i$, and all $m_{i,j} \in \{1, \ldots, n\}$ such that $\lambda \in L_{m_{i,j-1}, m_{i,j}}$ for all $j = 1, \ldots, r$.

If this condition is violated, Theorem 3.2 will yield a parametric representation of all solutions.

Note that in the construction in Theorem 3.2, we will obtain a regular expression (in terms of the constant languages) for each variable. In practice, one may be interested only in the solution for one specific variable. In particular, if one starts with a finite automaton N as in Section 3.1, one would only be interested in the solution corresponding to the automaton's initial state, as this solution would be identical to $L(\mathrm{N})$, the language accepted by the automaton; it should be clear that in this case, the solution expression is a true regular expression. All other solutions (languages corresponding to states other than the initial state of N) are identical to the set of words that the automaton would accept if that state were the initial state (the resulting automata may not be connected, but this is of no consequence here).

Consider the following system of three equations in the three variables X, Y, and Z. In preparation of our subsequent discussion of the substitution property, we will use B, C, D, E, F, G, and H to stand for the constant languages which may, of course, be completely arbitrary; however, we will have to state for some of them whether they contain the empty word λ. The equations are as follows:

$$X = B \cdot Y \cup C \cdot Z,$$
$$Y = D \cdot Y \cup E,$$
$$Z = F \cdot X \cup G \cdot Y \cup H \cdot Z.$$

We observe that only for D and H must we know whether they contain λ; let us assume that H does and D does not. We start the process with X; since there is no term with X in the equation for X, we need not apply Proposition 3.1 and can immediately substitute the expression $B \cdot Y \cup C \cdot Z$ for every occurrence of X in the remaining equations. There is only one such occurrence, in the equation for Z; thus, this equation becomes

$$Z = F \cdot (B \cdot Y \cup C \cdot Z) \cup G \cdot Y \cup H \cdot Z$$

or, after normalization,

$$Z = (F \cdot B \cup G) \cdot Y \cup (F \cdot C \cup H) \cdot Z.$$

So, we deal now with the following system of two equations in the two variables Y and Z:

$$Y = D \cdot Y \cup E,$$
$$Z = (F \cdot B \cup G) \cdot Y \cup (F \cdot C \cup H) \cdot Z.$$

Let us continue with the variable Y. Here, we must apply Proposition 3.1; this yields the following expression (recall the assumption that $\lambda \notin D$):

$$Y = D^* \cdot E.$$

Substituting this into the equation for Z yields

$$Z = (F \cdot C \cup H) \cdot Z \cup (F \cdot B \cup G) \cdot D^* \cdot E$$

and this equation can be solved directly, using Proposition 3.1 again:

$$Z = (F \cdot C \cup H)^* \cdot [(F \cdot B \cup G) \cdot D^* \cdot E \cup T]$$

for T any constant language (since H contains the empty word, by assumption). Now, we can obtain expressions in terms of the constant languages only for the other variables also. The expression that we determined for Y is already in the desired form; the expression for X is obtained by substituting the expressions for Y and Z:

$$X = B \cdot D^* \cdot E \cup C \cdot (F \cdot C \cup H)^* \cdot [(F \cdot B \cup G) \cdot D^* \cdot E \cup T].$$

Thus, we obtain as final solution

$$X = B \cdot D^* \cdot E \cup C \cdot (F \cdot C \cup H)^* \cdot [(F \cdot B \cup G) \cdot D^* \cdot E \cup T],$$
$$Y = D^* \cdot E,$$
$$Z = (F \cdot C \cup H)^* \cdot [(F \cdot B \cup G) \cdot D^* \cdot E \cup T].$$

Because of Proposition 3.1(c), these expressions represent all solutions; they are a parametrized representation, with T being the (unconstrained) parameter. In this case, there is only one such parameter, as only H contains λ but D does not. Were both D and H to contain λ, we would have two parameters, T_Y and T_Z, both of which would range over all permissible languages (languages in CONST).

We reiterate that the constant languages B, C, D, E, F, G, and H (as well as the parameter T) are completely arbitrary; they need not even be recursively enumerable. These expressions constitute valid solutions for any choice of languages. Of course, for certain language classes, we may not have effective constructions to carry out certain operations such as union, concatenation, or star, but this has no bearing on the fact that these expressions are representations of all solutions of these equations.

3.3   The Substitution Property

Suppose we have two expressions $\alpha, \beta \in \mathrm{EX}_A(\mathrm{CONST}; \mathrm{OP}; X_1, \ldots, X_n)$ for some class CONST and some set OP, and assume that α and β are equivalent $(\alpha \equiv \beta)$ (i.e., the functions defined by the two expressions are identical, $F_\alpha = F_\beta$). If we substitute for a specific letter of A an arbitrary language in both expressions, the substitution property postulates that the equivalence of the resulting two expressions be preserved.

As an example, consider the two equivalent equations over the alphabet $\{a, b\}$ from the previous chapter:

$$\alpha = (ab^*)^* X \cup a(aa)^* Y \cup aa(aaa)^* Y,$$
$$\beta = (a(a \cup b)^* \cup \lambda) X \cup (aaaaaa)^* (a \cup aa \cup aaa \cup aaaaa) Y.$$

If we systematically replace the letter a by the language a^*, we will obtain equivalent expressions:

$$\alpha' = (a^* b^*)^* X \cup a^* (a^* a^*)^* Y \cup a^* a^* (a^* a^* a^*)^* Y$$
$$= (a \cup b)^* X \cup a^* Y,$$
$$\beta' = (a^* (a^* \cup b)^* \cup \lambda) X \cup (a^* a^* a^* a^* a^* a^*)^* (a^* \cup a^* a^* \cup a^* a^* a^*$$
$$\cup a^* a^* a^* a^* a^*) Y$$
$$= (a \cup b)^* X \cup a^* Y.$$

It is easily seen that the substitution property always holds if OP contains union, concatenation (either type), and star. This follows directly from the elementary properties of language operations, in particular the distributivity of concatenation over union. It was the fact that the substitution property holds for these expressions that provided the theoretical foundation for the solving-by-parts approach that we used in the proof of Theorem 3.2. More specifically, the substitution property allowed us to ignore all other variables when we solved for the variable X_i.

In the solution derived in the previous section,

$$X = B \cdot D^* \cdot E \cup C \cdot (F \cdot C \cup H)^* \cdot [(F \cdot B \cup G) \cdot D^* \cdot E \cup T],$$
$$Y = D^* \cdot E,$$
$$Z = (F \cdot C \cup H)^* \cdot [(F \cdot B \cup G) \cdot D^* \cdot E \cup T],$$

the expressions are effectively over the alphabet $\{B, C, D, E, F, G, H\}$. (We still have the parameter T, but since it is completely arbitrary as long as it is a language over the appropriate alphabet, this does not create problems.) We may now substitute arbitrary languages for these seven letters (as long as we respect our original decision that D does not contain the empty word but H does) and obtain valid solutions of the corresponding language equations. For example, we may choose the alphabet $\{a, b\}$ and set

$$B = C = D = aa^* \quad \text{and} \quad E = F = G = H = b^*.$$

The resulting system of equations is therefore

$$X = aa^* \cdot Y \cup aa^* \cdot Z,$$
$$Y = aa^* \cdot Y \cup b^*,$$
$$Z = b^* \cdot X \cup b^* \cdot Y \cup b^* \cdot Z.$$

By strictly substituting the new languages for the old letters B through H in the original (universal) solution, we obtain

$$X = aa^* \cdot (aa^*)^* \cdot b^* \cup aa^* \cdot (b^* \cdot aa^* \cup b^*)^*$$
$$\cdot [(b^* \cdot aa^* \cup b^*) \cdot (aa^*)^* \cdot b^* \cup T],$$
$$Y = (aa^*)^* \cdot b^*,$$
$$Z = (b^* \cdot aa^* \cup b^*)^* \cdot [(b^* \cdot aa^* \cup b^*) \cdot (aa^*)^* \cdot b^* \cup T],$$

which simplifies to

$$X = a \cdot (a \cup b)^*,$$
$$Y = a^* \cdot b^*,$$
$$Z = (a \cup b)^*$$

using the identities $(aa^*)^* = a^*$, $b^* \cdot aa^* \cup b^* = b^* a^*$, and $(b^* \cdot aa^* \cup b^*)^* = (a \cup b)^*$, and observing that $(b^* \cdot aa^* \cup b^*)^* \cdot [(b^* \cdot aa^* \cup b^*) \cdot (aa^*)^* \cdot b^* \cup T] = (a \cup b)^* \cdot [b^* a^* \cdot a^* \cdot b^* \cup T]$ and since $\lambda \in b^* a^* \cdot a^* \cdot b^*$, $(a \cup b)^* \cdot [b^* a^* \cdot a^* \cdot b^* \cup T] = (a \cup b)^* \cup (a \cup b)^* \cdot T = (a \cup b)^*$, independent of any choice of T. It follows that for this particular choice for B through H, the solutions are, in fact, unique. For other choices, this need not be true. Consider

$$B = C = D = a, \quad E = F = G = b, \quad \text{and} \quad H = \lambda.$$

We obtain the following system:

$$X = a \cdot Y \cup a \cdot Z,$$
$$Y = a \cdot Y \cup b,$$
$$Z = b \cdot X \cup b \cdot Y \cup Z$$

with the following solutions

$$X = a \cdot a^* \cdot b \cup a \cdot (b \cdot a \cup \lambda)^* \cdot [(b \cdot a \cup b) \cdot a^* \cdot b \cup T]$$
$$= aa^* b \cup a(ba)^* [ba^* b \cup T],$$
$$Y = a^* \cdot b,$$
$$Z = (b \cdot a \cup \lambda)^* \cdot [(b \cdot a \cup b) \cdot a^* \cdot b \cup T] = (ba)^* [ba^* b \cup T]$$

and here, solutions will depend on the choice for T. For example, choosing $T = \emptyset$, we obtain

$$X = a(\lambda \cup (ba)^* b) a^* b, \quad Y = a^* b, \quad Z = (ba)^* ba^* b$$

and for the choice $T = (a \cup b)^*$, we obtain

$$X = (a \cup b)^*, \quad Y = a^* b, \quad Z = (a \cup b)^*.$$

Thus, one can see that different choices for T yield different solutions. Incidentally, the first of these two solutions is the smallest and the second the largest of all possible solutions. In fact, all possible solutions lie between these two extremal solutions. This is a direct consequence of the following statement which is quite complicated to formulate but in essence (if not entirely precisely) states that if a language for the parameter T contains another language, the resulting solutions preserve this containment relation.

Lemma 3.3. *Let $(\alpha_1, \ldots, \alpha_n)$ be the solution of the system (3.1) of classical language equations in n variables and let $\lambda \in L_{j,j}$ for all $j \in \{i_1, \ldots, i_k\}$. Denote the parameters corresponding to these equations by $T_{i_1}, \ldots, T_{i_k}$; thus each α_i can be viewed as a function $F_{\alpha_i}(T_{i_1}, \ldots, T_{i_k})$ for $i = 1, \ldots, n$. Now assume that $k \geq 1$ and let $t \in \{1, \ldots, k\}$. If $M, M' \in \mathrm{CONST}$ are languages such that $M \supset M'$, then for all $i = 1, \ldots, n$,*

$$F_{\alpha_i}(T_{i_1}, \ldots, T_{i_{t-1}}, M, T_{i_{t+1}}, \ldots, T_{i_k}) \supseteq F_{\alpha_i}(T_{i_1}, \ldots, T_{i_{t-1}}, M', T_{i_{t+1}}, \ldots, T_{i_k}).$$

The proof of this lemma is an easy exercise.

The substitution property appears to be very "natural". It is therefore interesting (and turns out to be very troublesome—see Chapter 4 and, even more so, Chapter 7) that the presence of operators other than union, concatenation, and star may invalidate the substitution property. To see this, consider the following two expressions over the alphabet $\{a\}$:

$$\alpha = \bar{a} \quad \text{and} \quad \beta = \lambda \cup aaa^*.$$

It is entirely obvious that α and β are equivalent since both contain all words except the word a. However, substituting a^* for the letter a (the same substitution that we carried out in the previous example) yields the following two expressions (after simplification):

$$\alpha' = \emptyset \quad \text{and} \quad \beta' = a^*$$

and, clearly, these two expressions are not equivalent.

Thus, the substitution property does not hold for complementation; it also does not hold for intersection, as the following two expressions over the alphabet $\{a\}$ demonstrate:

$$\alpha = a \cap aa \quad \text{and} \quad \beta = \emptyset.$$

Clearly, the two expressions are equivalent. However, substituting a^* for a again yields the following two expressions:

$$\alpha' = a^* \quad \text{and} \quad \beta' = \emptyset$$

and again, there is no equivalence.

3.4   Constructing Nondeterministic Finite Automata for the Solution Languages

This construction requires that all constant languages $L_{i,j}$ occurring in the system (3.1) be regular. Moreover, in order to simplify the exposition, we will assume that none of the languages $L_{i,j}$ for $i = 1, \ldots, n$ and $j = 1, \ldots, n$ contains the empty word.

[This assumption really has two parts, the first one being the condition that a solution is unique, a condition that can be formulated strictly in terms of $\lambda \notin L_{i,j}$, for some (i, j) pairs, and the second one the assumption that λ is also not contained in the other languages. The second part of our assumption is strictly because of laziness; it can be removed, although at the cost of vastly complicating the exposition. The first part, however, is necessary, in the following sense: We know from the discussion following Theorem 3.2 that there is a condition that implies that the system has a unique solution; on the other hand, if this condition is not satisfied, we will obtain a parametric representation of the solutions. It is not difficult to see that choosing the empty language for the parameters T_j in the solution expressions α_i is equivalent to removing the empty word from $L_{i,j}$ for $i = 1, \ldots, n$ and $j = 1, \ldots, n$ (see also Lemma 3.3). Since an automaton represents a single, uniquely determined language, and not a parametrized class of languages, the automaton approach will not be able to capture the fact that there may be many different solutions; it will only represent one of them. If we are interested in the minimal solution, then all we have to do is remove the empty word from all those languages $L_{i,j}$ (with $j \geq 1$) that contain it. This will satisfy the assumption we make for the construction in this section.]

For each (regular) language $L_{i,j}$, we assume there is a nondeterministic finite automaton

$$\mathbb{A}_{i,j} = (A, P_{i,j}, \mu_{i,j}, p_{0,i,j}, G_{i,j}) \quad \text{for all } i = 1, \ldots, n$$
$$\text{and all } j = 0, 1, \ldots, n \text{ such that } L(\mathbb{A}_{i,j}) = L_{i,j}.$$

Since $\lambda \notin L_{i,j}$ for all $i = 1, \ldots, n$ and all $j = 1, \ldots, n$, it follows that $p_{0,i,j} \notin G_{i,j}$. We now construct n nondeterministic finite automata

$$\mathbb{N}_i = (A, Q, \tau, q_{0,i}, F) \quad \text{for all } i = 1, \ldots, n$$

with the objective that

$(L(\mathbb{N}_1), \ldots, L(\mathbb{N}_n))$ is the unique solution of the system (3.1).

These automata will be completely defined by specifying Q, τ, and F:

$$Q = \bigcup_{i=1}^{n} \left[\bigcup_{j=0}^{n} P_{i,j} \cup \{q_{0,i}\} \right],$$

$$F' = \bigcup_{i=1}^{n} G_{i,0};$$

F is then F' plus all $q_{0,i}$ where $p_{0,i,0} \in G_{i,0}$, $i = 1, \ldots, n$. $\tau(q,a)$ for all $q \in Q$ and $a \in A$ is defined as follows:

For all $i = 1, \ldots, n$ and for all $h = 1, \ldots, n$:

if $q = q_{0,i}$, then $\tau(q,a) = \bigcup_{j=0}^{n} \mu_{i,j}(p_{0,i,j}, a)$

else if $q \in G_{i,h}$, then $\tau(q,a) = \bigcup_{k=0}^{N} \mu_{h,k}(p_{0,h,k}, a) \cup \mu_{i,h}(q,a)$

else if $q \in P_{i,h} - G_{i,h}$, then $\tau(q,a) = \mu_{i,h}(q,a)$

else if $q \in P_{i,0}$, then $\tau(q,a) = \mu_{i,0}(q,a)$

else $\tau(q,a) = \emptyset$.

Thus, we define essentially one nfa with n different starting states. The set of states Q is the union of the sets of states of all the automata $\mathbb{A}_{i,j}$, plus one initial state $(q_{0,i})$ for each variable X_i. The set of final states consists precisely of all the final states of the automata $\mathbb{A}_{i,0}$ (they represent the languages that are not concatenated with any variable). [Here, we are greatly helped by the assumption that $\lambda \notin L_{i,j}$ for all i and all j.] Finally, the transition function: To start things, we have, for each initial state $q_{0,i}$, all those transitions that each corresponding automaton $\mathbb{A}_{i,j}$ takes from its initial state under the letter a, for all $j = 0, 1, \ldots, n$. Then, if we reach a final state of an automaton $\mathbb{A}_{i,j}$ $(j \neq 0)$, we must branch over to allow the nfa to do whatever X_j will do (in addition to continuing in $\mathbb{A}_{i,j}$). On the other hand, if we are in any rejecting state or in any state of $\mathbb{A}_{i,0}$ we merely continue without any branching.

By inspecting the function of each state in the above construction, it is rather easy to verify that the objective is achieved; $(L(\mathbb{N}_1), \ldots, L(\mathbb{N}_n))$ is the unique solution of the system (3.1). We summarize:

Theorem 3.4. *Let a system (3.1) of n classical language equations in n variables X_i be given, where the constant languages $L_{i,j}$ for $i = 1, \ldots, n$ and $j = 0, 1, \ldots, n$ are regular and $\lambda \notin L_{i,j}$ for all i and all j. Then, $(L(\mathbb{N}_1), \ldots, L(\mathbb{N}_n))$ is the unique solution of the system where the n nfa's $\mathbb{N}_i$ are constructed as defined above.*

[It is easy to see how we have to modify the construction if $\lambda \in L_{i,j}$ for any $i \neq j$. In addition to the change of F mentioned above, this implies that the transitions for the initial state $q_{0,i}$ have to contain all the transitions for the initial state $q_{0,j}$ as well. It does, however, complicate the general description of the construction. In specific cases, the modification is easily supplied.]

We give an example of a system with three equations in the three variables X, Y, and Z:

$$X = L_1 \cdot X \cup L_2 \cdot Y,$$
$$Y = L_3 \cdot Y \cup L_4 \cdot Z,$$
$$Z = L_5 \cdot X \cup L_6.$$

The six regular languages L_i over the alphabet $\{a, b\}$ are given by the following nfa's (the first state is always assumed to be the initial state):

A_1:

	a	b	
1	2	3	0
2	/	1	1
3	1	/	1

A_2:

	a	b	
4	5	6	0
5	4	/	1
6	/	4	1

A_3:

	a	b	
7	/	7, 8	0
8	7	8	1

A_4:

	a	b	
9	9	10	0
10	10	9	1

A_5:

	a	b	
11	12, 13	/	0
12	12, 13	11	1
13	11	/	0

A_6:

	a	b	
14	/	15	0
15	/	15	1

We therefore obtain the following automata N_X, N_Y, and N_Z:

$$Q = \{1, 2, 3, 4, 5, 6, 7, 8, 9, 10, 11, 12, 13, 14, 15; x, y, z\},$$
$$F = \{15\},$$

τ :	a	b
x	2, 5	3,6
y	9	7, 8, 10
z	12, 13	15
1	2	3
2	2, 5	1, 3, 6
3	1, 2, 5	3, 6
4	5	6
5	4, 9	7, 8, 10
6	9	4, 7, 8, 10
7	/	7, 8
8	7, 9	7, 8, 10
9	9	10
10	10, 12, 13	9, 15
11	12, 13	/
12	2, 5, 12, 13	3, 6, 11
13	11	/
14	/	15
15	/	15

It is important to note that this automaton represents all three nfa's,

$$N_X = (A, Q, \tau, x, F), \quad N_Y = (A, Q, \tau, y, F), \quad N_Z = (A, Q, \tau, z, F).$$

While, in general, the resulting automata may not be connected (i.e., there may be states in F that cannot be reached from the initial state), in this particular case the three resulting automata are in fact connected, provided one removes state 14, which does not occur as a target of any transition in the table for τ.

One should be aware that this construction greatly reduces the rather laborious work required to obtain the actual solution languages in all but the most banal cases. Compare this example with what one would obtain from an application of Theorem 3.2. Of the three variables, Z has the simplest expression; it can be determined to be

$$(L_5 \cdot L_1^* \cdot L_2 \cdot L_3^* \cdot L_4)^* \cdot L_6.$$

To obtain from this the actual language involves numerous constructions. We first must construct automata for L_1^* and L_3^*, then we have to concatenate the five automata to get an automaton for $L_5 \cdot L_1^* \cdot L_2 \cdot L_3^* \cdot L_4$, then this automaton must be starred, and finally the resulting automaton must be concatenated with L_6. For the variable Y, one must construct an automaton for

$$L_3^* \cdot L_4 \cdot (L_5 \cdot L_1^* \cdot L_2 \cdot L_3^* \cdot L_4)^* \cdot L_6,$$

and to get an automaton for the solution for X, one must construct one for

$$L_1^* \cdot L_2 \cdot L_3^* \cdot L_4 \cdot (L_5 \cdot L_1^* \cdot L_2 \cdot L_3^* \cdot L_4)^* \cdot L_6.$$

It is quite clear that the above direct construction, while be no means quick, nevertheless saves a good deal of time, compared with applying Theorem 3.2. Thus, if it is possible to apply this construction, it is definitely preferable.

3.5   A Note on Context-Free Grammars

Context-free grammars also give rise to language equations, in the obvious way: Let $G = (N, T, P, S)$ be a context-free grammar. If for a variable X, all X productions are given by

$$X \rightarrow \alpha_1 | \cdots | \alpha_s$$

with the α_i strings over the variables N and terminals T, then the equation for the variable (corresponding to) X is precisely

$$X = \alpha_1 \cup \cdots \cup \alpha_s$$

and, clearly, the operations involved are union and unrestricted concatenation. Just as clearly, one solution of the system of language equations corresponding to the grammar G is

$$(L(G_X) \mid X \in N),$$

where $G_X = (N, T, P, X)$ is the context-free grammar obtained from G by changing the starting symbol from S to X, for $X \in N$. However, note that $(L(G_X) \mid X \in N)$ need not be the only solution; this was illustrated by the discussion of the first example in Chapter 1. It is fairly easy to see that the uniqueness of this solution is guaranteed if for all variables $X \in N$, it is impossible to derive X from X: $X \overset{+}{\Rightarrow} X$. This criterion is an obvious analogue of the uniqueness condition following Theorem 3.2.

If one is interested in a representation of all context-free solutions, it suffices to do the following: Determine the set of all variables X for which $X \overset{+}{\Rightarrow} X$. Then, starting from G, construct a new context-free grammar which contains all productions of G plus, for each such variable X, a production $X \rightarrow S_{T_X}$, where S_{T_X} is the starting symbol of a context-free grammar for the arbitrary context-free language T_X. Thus, T_X again plays the role of a parameter. The only restriction in this construction of the new context-free grammar is that T_X must be context-free. If one wants to do away with this restriction, the construction is still valid but will no longer yield a context-free grammar; instead, S_{T_X} must be the starting variable of a grammar that generates T_X (possibly a Type 0 grammar). Because this effectively completes the coverage of equations corresponding to context-free grammars, we will pay no more attention to these equations for the remainder of this book.

3.6   Bibliographical Notes

Classical language equations occur in many introductory textbooks on automata theory since they provide one-half of the usual way of proving that regular expressions and finite automata are equally powerful. We refer for instance to [Salom 69]. The substitution property is one of those results that many people know about but on which there is little literature. Robert McNaughton many years ago wrote a paper in which he discussed its implications. [Leiss 94a] made reference to it in the context of solving equations over a one-letter alphabet. The construction of Section 3.4 is closely related to that for boolean automata, first described in [Leiss 81a]; we will present it in the next chapter. It was inspired by work by B. G. Mirkin [Mirki 66]; see also [Leiss 81c]. To work on Problem 4 below, it may be useful to use a nonstandard definition of the length of regular expressions, as outlined in [Leiss 81c].

3.7 Problems

1. Solve the following system of classical equations for the variables X and Y,

$$X = L_1 \cdot X \cup L_2 \cdot Y \cup L_3,$$
$$Y = L_3 \cdot X \cup L_2 \cdot Y \cup L_1,$$

where the constant languages are given by

   a. $L_1 = aa^*$, $L_2 = bb^*$, and $L_3 = cc^*$

      i. using the construction of Section 3.2.
     ii. using the construction of Section 3.4.

   b. $L_1 = \{a^n b^n \mid n \geq 1\}$, $L_2 = aa^* bb^*$, and $L_3 = \lambda$.

2. Define a class of systems of classical language equations as follows. Let $k \geq 2$ and $m_j \geq 1$ for $j = 1, \ldots, k$, and define the positive integer $M = m_1 \cdots \cdots m_k$. Consider the set of M equations over the alphabet $\{a_1, \ldots, a_k\}$ in the M variables $X_{i_1, \ldots, i_k}$ with $0 \leq i_j \leq m_j - 1$ for $j = 1, \ldots, k$:

$$X_{i_1, \ldots, i_s, \ldots, i_k} = \bigcup_{\substack{j=1,\ldots,k \\ j \neq s}} a_j \cdot X_{i_1, \ldots, i_s, \ldots, i_k}$$
$$\cup \ as \cdot X_{i_1, \ldots, (i_s+1) \bmod m_s, \ldots, i_k}$$
$$\cup \ \delta(X_{i_1, \ldots, i_s, \ldots, i_k})$$

   for all $0 \leq i_j \leq m_j - 1$ for $j = 1, \ldots, k$ and $s \in \{1, \ldots, k\}$. Choose specific values for k and the m_j's and construct the corresponding solutions for this system of equations

      i. using the construction of Section 3.2.
     ii. using the construction of Section 3.4.

3. Assume that a system (3.1) is given, but you only know that $\lambda \notin L_{i,i}$ for all $i = 1, \ldots, n$. Is this sufficient for guaranteeing uniqueness of the solution? If not, show why not and indicate what additional restrictions must be imposed? Under this condition, formulate the construction of the n automata $\mathbb{N}_i$ (i.e., you will have to deal with the case $\lambda \in L_{i,j}$ for some $i \neq j$).

4. Let all languages in (3.1) be regular and assume they are given as regular expressions of length $l_{i,j}$. Determine an upper bound on the length of the regular expressions α_i representing the solution according to Theorem 3.2. Compare this with the number of states of the nondeterministic finite automata representing the solution that we constructed in Section 3.4.

5. Consider a system (3.1) of n classical equations. Assume that for some $s \in \{1, \ldots, n\}$, $\lambda \in L_{s,s}$ and let T_s be the corresponding parameter. Let

$(\gamma_1(T_1, \ldots, T_s), \ldots, \gamma_n(T_1, \ldots, T_s))$ be the parametrized representation of the solution of (3.1) where the T_j are all parameters that occur in the construction. Clearly, $\gamma_i(L_1, \ldots, L_s)$ is a uniquely determined language, for any choice of languages $L_1, \ldots, L_s$. Consider a second system of n classical equations defined as follows: All equations of the new systems are identical to those of the old one, except that any language $L_{i,j}$ is replaced by $L_{i,j} - \{\lambda\}$, for all $i = 1, \ldots, n$ and all $j = 1, \ldots, n$ (but not $j = 0$). Prove:

$$(\alpha_1(\emptyset, \ldots, \emptyset), \ldots, \alpha_n(\emptyset, \ldots, \emptyset))$$

is the unique solution representation of the new system.

4

Boolean Language Equations

About This Chapter: We define boolean language equations and relate them to boolean automata. Boolean language equations are explicit equations over an arbitrary alphabet in which union, left-concatenation, and complementation may occur. Boolean automata are a generalization of nondeterministic finite automata that are able to accommodate, in a natural way, the complementation operation. We first show that not every boolean equation has a solution. Then, we give a constructive approach to solving any system of boolean equations that has a solution. We also give a complete characterization of the existence of solutions, decide whether more than one solution exists, give a representation of all solutions if more than one exists, and show that any boolean equation whose constant languages are regular must have a regular solution, if it has any.

Boolean language equations are explicit language equations over an arbitrary alphabet A where the constant languages and the variables are operated upon by union, left-concatenation, and unrestricted complementation. Thus, a system of n boolean equations in n variables is given by

$$X_i = \alpha_i(X_1, \ldots, X_n), \quad i = 1, \ldots, n,$$

where $\alpha_i \in \text{EX}_A(\text{CONST}; \text{OP}; X_1, \ldots, X_n)$ for all $i = 1, \ldots, n$ and CONST is the class of constant languages, and OP consists of the following operations throughout this chapter:

- Union
- Left-concatenation

- Unrestricted complementation

For convenience, we will also use the intersection operator occasionally, even though it can be expressed in terms of union and complementation.

In much of what follows, we will assume that CONST is the class REG of all regular languages. This is because if CONST = REG, we can effectively construct the solutions of the equations we will discuss. These constructions are based on boolean automata, a generalization of finite automata which permit the treatment of complementation. Boolean automata will be defined and discussed in Section 4.1.

The existence and uniqueness of solutions of boolean equations depends heavily on a syntactic property of the underlying expressions, the λ-property. Using it, we can formulate a normal form theorem for boolean expressions. This normal form then provides the basis for tests for existence and for uniqueness of solutions of the corresponding boolean equations. Equations with multiple solutions will also be covered, in a later section.

4.1   Boolean Automata

A boolean automaton $\mathbb{B}$ is a quintuple (A, Q, τ, f_0, F), where

- A is (as always) the underlying alphabet
- Q is the finite, nonempty set of states, $Q = \{q_0, \ldots, q_{n-1}\}$
- f_0 is the (single) initial state function ($f_0 \in B_Q$)
- F, a subset of Q, is the set of final states
- τ is the transition function

$$\tau : Q \times A \to B_Q,$$

where B_Q is the set of all boolean functions in the variables $q_0, \ldots, q_{n-1}$.

Note that we treat the n states of the automaton also as variables of the functions in the set B_Q which has, of course, 2^{2^n} elements. Each element $f \in B_Q$ is a function from Q to $\{0, 1\}$, where 0 and 1 represent the two truth values in (classical, two-valued) boolean algebra. We define the relation $=_F$ on $B_Q \times \{0, 1\}$ as follows. Given a function $f \in B_Q$, $F =_F z$ with $z \in \{0, 1\}$ if after substituting 0 in f for every variable $q \in Q - F$ and substituting 1 for every variable $q \in F$, the function f evaluates to z.

In complete analogy to the usual extension of the transition function of an nfa to words, we extend our transition function $\tau : Q \times A \to B_Q$ to

$$\tau : B_Q \times A^* \to B_Q$$

as follows:

a. $\tau(f, \lambda) = f$ for all $f \in B_Q$.
b. For all $f \in B_Q$ and for all $a \in A$,
$\tau(f, a) = f(\tau(q_0, a), \tau(q_1, a), \ldots, \tau(q_{n-1}, a))$.

c. For all $f \in B_Q$ and for all $a \in A$, $v \in A^*$, $\tau(f, av) = \tau(\tau(f, a), v)$.

Given a word $w \in A^*$, w is accepted by the boolean automaton $\mathbb{B} = (A, Q, \tau, f_0, F)$ if and only if

$$\tau(f_0, w) =_F 1.$$

Thus, if $w = a_1 \cdot a2 \cdots a_m$ for $m \geq 1$ and all the a_i are elements of the alphabet A, one constructs successively, starting from the initial function f_0, the following sequence of boolean functions:

$$f_1 = \tau(f_0, a_1),$$
$$f_2 = \tau(f_1, a_2),$$
$$\vdots$$
$$f_m = \tau(f_{m-1}, a_m).$$

This is independent of the set of final states F. Only when one wants to determine whether the word is accepted does one subject the last function, f_m, to the test $=_F$ which evaluates whether f_m is true or false. The word w is then accepted if and only if (iff) this evaluation yields true (represented by 1). Finally, the language $L(\mathbb{B})$ consisting of all words accepted by the boolean automaton $\mathbb{B} = (A, Q, \tau, f_0, F)$ is defined by

$$L(\mathbb{B}) = \{w \in A^* \mid \tau(f_0, w) =_F 1\}.$$

In the remainder of this section, we first establish that each boolean automaton accepts a regular language; then, we discuss the economy with which boolean automata represent regular languages.

Theorem 4.1. *The class of all languages accepted by boolean automata is exactly the class of all regular languages.*

PROOF.   We first observe that each regular language L can be accepted by a boolean automaton. Let $\mathbb{D}$ be a deterministic finite automaton accepting L. It is easily verified that $\mathbb{D}$ can be viewed as a boolean automaton: The transition function of $\mathbb{D}$ yields exactly a single state for each (state, letter) pair, which can be interpreted as a function yielding just that state, and both the extension of the transition function to words and the definition of acceptance of a word are completely compatible.

To show that $L(\mathbb{B})$ for a given boolean automaton $\mathbb{B}$ is a regular language, we construct a deterministic finite automaton $\mathbb{D}_\mathbb{B}$ for $\mathbb{B} = (A, Q, \tau, f_0, F)$. This is done by adapting the well-known subset construction from unions (sets) of states to boolean functions of states:

$$\mathbb{D}_\mathbb{B} = (A, P, \mu, f_0, G),$$

where A and f_0 are already fixed and P, μ, and G are defined as follows:

$$P = \{f \in B_Q \mid f = \tau(f_0, w) \text{ for some } w \in A^*\},$$

$$G = \{f \in P \mid f =_F 1\},$$
$$\mu(f,a) = \tau(f,a) \text{ for all } f \in P \text{ and all } a \in A.$$

It is obvious that $w \in L(\mathbb{B})$ iff $w \in L(\mathbb{D}_{\mathbb{B}})$. Furthermore, P is finite (it cannot have more elements than B_Q has functions, namely 2^{2^n}), and therefore our claim follows. $\square$

Let us define the deterministic (nondeterministic, boolean) complexity of a regular language L as the least number of states of any deterministic (nondeterministic, boolean) automaton accepting L. [While for deterministic finite automata (dfa), there is a unique automaton—up to renaming of states—with the least number of states, namely the reduced automaton, for nondeterministic and boolean automata, there may be several different automata with the least number of states.][1] It follows immediately from Theorem 4.1 that the deterministic complexity of $L(\mathbb{B})$ for any boolean automaton $\mathbb{B}$ is bounded from above by 2^{2^n}, which raises the question of whether this upper bound can be attained. The following theorem provides the answer.

Theorem 4.2.   *There exists an n-state boolean automaton of deterministic complexity 2^{2^n}. There exists an n-state boolean automaton of nondeterministic complexity 2^n.*

PROOF.   Let us first define L^R as the reverse of the language L,

$$L^R = \{a_n \cdot a_{n-1} \cdots \cdot a_1 \mid a_1 \cdot a_2 \cdots \cdot a_n \in L \text{ for some } n \geq 0\}.$$

We use without proof the fact that for any regular language L of deterministic complexity N, one can construct a boolean automaton accepting the reverse L^R that has exactly $\lceil \log_2(N) \rceil$ states. Since for any $n \geq 2$, there exists a reduced automaton $\mathbb{D}$ with the property that $L(\mathbb{D})^R$ has deterministic complexity 2^n, the first claim follows by taking $L(\mathbb{D})^R$ as the desired language. The second claim derives from the observation that an arbitrary single word w of length $n-1$ is of nondeterministic complexity n; thus, the deterministic and the nondeterministic complexities are identical for $L(\{w\})$. However, if we choose for w a palindrome, $w = w^R$, the result

---

[1]Consider $a^n a^*$; here are two nfa's accepting this language. Since an nfa is also a boolean automaton, the claim also holds for boolean automata.

	a				a	
0	0, 1	0		0	1	0
1	2	0		1	2	0
$\cdots$				$\cdots$		
i	$i+1$	0		i	$i+1$	0
$\cdots$				$\cdots$		
n	/	1		n	n	1

cited yields a boolean automaton for w^R ($=w$) with $\lceil \log_2(n) \rceil$ states. Thus, the second claim is proven.   □

We can paraphrase this theorem as follows. In the best case, boolean automata provide an exponential increase in efficiency over nfa and a doubly exponential efficiency increase over dfa. This way of stating it raises the question of the worst case immediately. This is answered in the following theorem which we give without proof.

Theorem 4.3. *There exist infinitely many languages whose deterministic complexity is identical to their boolean complexity.*

4.2 The λ-Property and the Normal Form Theorem

Consider an expression $a \in \mathrm{EX}_A(\mathrm{CONST}; \mathrm{OP}; X_1, \ldots, X_n)$, where OP, as throughout this entire chapter, consists of

- Union
- Left-concatenation
- Unrestricted complementation

The λ-property for such expressions α is defined as follows. First, we define the λ-property of α with respect to the variable X_i by induction on the structure of α:

a. *Basis:* If $\alpha \in \mathrm{CONST}$, then α has the λ-property with respect to X_i.

If $\alpha = X_j$ for $j \neq i$, then α has the λ-property with respect to X_i.

If $\alpha = X_i$, then α does not have the λ-property with respect to X_i.

b. *Inductive step:* Let $\alpha, \beta \in \mathrm{EX}_A(\mathrm{CONST}; \mathrm{OP}; X_1, \ldots, X_n)$.

- $\alpha \cup \beta$ has the λ-property with respect to X_i iff both α and β have the λ-property with respect to X_i.
- $\bar{\alpha}$ has the λ-property with respect to X_i iff α has the λ-property with respect to X_i.
- $L \cdot \alpha$ has the λ-property with respect to X_i iff α has the λ-property with respect to X_i or $\lambda \notin L$.

Then we say that $\alpha \in \mathrm{EX}_A(\mathrm{CONST}; \mathrm{OP}; X_1, \ldots, X_n)$ has the λ-property iff α has the λ-property with respect to X_i for all $i = 1, \ldots, n$.

The λ-property is a syntactic property of expressions; very informally, it captures the idea that a variable may "occur on the left end of an expression". For example, the expression a^*X does not have the λ-property (with respect to X), nor does $aX \cup b^*\bar{X}$. On the other hand, the expression

$$\overline{a \cdot \bar{X} \cup b^*(a\overline{X} \cup b \cdot \overline{a^*X})}$$

has the λ-property (with respect to X).

Define for any language L and any nonnegative integer n

$$L|_{\leq n} = \{u \in L \mid |u| \leq n\}.$$

The notation $L|_{<n}$ is defined analogously. A useful observation that can easily be verified by structural induction on α (see also Propositions 5.2 and 5.3) is the following:

Proposition 4.4. *Let $\alpha \in \mathrm{EX}_A(\mathrm{CONST}; \mathrm{OP}; X_1, \ldots, X_n)$. Then, for any languages $L_1, \ldots, L_n$ over A and any word $w \in A^*$,*

$$w \in \alpha(L_1, \ldots, L_n) \quad \textit{iff} \ w \in \alpha(L_1|_{\leq|w|}, \ldots, L_n|_{\leq|w|}).$$

Furthermore, if α has the λ-property, then

$$w \in \alpha(L_1, \ldots, L_n) \quad \textit{iff} \ w \in \alpha(L_1|_{<|w|}, \ldots, L_n|_{<|w|}).$$

In other words, determining whether a word w is contained in $\alpha(L_1, \ldots, L_n)$ depends only on those words in the L_i that are no longer than w; moreover, if the expression has the λ-property, it depends only on strictly shorter words. Note that this holds even though the complementation operator may occur in these expressions.

The significance of the λ-property is indicated by the following result:

Proposition 4.5. *Let $\alpha \in \mathrm{EX}_A(\mathrm{CONST}; \mathrm{OP}; X)$ and consider the boolean language equation*

$$X = \alpha(X).$$

If α does not have the λ-property, the equation need not have a solution.

PROOF.   Consider the equation $X = a^* \cdot \bar{X}$ over the alphabet $A = \{a, b\}$. The expression does not have the λ-property. Clearly, as

$$a^* \cdot \bar{X} = \bar{X} \cup a^* \cdot \bar{X},$$

we must have

$$X \supseteq \bar{X}.$$

Since $X \cap \bar{X} = \emptyset$, this necessarily implies that $\bar{X} = \emptyset$ or $X = A^*$. However, $X = A^*$ is not a solution of this equation:

$$a^* \cdot \overline{A^*} = a^* \emptyset = \emptyset$$

which is not equal to A^*.   □

Note: We will show later that the equation will always have a solution if α has the λ-property with respect to X. For example, if we change the equation in the proof of the proposition to $X = aa^* \cdot \bar{X}$, there is a (unique) solution given by $X = aA^*$.

Based on the λ-property, we obtain the following normal form result for expressions in $\mathrm{EX}_A(\mathrm{CONST}; \mathrm{OP}; X_1, \ldots, X_n)$:

Theorem 4.6. *Consider $\alpha \in \mathrm{EX}_A(\mathrm{CONST}; \mathrm{OP}; X_1, \ldots, X_n)$. Then α can be written as*

$$\alpha_1 \cup (X_i \cap \alpha_2) \cup (\overline{X}_i \cap \alpha_3),$$

where α_1, α_2, and α_3 possess the λ-property with respect to X_i and

$$F_\alpha(X_1, \ldots, X_n) \equiv F_{\alpha_1}(X_1, \ldots, X_n) \cup (X_i \cap F_{\alpha_2}(X_1, \ldots, X_n))$$
$$\cup (\overline{X}_i \cap F_{\alpha_3}(X_1, \ldots, X_n)).$$

PROOF. By induction on the structure of α.

1. *Basis*:

   - If $\alpha \in \mathrm{CONST}$, then α has the λ-property with respect to X_i; therefore,

     $$\alpha_1 = L, \qquad \alpha_2 = \alpha_3 = \emptyset$$

     yields the desired representation.
   - If $\alpha = X_j$ for $j \neq i$, then α has the λ-property with respect to X_i; therefore,

     $$\alpha_1 = X_j, \qquad \alpha_2 = \alpha_3 = \emptyset$$

     yields the desired representation.
   - If $\alpha = X_i$, then α does not have the λ-property with respect to X_i; therefore,

     $$\alpha_1 = \emptyset, \qquad \alpha_2 = A^*, \qquad \alpha_3 = \emptyset$$

     yields the desired representation.

2. *Inductive step*: Assume inductively that β and γ have the desired representations

   $$\beta_1 \cup (\overline{X}_i \cap \beta_2) \cup (\overline{X}_i \cap \beta_3), \qquad \gamma_1 \cup (X_i \cap \gamma_2) \cup (\overline{X}_i \cap \gamma_3)$$

   with β_1, β_2, β_3, γ_1, γ_2, and γ_3 all having the λ-property with respect to X_i.

   - If $\alpha = \beta \cup \gamma$, then the desired representation is given by

     $$\alpha_t = \beta_t \cup \gamma_t \quad \text{for } t = 1, 2, 3.$$

   - If $\alpha = \bar{\beta}$, then the desired representation is given by

     $$\alpha_1 = \overline{\beta_1 \cup \beta_2 \cup \beta_3}, \qquad \alpha_2 = \overline{\beta_1 \cup \beta_2}, \qquad \alpha_3 = \overline{\beta_1 \cup \beta_3}.$$

   - If $\alpha = L \cdot \beta$ with $L \in \mathrm{CONST}$, then the desired representation is given as follows:

     If $\lambda \notin L$, then

     $$\alpha_1 = L \cdot \beta, \qquad \alpha_2 = \alpha_3 = \emptyset.$$

If $\lambda \in L$, then we have $L = \{\lambda\} \cup (L - \{\lambda\})$; thus, the desired representation is

$$\alpha_1 = L \cdot \beta_1 \cup (L - \{\lambda\}) \cdot \beta, \qquad \alpha_2 = \beta_2, \qquad \alpha_3 = \beta_3.$$

It is easily verified that the given representation satisfy the claim of the theorem. □

Note: Since each of the α_t have a normal form with respect to X_j for $j \neq i$, Theorem 4.6 can be applied until all expressions have the λ-property (with respect to all variables).

Example: Consider the expression

$$\alpha = c^* \left[(a^* X \cup b^* \cdot \bar{Y}) \cup \overline{d^*(\bar{X} \cup a^* Y)} \right]$$

in the two variables X and Y. We first apply Theorem 4.6 on X and obtain

$$\alpha = \alpha_1 \cup (X \cap \alpha_2) \cup (\bar{X} \cap \alpha_3),$$

where

$$\alpha_1 = cc^* \overline{\left[a^* X \cup b^* \cdot \bar{Y} \right) \cup \overline{d^*(\bar{X} \cup a^* Y)} \right]},$$
$$\alpha_2 = \overline{a^* Y \cup dd^*(\bar{X} \cup a^* Y)},$$
$$\alpha_3 = \overline{aa^* X \cup b^* \cdot \bar{Y}}.$$

Then we apply Theorem 4.6 for Y to these expressions and obtain

$$\alpha_{1,1} = \alpha_1, \qquad \alpha_{1,2} = \alpha_{1,3} = \emptyset, \qquad \alpha_{2,1} = \alpha_{2,2} = \emptyset.$$

$$\alpha_{2,3} = \overline{aa^* Y \cup dd^*(\bar{X} \cup a^* Y)},$$
$$\alpha_{3,1} = \alpha_{3,3} = \emptyset,$$
$$\alpha_{3,2} = \overline{aa^* X \cup bb^* \cdot \bar{Y}}.$$

Thus, we get the following final representation for α:

$$\alpha = \alpha_1 \cup (X \cap \bar{Y} \cap \alpha_{2,3}) \cup (\bar{X} \cap Y \cap \alpha_{3,2}),$$

where α_1, $\alpha_{2,3}$, and $\alpha_{3,2}$ all have the λ-property.

We formulate our normal form theorem for expressions in $\mathrm{EX}_A(\mathrm{CONST}; \mathrm{OP}; X_1, \ldots, X_n)$.

Theorem 4.7. *Let* $\alpha \in \mathrm{EX}_A(\mathrm{CONST}; \mathrm{OP}; X_1, \ldots, X_n)$. *Then* α *can be written as*

$$\bigcup_{s \in \{1,2,3\}^n} P(s) \cap \alpha_s,$$

where $P(s_1 \cdot \ldots \cdot s_n) = p_1 \cap \cdots \cap p_n$ *for* $s_i \in \{1,2,3\}$ *and* $p_i = A^*$ *if* $s_i = 1$, $p_i = X_i$ *if* $s_i = 2$, *and* $p_i = \bar{X}_i$ *if* $s_i = 3$, *and each* α_s *has the λ-property for all* $s \in \{1,2,3\}^n$.

4.3   The Uniqueness Criterion for Boolean Equations

In this section, we show that any system of n boolean equations

$$X_i = \alpha_i \quad \text{for } i = 1, \ldots, n,$$

where $\alpha_i \in \mathrm{EX}_A(\mathrm{REG}; \mathrm{OP}; X_1, \ldots, X_n)$ for $i = 1, \ldots, n$, cannot have more than one solution if an easily verified criterion is satisfied. Note that we are assuming here that all constants are arbitrary languages. This criterion is based on the λ-property and is stated in the following theorem.

Theorem 4.8. *Consider the system of boolean language equations*

$$X_i = \alpha_i \quad \text{with } \alpha_i \in \mathrm{EX}_A(\mathrm{REG}; \mathrm{OP}; X_1, \ldots, X_n), \quad i = 1, \ldots, n.$$

If α_i has the λ-property for all $i = 1, \ldots, n$, then there exists at most one solution of this system.

PROOF.   Assume there are two different solutions, namely

$$(X_1, \ldots, X_n) = (S_1, \ldots, S_n) \quad \text{and} \quad (X_1, \ldots, X_n) = (T_1, \ldots, T_n)$$

such that

$$S_i = \alpha_i(S_1, \ldots, S_n) \quad \text{and} \quad T_i = \alpha_i(T_1, \ldots, T_n)$$

and there exists a $j \in \{1, \ldots, n\}$ with $S_j \neq T_j$. Let v be a shortest word in the difference,

$$v \in \bigcup_{i=1,\ldots,n} (S_i - T_i) \cup (T_i - S_i).$$

Without loss of generality, $v \in S_t - T_t$ for some t. Thus,

$$v \in S_t = \alpha_t(S_1, \ldots, S_n), \quad \text{but } v \notin T_t = \alpha_t(T_1, \ldots, T_n).$$

However, since α_t has the λ-property, $v \in \alpha_t(S_1, \ldots, S_n)$ implies by Proposition 4.4 that v is expressed by α_t using only words in $S_1, \ldots, S_n$ that are shorter than v. By the minimality of v, all these words must however be also in the T_i's. Thus,

$$v \in \alpha_t(T_1, \ldots, T_n)$$

and since $T_t = \alpha_t(T_1, \ldots, T_n)$, $v \in T_t$, in contradiction to the assumption. Thus, two different solutions cannot exist.   □

Note that this result holds for any class of languages. However, for the constructions in the following sections, we must assume that CONST is equal to the class REG of regular languages.

4.4   Generalized Derivatives of Expressions

Assume we are given an expression $\alpha \in EX_A(REG; OP; X_1, \ldots, X_n)$ and a word $w \in A^*$. The generalized derivative of α with respect to w is written as α/w and defined as follows:

Definition.

A. For all $\alpha \in EX_A(REG; OP; X_1, \ldots, X_n)$, $\alpha/\lambda = \alpha$.

B. If $w = av$ with $a \in A$ and $v \in A^*$, then $\alpha/w = (\alpha/a)/v$.

C. For all $\alpha \in EX_A(REG; OP; X_1, \ldots, X_n)$ and all $a \in A$, α/a is defined inductively:

    a. *Basis*: If $\alpha = L \in CONST$, then $\alpha/a = L/a = \{u \in A^* \mid au \in L\}$.
        If $\alpha = X_i$ for some $i \in \{1, \ldots, n\}$, then $\alpha/a = X_{i,a}$.

    b. *Inductive step*: If $\alpha = \beta \cup \gamma$, then $\alpha/a = \beta/a \cup \gamma/a$.
        If $\alpha = \bar{\beta}$, then $\alpha/a = \overline{\beta/a}$.
        If $\alpha = L \cdot \beta$ with $L \in CONST$, then if $\lambda \notin L$, $\alpha/a = (L/a) \cdot \beta$, and
        if $\lambda \in L$, $\alpha/a = (L/a) \cdot \beta \cup \beta/a$.

Derivatives of expressions are an analogue to quotients of languages. What distinguishes our derivatives is the fact that variables may occur in them. Note that nothing is said at this point about the terms $X_{s,a}$ that occur in the definition; they are just symbols for now.

Example: Consider the expression $\alpha \in EX_A(REG; OP; X)$ given by

$$\alpha = \overline{a \cdot \bar{X} \cup b^*(a \cdot \bar{X} \cup b \cdot \overline{a^* X})};$$

$$\alpha/a = X \quad \text{(after simplification)},$$

$$\alpha/b = \overline{a/b \cdot \bar{X} \cup b^*/b \cdot (a \cdot \bar{X} \cup b \cdot \overline{a^* X}) \cup (a/b \cdot \bar{X} \cup b/b \cdot \overline{a^* X})}$$

$$= \overline{b^* a \cdot \bar{X} \cup b^* \cdot \overline{a^* X}}.$$

Of importance is the following result:

Proposition 4.9. *If the expression* $\alpha \in EX_A(REG; OP; X_1, \ldots, X_n)$ *has the λ-property, then* $\alpha/a \in EX_A(REG; OP; X_1, \ldots, X_n)$ *for all* $a \in A$.

In other words, none of the symbols $X_{s,a}$ will occur in the generalized derivative α/a.

PROOF.   By structural induction on α.

    a. *Basis*: If $\alpha = L \in CONST$, then $\alpha/a = L/a$, and the claim follows. X_i does not have the λ-property.

    b. *Inductive step*: Let $\alpha = \beta \cup \gamma$, then α has the λ-property iff β and γ have it. Thus,

$$\alpha/a \in EX_A(REG; OP; X_1, \ldots, X_n)$$
$$\text{iff } \beta/a, \gamma/a \in EX_A(REG; OP; X_1, \ldots, X_n).$$

Let $\alpha = \bar{\beta}$; α has the λ-property iff β has it. Thus,

$$\alpha/a \in \mathrm{EX}_A(\mathrm{REG}; \mathrm{OP}; X_1, \ldots, X_n)$$
$$\text{iff } \beta/a \in \mathrm{EX}_A(\mathrm{REG}; \mathrm{OP}; X_1, \ldots, X_n).$$

Let $\alpha = L \cdot \beta$; then α has the λ-property iff $\lambda \notin L$ or β has the λ-property. By definition, we have the following. If $\lambda \notin L$, then $\alpha/a = (L/a) \cdot \beta$, and therefore, we have

$$\alpha/a \in \mathrm{EX}_A(\mathrm{REG}; \mathrm{OP}; X_1, \ldots, X_n)$$
$$\text{iff } \beta \in \mathrm{EX}_A(\mathrm{REG}; \mathrm{OP}; X_1, \ldots, X_n),$$

which is satisfied by assumption.

If $\lambda \in L$, then $\alpha/a = (L/a) \cdot b \cup \beta/a$, and therefore, we have

$$\alpha/a \in \mathrm{EX}_A(\mathrm{REG}; \mathrm{OP}; X_1, \ldots, X_n)$$
$$\text{iff } \beta, \beta/a \in \mathrm{EX}_A(\mathrm{REG}; \mathrm{OP}; X_1, \ldots, X_n).$$

Thus, the claim follows.   □

We now present the algorithm GEN-DERIV$(\alpha_1, \ldots, \alpha_n)$ which constructs, for given expressions $\alpha_1, \ldots, \alpha_n \in \mathrm{EX}_A(\mathrm{REG}; \mathrm{OP}; X_1, \ldots, X_n)$, all possible derivations with respect to all words $w \in A^*$, provided the expressions $\alpha_1, \ldots, \alpha_n$ all have the λ-property. Note that the constants must be REG.

GEN-DERIV$(\alpha_1, \ldots, \alpha_n)$

for all $i = 1, \ldots, n$ and for all $a \in A$ **do**
    { Construct α_i/a;
     Place each α_i/a into a queue Q;
     Place each α_i/a into a look-up table T
    }
                          // By Prop. 4.9, no $X_{i,a}$ occurs in α_j/a.

while Q not empty **do**
    { α=front(Q);
     for all $a \in A$ **do**
        { 1. Construct α/a;
         2. For any $X_{i,a}$ occurring in α/a after Step 1., substitute α_i/a.
           // Since $\alpha_i/a \in \mathrm{EX}_A(\mathrm{REG}; \mathrm{OP}; X_1, \ldots, X_n)$ by Prop. 4.9,
       // the result for α/a must also be in $\mathrm{EX}_A(\mathrm{REG}; \mathrm{OP}; X_1, \ldots, X_n)$
         3. Simplify the expression from Step 2., using the following
           identities:

$$\alpha \cup \alpha = \alpha. \quad \alpha \cup \bar{\alpha} = A^*. \quad\quad \alpha \cup \beta = \beta \cup \alpha.$$
$$\bar{\emptyset} = A^*. \quad\quad \emptyset \cdot \alpha = \alpha \cdot \emptyset = \emptyset. \quad \bar{\bar{\alpha}} = \alpha.$$

           All boolean identities.
           Let the result be β.
         4. If β is not in T, then append β to Q.

    }.

We will show indirectly in the next section that there are finitely many generalized derivatives α/w for any expression $\alpha \in \mathrm{EX}_A(\mathrm{REG}; \mathrm{OP}; X_1, \ldots, X_n)$ (for all $w \in A^*$). Let us assume for now that we know this already. Then, we can obtain n dfa for the solution of the system $X_i = \alpha_i$, $i = 1, \ldots, n$, of boolean language equations. This set of dfa is defined as

$$\mathbb{D}_i = (A, Q, \tau, X_i, F),$$

where

$Q = T$, where T is the look-up table of GEN-DERIV; thus, there is a state in Q for every derivative α/w with $w \in A^*$.

$\tau(q, a) = q/a$ for all $q \in Q$ and all $a \in A$, where q/a is the generalized derivative obtained after executing Steps 1, 2, and 3 of GEN-DERIV.

This leaves the definition of the set F of final states. By Proposition 4.4, it follows that we can determine whether the unique solution for X_i contains the empty word by simply constructing the language $\alpha_i(\emptyset, \ldots, \emptyset)$ and checking whether it contains the empty word. Let us define the set Λ to contain precisely those X_i that contain the empty word. Furthermore, define Λ_i to be $\{\lambda\}$ if $X_i \in \Lambda$ and to be $\emptyset$ otherwise. Then, by the same proposition, we can determine whether β contains λ by determining whether $\beta(\Lambda_1, \ldots, \Lambda_n)$ contains λ even if the expression β does not have the λ-property. Thus, the set of final states of the deterministic finite automaton $\mathbb{D}_i = (A, Q, \tau, X_i, F)$ is defined as

$$F = \{q \in Q \mid \lambda \in q(\Lambda_1, \ldots, \Lambda_n)\}.$$

This concludes the definition of the dfa for the solution.

Example: Consider the equation over the alphabet $A = \{a, b\}$:

$$X = \overline{a \cdot \bar{X} \cup b^*(a \cdot \bar{X} \cup b \cdot \overline{a^* X})}.$$

Let us determine all possible generalized derivatives:

$$X_a = X \cap \bar{\bar{X}} = X;$$
$$X_b = \overline{b^*(a \cdot \bar{X} \cup b \cdot \overline{a^* X}) \cup \overline{a^* X}} = \overline{b^* a \cdot \bar{X} \cup b^* \cdot \overline{a^* X}};$$
$$X_{ba} = \overline{\bar{X} \cup \overline{a^* X} \cup \overline{X_a}} = X \cap a^* X = X;$$
$$X_{bb} = \overline{b^* a \cdot \bar{X} \cup b^* \cdot \overline{a^* X} \cup \bar{X}_b} = \overline{b^* a \cdot \bar{X} \cup b^* \cdot \overline{a^* X}} = X_b.$$

It is now easily verified that X and X_b contain the empty word. Therefore, we have

$$X = a \cdot X \cup b \cdot X_b \cup \lambda,$$
$$X_b = a \cdot X \cup b \cdot X_b \cup \lambda$$

and, from this, one concludes immediately that

$$X = A^*$$

is a solution of the given equation. It is easy to verify by direct substitution that this language is indeed a solution. By Theorem 4.8, this solution must therefore be the only one, since the expression has the λ-property.

4.5 Constructing a Boolean Automaton for the Solution of Boolean Equations

In this section, we finally show how to construct a solution of any system of n boolean equations

$$X_i = \alpha_i \quad \text{for } i = 1, \ldots, n,$$

where all $\alpha_i \in \text{EX}_A(\text{REG}; \text{OP}; X_1, \ldots, X_n)$ for $i = 1, \ldots, n$ have the λ-property. Note that by Theorem 4.8, this solution must then be unique.

We define boolean automata $\mathbb{B}_i = (A, Q, \tau, X_i, F)$ for $i = 1, \ldots, n$; note that only the initial state varies, while all other components of the n boolean automata are identical. The boolean automata have the property that $(L(\mathbb{B}_1), \ldots, L(\mathbb{B}_n))$ is the unique solution of the given system of boolean language equations.

The first step in our construction is replacing each equation $X_i = \alpha_i$ by

$$X_i = \bigcup_{a \in A} a \cdot \alpha_i/a \cup \Lambda_i,$$

where Λ_i was defined in the last section.

Now we can define the components of the automata $\mathbb{B}_i$. The set of states Q of the n boolean automata $\mathbb{B}_i$ contains a state q_β for every subexpression β of any of these expressions α_i/a for $i = 1, \ldots, n$, plus possibly additional states that are required during the construction. Recall that by Proposition 4.9, all the expressions α_i/a are elements of $\text{EX}_A(\text{REG}; \text{OP}; X_1, \ldots, X_n)$ since each α_i has the λ-property. Therefore, we define for $i = 1, \ldots, n$

$$\tau(X_i, a) = q_{\alpha_i/a} \quad \text{for all letters } a \in A$$
$$X_i \in F \quad \text{iff } X_i \in \Lambda.$$

Then we specify the construction of a boolean automaton for each subexpression β of any of the expressions α_i/a for $i = 1, \ldots, n$. This is done by structural induction.

Basis, A: If $\beta = L \in \text{REG}$, then construct a nonreturning nondeterministic finite automaton $\mathbb{B}_L = (A, Q_L, \tau_L, q_L, F_L)$ for the regular language L. An nfa $\mathbb{N} = (A, Q, \tau, q_0, F)$ is called nonreturning iff $q_0 \notin \tau(q_0, aw)$ for all $a \in A$ and all $w \in A^*$. In other words, every transition from the initial state must leave it and no transition may return to it.

Lemma A. *For each language $L \in \text{REG}$, there exists a nonreturning boolean automaton $\mathbb{B}_L = (A, Q_L, \tau_L, q_L, F_L)$ such that $L(\mathbb{B}_L) = L$.*

PROOF. For any regular language, there exists an nfa accepting it. If this nfa is not nonreturning, it is easily converted in one, by adding a new initial state. □

Basis, B: If $\beta = X_i$, then $\mathbb{B}_\beta = (A, Q_\beta, \tau_\beta, q_\beta, F_\beta)$, where

$$Q_\beta = \{q_\beta\} \cup \{q_{\alpha_i/a} \mid a \in A\},$$
$$F_\beta = \{q_\beta \quad \text{if } X_i \in \Lambda \text{ and } F_\beta = \emptyset \quad \text{if } X_i \notin \Lambda,$$
$$\tau_\beta(q_\beta, a) = q_{\alpha_i/a} \quad \text{for all } a \in A.$$

Lemma B. *If there is a boolean automaton* $\mathbb{B}_{X_i}$ *accepting a language, then* $\mathbb{B}_\beta$ *accepts the same language.*

PROOF. By construction. □

Inductive step: Assume for the inductive step that we have boolean automata $\mathbb{B}_\gamma = (A, Q_\gamma, \tau_\gamma, q_\gamma, F_\gamma)$ for γ and $\mathbb{B}_\delta = (A, Q_\delta, \tau_\delta, q_\delta, F_\delta)$ for δ.

Union, C: If $\beta = \gamma \cup \delta$, then $\mathbb{B}_\beta = (A, Q_\beta, \tau_\beta, q_\beta, F_\beta)$, where

$$Q_\beta = (Q_\gamma - \{q_\gamma\}) \cup (Q_\delta - \{q_\delta\}) \cup \{q_\beta\},$$
$$F_\beta = (F_\gamma - \{q_\gamma\}) \cup (F_\delta - \{q_\delta\}) \text{ if } q_\gamma \notin F_\gamma \text{ and } q_\delta \notin F_\delta, \text{ and}$$
$$F_\beta = (F_\gamma - \{q_\gamma\}) \cup (F_\delta - \{q_\delta\}) \cup \{q_\beta\} \text{ otherwise,}$$
$\tau_\beta(q, a)$ for all $a \in A$ and all $q \in Q_\beta$ is defined as follows:

If $q = q_\beta$, then $\tau_\beta(q, a) = \tau_\gamma(q_\gamma, a) \cup \tau_\delta(q_\delta, a)$.
If $q \in Q_\gamma - \{q_\gamma\}$, then $\tau_\beta(q, a) = \tau_\gamma(q, a)$.
If $q \in Q_\delta - \{q_\delta\}$, then $\tau_\beta(q, a) = \tau_\delta(q, a)$.

Lemma C. *If* $\mathbb{B}_\gamma$ *accepts a language* L_γ *and* $\mathbb{B}_\delta$ *accepts a language* L_δ, *then* $\mathbb{B}_\beta$ *accepts the language* $L_\gamma \cup L_\delta$.

PROOF. By construction of $\mathbb{B}_\beta$. □

Complement, D: If $\beta = \bar{\gamma}$, then $\mathbb{B}_\beta = (A, Q_\beta, \tau_\beta, q_\beta, F_\beta)$, where

$$Q_\beta = (Q_\gamma - \{q_\gamma\}) \cup \{q_\beta\},$$
$$F_\beta = F_\gamma \cup \{q_\beta\} \text{ if } q_\gamma \notin F_\gamma, \text{ and } F_\beta = F_\gamma - \{q_\gamma\} \text{ if } q_\gamma \in F_\gamma,$$
$\tau_\beta(q, a)$ for all $a \in A$ and all $q \in Q_\beta$ is defined as follows:

If $q = q_\beta$, then $\tau_\beta(q, a) = \overline{\tau_\gamma(q_\gamma, a)}$.
If $q \in Q_\gamma - \{q_\gamma\}$, then $\tau_\beta(q, a) = \tau_\gamma(q, a)$.

Lemma D. *If* $\mathbb{B}_\gamma$ *accepts a language* L_γ, *then* $\mathbb{B}_\beta$ *accepts the language* $\bar{L}_\gamma$.

PROOF. By construction of $\mathbb{B}_\beta$. □

Left-Concatenation, E: If $\beta = L \cdot \gamma$, then $\mathbb{B}_\beta = (A, Q_\beta, \tau_\beta, q_\beta, F_\beta)$, where

$$Q_\beta = (Q_L - \{q_L\}) \cup (Q_\gamma - \{q_\gamma\}) \cup \{q_\beta\},$$

$F_\beta = F_\gamma$ if $q_\gamma \notin F_\gamma$, $F_\beta = F_L \cup (F_\gamma - \{q_\gamma\})$ if $q_L \notin F_L$ and $q_\gamma \in F_\gamma$, and
$F_\beta = (F_L - \{q_L\}) \cup (F_\gamma - \{q_\gamma\}) \cup \{q_\beta\}$ if $q_L \in F_L$ and $q_\gamma \in F_\gamma$.
$\tau_\beta(q, a)$ for all $a \in A$ and all $q \in Q_\beta$ is defined as follows:

If $q \in F_L - \{q_L\}$, then $\tau_\beta(q, a) = \tau_L(q, a) \cup \tau_\gamma(q_\gamma, a)$.
If $q \in Q_L - (F_L \cup \{q_L\})$, then $\tau_\beta(q, a) = \tau_L(q, a)$.
If $q \in Q_\gamma - \{q_\gamma\}$, then $\tau_\beta(q, a) = \tau_\gamma(q, a)$.
If $q = q_\beta$ and $q_L \in F_L$, then $\tau_\beta(q, a) = \tau_L(q_L, a) \cup \tau_\gamma(q_\gamma, a)$.
If $q = q_\beta$ and $q_L \notin F_L$, then $\tau_\beta(q, a) = \tau_L(q_L, a)$.

Lemma E. *If $\mathbb{B}_L$ accepts the language L and $\mathbb{B}_\gamma$ accepts a language L_γ, then $\mathbb{B}_\beta$ accepts the language $L \cdot L_\gamma$.*

PROOF.   By construction of $\mathbb{B}_\beta$. $\square$

Theorem 4.10. *Let $X_i = \alpha_i$ be a system of boolean language equations for $i = 1, \ldots, n$, where all $\alpha_i \in \mathrm{EX}_A(\mathrm{REG}; \mathrm{OP}; X_1, \ldots, X_n)$ for $i = 1, \ldots, n$ have the λ-property. Then, $(L(\mathbb{B}_1), \ldots, L(\mathbb{B}_n))$ is the unique solution of this system of boolean equations.*

PROOF.   In constructing the boolean automata $\mathbb{B}_i$, five lemmas stated the correctness of the individual steps of the inductive construction. In the case of Lemmas B, C, D, and E, the lemmas assumed that the automata involved accepted languages. At the conclusion of the entire construction of all the $\mathbb{B}_i$, this assumption is obviously satisfied. Therefore, revisiting the inductive construction and collecting the statements of the lemmas in the aggregate yields the claim of the theorem. $\square$

Note that $\mathrm{EX}_A(\mathrm{REG}; \mathrm{OP}; \emptyset)$ is a special subclass of $\mathrm{EX}_A(\mathrm{REG}; \mathrm{OP}; X_1, \ldots, X_n)$; they are also a subclass of the class of extended regular expressions $\mathrm{EX}_A(\mathrm{REG}; \mathrm{OP}'; \emptyset)$ where OP' contains union, unrestricted concatenation, star, and unrestricted complementation. It is well known that expressions in $\mathrm{EX}_A(\mathrm{REG}; \mathrm{OP}'; \emptyset)$ denote regular languages of nonelementary deterministic complexity; i.e., there exist expressions α of length n, where the number of states of the reduced deterministic automaton for $L(\alpha)$ exceeds $2^{2^{\cdot^{\cdot^{2^n}}}}$ for any fixed-sized stack of powers of 2. However, the expressions in $\mathrm{EX}_A(\mathrm{REG}; \mathrm{OP}; \emptyset)$ have elementary complexity, since any such expression of length n denotes a language of boolean complexity $O(n)$ which translates to a deterministic complexity of $2^{2^{O(n)}}$. More specifically, we define the length $|\alpha|$ of an expression α in $\mathrm{EX}_A(\mathrm{REG}; \mathrm{OP}'; \emptyset)$ as follows:

a. If $\alpha = L$, then $|\alpha|$ is one less than the least number of states of a nonreturning nfa accepting L.
b. For all $\beta, \gamma \in \mathrm{EX}_A(\mathrm{REG}; \mathrm{OP}'; \emptyset)$:

$$|\beta \cup \gamma| = |\beta| + |\gamma|,$$
$$|\bar{\beta}| = |\beta|,$$
$$|\beta^*| = |\beta|,$$

$$|\beta \cdot \gamma| = |\beta| + |\gamma|.$$

Note that $\text{EX}_A(\text{REG}; \text{OP}; \emptyset)$ is a subset of $\text{EX}_A(\text{REG}; \text{OP}'; \emptyset)$. Also, we observe that the definition in (a) is consistent with the usual definition of the length of an expression. Usually, one defines the basis only for single letters, in which case the length of a letter is 1—which is consistent with the definition here, as the smallest nfa accepting a letter has two states and is nonreturning. Furthermore, it is known that for any expression β using union, concatenation, and star only and whose length is n by the usual definition, there exists a nonreturning nfa with $n + 1$ states that accepts $L(\beta)$. Then we can state:

Corollary 4.11. *Let* $\alpha \in \text{EX}_A(\text{REG}; \text{OP}; \emptyset)$ *and* $|\alpha| = n$. *Then, the boolean automaton for* α *constructed in this section has exactly* $n+1$ *states.*

PROOF. The construction parallels the definition of length. The basis is obvious (Case A only; Case B cannot occur). As to the induction step (Cases C, D, and E), we observe that for union and concatenation, the noninitial states of the resulting automaton are exactly the union of the noninitial states of the component automata, whereas for complementation, the noninitial states of the two automata are identical. Therefore, each step is additive in the number of noninitial states of the automata occurring. This accounts for the n states. The addition of 1 comes from the fact that each automaton has to have an initial state. $\square$

Corollary 4.12. *Let* $\alpha \in \text{EX}_A(\text{REG}; \text{OP}; \emptyset)$ *and* $|\alpha| = n$. *Then, the deterministic complexity of* $L(\alpha)$ *is at most* $2^{2^n} + 1$.

PROOF. By Corollary 4.11, the boolean automaton for $L(\alpha)$ has $n + 1$ states. This boolean automaton is nonreturning, as can be verified by induction. The basis case is obvious, and each of the inductive steps yields clearly a nonreturning boolean automaton when applied to nonreturning boolean automata. Therefore, the initial state can never occur together with other states in a boolean function; the only boolean function in which it can occur when one constructs a dfa is the function that is the state itself. Therefore, the obvious bound of $2^{2^{n+1}}$ is reduced to $2^{2^n} + 1$. $\square$

We now return to the algorithm GEN-DERIV. We still have to demonstrate that this procedure terminates. This is shown in the following theorem whose proof relies on a correspondence between transitions in the boolean automaton associated with a system of boolean language equations and the generalized derivatives of the expressions involved in the system of equations.

Theorem 4.13. *Let* $X_i = \alpha_i$, $i = 1, \ldots, n$, *be a system of boolean language equations where all* $\alpha_i \in \text{EX}_A(\text{REG}; \text{OP}; X_1, \ldots, X_n)$ *have the* λ-*property,* $i = 1, \ldots, n$. *Then the algorithm GEN-DERIV*$(\alpha_1, \ldots, \alpha_n)$ *terminates in finitely many steps.*

PROOF.   Given a system $X_i = \alpha_i$, $i = 1,\ldots,n$, we construct the corresponding boolean automata $\mathbb{B}_i = (A, Q, \tau, X_i, F)$ for $i = 1,\ldots,n$. We also execute GEN-DERIV$(\alpha_1,\ldots,\alpha_n)$. Then, there exists a correspondence between

$$\alpha_i/w \quad \text{and} \quad \tau(X_i, w) \quad \text{for all words } w \in A^*$$

such that

$$\text{if for any words } u, v \in A^*, \quad \tau(X_i, u) = \tau(X_i, v),$$

then this implies

$$\alpha_i/u = \alpha_i/v.$$

Here, the transitions $\tau(X_i, u)$ are treated as boolean functions and equality is that of boolean functions; equality between two expressions in $\text{EX}_A(\text{REG}; \text{OP}; X_1,\ldots,X_n)$ means that one can be transformed into the other using only the identities listed in Step 3 of the algorithm GEN-DERIV.

This correspondence is established by induction on the length of the words involved. Specifically, the generalized derivative $\alpha_i/\lambda = \alpha_i$ corresponds to the transition $\tau(X_i, \lambda) = X_i$; if a generalized derivative α_i/u (for some word $u \in A^*$) corresponds to a transition $\tau(X_i, v)$ (for some word $v \in A^*$), then for all $\alpha \in A$, $(\alpha_i/u)/a = \alpha_i/ua$ corresponds to $\tau(\tau(X_i, v), a) = \tau(X_i, va)$. That this correspondence satisfies the stated property follows directly by construction of the transition function τ and the definition of generalized derivatives. Since there are only finitely many different functions $\tau(X_i, u)$ for $i = 1,\ldots,n$ and $u \in A^*$, there can also be only finitely many generalized derivatives; hence, the claim follows. $\square$

Example: We will work out an example in detail. Consider the following boolean language equations in the variable X over the alphabet $A = \{a, b\}$:

$$X = \overline{a^* \cdot b * \cdot \overline{a^* b X}}.$$

Clearly, the expression has the λ-property. Let us construct the boolean automaton representing the unique solution of this equation. First, we determine whether the empty word λ will be in the solution:

$$X = \overline{a^* \cdot \overline{b^* \cdot \overline{a^* b \emptyset}}} = A^*;$$

thus, λ must be in the solution. Next we rewrite the equation as

$$X = a \cdot X_a \cup b \cdot X_b \cup \lambda,$$

where

$$X_a = \overline{a^* \cdot \overline{b^* \cdot \overline{a^* b X}}}/a$$
$$= \overline{a^* \cdot \overline{b^* \cdot \overline{a^* b X}}} \cup a^* b X,$$

$$X_b = \overline{a^* \cdot b^* \cdot \overline{\overline{a^*bX}}/b}$$
$$= b^* \cdot \overline{a^*bX} \cup \overline{X}.$$

We now construct automata for the expressions X_a and X_b inductively; we use numbers 10, 11, 12, ... for the states of the various boolean automata. We start with the simplest subexpressions and use them to construct automata for the more complicated ones. Note that 0 represents the boolean function that returns always 0, and 1 represents the boolean function that returns always 1.

First, we let state 10 correspond to X_a and state 11 to X_b; thus, we have

	a	b	
X	10	11	1

Now, we have to apply the construction: We must start with the simplest subexpressions and build up the more complicated ones, until we have the automata for the expressions X_a and X_b.

Let state 12 correspond to a^*b; we obtain the following automaton (recall that it must be nonreturning):

	a	b	
12	13	14	0
13	13	14	0
14	0	0	1

Let state 15 correspond to a^*bX; since we have the transitions for X under a and b, we get the following automaton:

	a	b	
15	13	14	0
13	13	14	0
14	10	11	1

Let state 16 correspond to $\overline{a^*bX}$; we get the following automaton:

	a	b	
16	$\overline{13}$	$\overline{14}$	1
13	13	14	0
14	10	11	1

Let state 17 correspond to b^*; we get the following nonreturning automaton:

	a	b	
17	0	18	1
18	0	18	1

Let state 19 correspond to $b^* \cdot \overline{a^*bX}$; we get the following automaton:

	a	b	
19	$\overline{13}$	$\overline{14}\cup 18$	1
18	$\overline{13}$	$\overline{14}\cup 18$	1
13	13	14	0
14	10	11	1

Let state 20 correspond to $b^* \cdot \overline{a^*bX}$; we get the following automaton:

	a	b	
20	13	$\overline{14}\cup 18$	0
18	$\overline{13}$	$\overline{14}\cup 18$	1
13	13	14	0
14	10	11	1

Let state 21 correspond to a^*; we get the following nonreturning automaton:

	a	b	
21	22	0	1
22	22	0	1

Let state 23 correspond to $a^* \cdot b^* \cdot \overline{a^*bX}$; we get the following automaton:

	a	b	
23	$13\cup 22$	$\overline{14}\cup 18$	0
22	$13\cup 22$	$\overline{14}\cup 18$	0
18	$\overline{13}$	$\overline{14}\cup 18$	1
13	13	14	0
14	10	11	1

Let state 24 correspond to a^*bX; we get the following automaton:

	a	b	
24	25	26	0
25	25	26	0
26	10	11	1

Let state 27 correspond to $a^* \cdot b^* \cdot \overline{a^*bX} \cup a^*bX$; we get the following automaton:

	a	b	
27	$13\cup 22\cup 25$	$\overline{14}\cup 18\cup 26$	0
22	$13\cup 22$	$\overline{14}\cup 18$	0
18	$\overline{13}$	$\overline{14}\cup 18$	1
13	13	14	0
14	10	11	1
25	25	26	0
26	10	11	1

Now it follows that state 10 corresponds to $\overline{a^* \cdot b^* \cdot \overline{a^*bX} \cup a^*bX}$; here is the automaton:

	a	b	
10	$\overline{13 \cup 22 \cup 25}$	$\overline{14} \cup 18 \cup 26$	1
22	$13 \cup 22$	$\overline{14} \cup 18$	0
18	$\overline{13}$	$\overline{14} \cup 18$	1
13	13	14	0
14	10	11	1
25	25	26	0
26	10	11	1

We now must carry out a similar construction for state 11. We obtain for $b^* \cdot \overline{a^* b X}$

	a	b	
29	$\overline{31}$	$\overline{32} \cup 30$	1
30	$\overline{31}$	$\overline{32} \cup 30$	1
31	31	32	0
32	10	11	1

The automaton for $\bar{X}$ is given by

	a	b	
33	$\overline{10}$	$\overline{11}$	0

Therefore, the automaton corresponding to state 11 for the expression $b^* \cdot \overline{a^* b X} \cup \bar{X}$ is

	a	b	
11	$\overline{31} \cup \overline{10}$	$\overline{32} \cup 30 \cup \overline{11}$	1
30	$\overline{31}$	$\overline{32} \cup 30$	1
31	31	32	0
32	10	11	1

We now can write down the entire boolean automaton for the solution of the given equation:

	a	b	
X	10	11	1
10	$\overline{13 \cup 22 \cup 25}$	$\overline{14} \cup 18 \cup 26$	1
11	$\overline{10} \cup \overline{31}$	$\overline{11} \cup 30 \cup \overline{32}$	1
13	13	14	0
14	10	11	1
18	$\overline{13}$	$\overline{14} \cup 18$	1
22	$13 \cup 22$	$\overline{14} \cup 18$	0
25	25	26	0
26	10	11	1
30	$\overline{31}$	$30 \cup \overline{32}$	1
31	31	32	0
32	10	11	1

It is now obvious that the following groups of states are identical and can be replaced by one of them:

States 14, 26, and 32: replaced by 14
States 13, 25, and 31: replaced by 13

This yields, after suitable simplification of the resulting boolean functions, the following boolean automaton for the unique solution of the given equation in X over $\{a, b\}$:

	a	b	
X	10	11	1
10	$\overline{13 \cup 22}$	$\overline{14}$	1
11	$\overline{10} \cup \overline{13}$	$\overline{11} \cup \overline{14} \cup 30$	1
13	13	14	0
14	10	11	1
18	$\overline{13}$	$\overline{14} \cup 18$	1
22	$13 \cup 22$	$\overline{\overline{14} \cup 18}$	0
30	$\overline{13}$	$\overline{14} \cup 30$	1

Carrying out the conversion of a boolean automaton to a deterministic finite automaton (see Section 4.1) yields the following correspondence between dfa states and boolean functions:

dfa states		boolean functions			
1	::	X		2 :: 10	3 :: 11
4	::	$\overline{13 \cup 22}$			
5	::	$\overline{14}$			
6	::	$\overline{10} \cup \overline{13}$			
7	::	$\overline{11} \cup \overline{14} \cup 30$			
8	::	$\overline{10}$			
9	::	$\overline{11}$		10 :: 1	11 :: $13 \cup 22$
12	::	14			
13	::	$\overline{10} \cup \overline{13}$			
14	::	$\overline{11} \cup \overline{14} \cup 30$		15 :: 0	

The resulting dfa is given by:

	a	b	
$\rightarrow$ 1	2	3	1
2	4	5	1
3	6	7	1
4	4	5	1
5	8	9	0
6	10	10	1
7	10	10	1
8	11	12	0
9	12	13	0
10	10	10	1
11	11	12	0
12	2	3	1
13	15	15	0
14	15	15	0
15	15	15	0

To conclude the example, we present the reduced automaton; it can be verified by direct substitution into the given equation that the language accepted by this reduced automaton is indeed a solution:

	a	b	
1	2	3	1
2	2	4	1
3	3	3	1
4	5	6	0
5	5	1	0
6	1	7	0
7	7	7	0

Additional Examples: We give two more examples, but not nearly in as much detail as the last one.

1. Consider the single equation in the variable X over the alphabet $\{a, b\}$:

$$X = a \cdot b \cdot \overline{X} \cup a \cdot \overline{X}.$$

Applying the construction, we obtain the following boolean automaton:

	a	b	
X	10	0	0
10	1	$\overline{11}$	1
11	$\overline{10 \cup 12}$	$\overline{1}$	1
12	$\overline{10}$	1	1

The resulting reduced automaton for the solution in X has five states and accepts precisely

$$a(\lambda \cup (a \cup ba)A^*).$$

2. Consider the system of three equations in the variables X, Y, and Z, over the alphabet $\{a, b\}$:

$$X = a \cdot \bar{X} \cup bb^*Y \cup a^*,$$
$$Y = a \cdot \bar{Z} \cup \lambda,$$
$$Z = \overline{a \cdot \bar{Z} \cup X}.$$

The resulting boolean automaton is then as follows:

	a	b	
X	10	11	1
Y	$\overline{Z}$	0	1
Z	$\overline{\bar{Z} \cup X}$	0	0
10	$\overline{10} \cup 12$	$\overline{11}$	1
11	$\overline{Z}$	13	1
12	12	0	1
13	$\overline{Z}$	13	1

One obtains the following solution:

$$X = (aa)^*(\lambda \cup a \cup bA^*),$$
$$Y = aA^* \cup \lambda,$$
$$Z = \emptyset.$$

4.6   Boolean Equations with Multiple Solution

Theorem 4.6 established a normal form of an expression $\alpha \in \mathrm{EX}_A(\mathrm{REG};$ $\mathrm{OP}; X_1, \dots, X_n)$. The construction in Section 4.5 and Theorem 4.10 yielded regular languages that solved a system of boolean equations $X_i = \alpha_i$ for $i = 1, \dots, n$, provided the α_i have the λ-property. By Theorem 4.8, this solution is unique under the same condition. In this section, we address the question of what happens if the uniqueness criterion is not satisfied. To simplify the results, we will consider a single equation in the variable X.

Theorem 4.14. *Let $X = \alpha$ be a boolean language equation over the alphabet A with $\alpha \in \mathrm{EX}_A(\mathrm{REG}; \mathrm{OP}; X)$ and let $\alpha_1 \cup X \cap \alpha_2 \cup \bar{X} \cap \alpha_3$ be its normal form so that α_1, α_2, and α_3 have the λ-property.*

a. *If $\alpha_2 = \emptyset$ and $\alpha_3 = \emptyset$, then there exists exactly one solution of the equation; this solution is regular.*

b. *If $\alpha_1 = \emptyset$ and $\alpha_2 = \emptyset$, then there does not exist any solution of the equation, unless $\alpha_3 = \emptyset$.*

c. *If $\alpha_3 = \emptyset$, then the class of all solutions is given by*

$$\{L \in \mathrm{REG} \mid L \text{ is the unique solution of}$$
$$X = \alpha_1 \cup T \cap \alpha_2 \text{ for } T \in \mathrm{REG}\}.$$

There exists a minimal solution contained in all solutions and a maximal solution containing all solution of the equation.

d. *If $\alpha_2 = \emptyset$, then there exists at most one solution of the equation. If one exists, it is the unique solution of $X = \alpha_1$.*

PROOF.   Case (a) is covered by Theorems 4.8 and 4.10.

Case (b): We have $X = \bar{X} \cap \alpha_3$; thus, $\bar{X} \supseteq X$ and necessarily $X = \emptyset$, which converts the given equation into $\bar{\emptyset} \cap \alpha_3 = \alpha_3$. It follows that we must have $\emptyset = \alpha_3$, where α_3 has the λ-property. This, however, is impossible unless $\alpha_3 = \emptyset$.

Case (c): If S is a solution of $X = \alpha_1 \cup T \cap \alpha_2$ for some regular language T over A [i.e., $S = \alpha_1(S) \cup T \cap \alpha_2(S)$], then it must also be true that $S = \alpha_1(S) \cup S \cap T \cap \alpha_2(S)$, and, therefore, $S = \alpha_1(S) \cup S \cap \alpha_2(S)$. Conversely, if S is a solution of $X = \alpha_1 \cup X \cap \alpha_2$, then setting $T := S$ proves the claim. The minimal solution $S_{\min}$ is obtained by setting $T = \emptyset$, the maximal, $S_{\max}$, by setting $T = A^*$. Thus, $S_{\min}$ is the unique solution of the equation $X = \alpha_1$ and $S_{\max}$ is the unique solution of $X = \alpha_1 \cup \alpha_2$.

Case (d): If $\alpha_2 = \emptyset$, then $X = \alpha_1 \cup \bar{X} \cap \alpha_3$. Assume now that S is a solution of this equation: $S = \alpha_1(S) \cup \bar{X} \cap \alpha_3(S)$. Therefore, $S \supseteq \bar{S} \cap \alpha_3(S)$. We claim that $\bar{S} \cap \alpha_3(S)$ must be empty; for if there is a word w in $\bar{S} \cap \alpha_3(S)$, then w must also be in $\bar{S}$, and since $S \supseteq \bar{S} \cap \alpha_3(S)$, w must also be in S. This is impossible; therefore, $\bar{S} \cap \alpha_3(S)$ must be empty. Consequently, $S = \alpha_1(S) \cup \bar{S} \cap \alpha_3(S)$ implies that $S = \alpha_1(S)$. Thus, S must be the unique solution of $X = \alpha_1$. It is, of course, possible that no solution exists; this was shown in the proof of Proposition 4.5.   □

Note: Maximal and minimal solutions are guaranteed to exist only for equations in one variable. To see this, consider the following two equations:

$$X = a^* X, \qquad Y = a \cdot \bar{X}.$$

It follows that the minimal solution for X is $\emptyset$, and the maximal is A^*, but this does not hold for Y: the solution for Y that corresponds to $X = \emptyset$ is $Y = aA^*$ and that corresponding to $X = A^*$ is $Y = \emptyset$.

Let us derive a final result about the structure of these multiple solutions. We claim that the lattice under inclusion of the languages T in REG is exactly mirrored in a corresponding lattice of solutions of the equation $X = \alpha_1 \cup X \cap \alpha_2$. Note that the expressions α_1 and α_2 may contain arbitrarily nested complementations. This claim is a direct consequence of the following proposition:

Proposition 4.15. *Let T_1 and T_2 be languages over A. If S_i is the solution of $X = \alpha_1 \cup T_i \cap \alpha_2$ for $i = 1, 2$, then $T_1 \subseteq T_2$ implies $S_1 \subseteq S_2$.*

PROOF.   Indirectly. Assume $T_1 \subseteq T_2$, but that S_1 is not contained in S_2. Let w be a shortest word in $S_1 - S_2$. Therefore, $w \in \alpha_1(S_1) \cup T_1 \cap \alpha_2(S_1)$, but $w \notin \alpha_1(S_2) \cup T_2 \cap \alpha_2(S_2)$. By Proposition 4.4, $w \in \alpha_1(S_1|_{<|w|}) \cup T_1|_{\leq|w|} \cap \alpha_2(S_1|_{<|w|})$ since α_1 and α_2 have the λ-property. However, by definition of w,

$$S_1|_{<|w|} = S_2|_{<|w|},$$

and therefore the only way $w \notin S_2$ is possible is if $w \notin T_2$. This, however, is not possible since, by assumption, $T_1 \subseteq T_2$.   □

4.7   Bibliographical Notes

This chapter is based on a number of papers by the author. In particular, the original definition of boolean automata and boolean language equations was given in [Brzoz/Leiss 80]; this paper also contains the construction of a boolean automaton with n states for the reverse of a regular language with 2^n states as well as an application of boolean language equation to the problem of describing the language defined by a sequential network. Questions related to the complexity of boolean automata are discussed in [Leiss

81b] and [Leiss 85b]; in particular, these papers show that there exist regular languages of deterministic complexity 2^{2^n} whose boolean complexity is n and that there exist regular languages whose deterministic complexity equals their boolean complexity. The basic results for boolean language equations are reported in [Leiss 81a] for boolean equations with unique solutions and in [Leiss 86] for boolean equations with multiple solutions. However, the construction in [Leiss 81a] was not completely specified; the construction given in Section 4.5 is essentially new. [Leiss 86] also discusses the case of systems of several equations with multiple solutions; among other results, it characterizes those systems for which a substitution procedure allows one to reduce uniqueness and existence questions about several equations to those about one equation. However, since this approach does not provide a complete treatment of the uniqueness question for equations with multiple solutions, we elected not to present it here. The interested reader is referred to the original paper [Leiss 86]. Finally, questions related to unrestricted regular expressions are covered in [Leiss 85a]; the construction given in Section 4.5 is related to the construction presented in this paper.

4.8 Problems

1. For the following expressions in $\text{EX}_A(\text{REG}; \text{OP}; X, Y)$, determine whether they have the λ-property:

   a. $a^*(X \cap aY)$ with respect to X, with respect to Y.

   b. $a^* \cap b^* \cdot a \cdot \overline{X}$ with respect to X.

   c. $\overline{\overline{a^* \cdot b^* \cdot c^* \cdot a^*} \cdot \overline{X \cup Y}}$ with respect to X, with respect to Y.

2. Construct equivalent deterministic finite automata for the following boolean automata:

   a. $\mathbb{B} = (\{a, b\}, \{p, q, r\}, \tau, f_0, \emptyset)$, where the initial function f_0 is $p \cup \bar{q} \cup \bar{r}$ and the transition function is given by

	a	b
p	$p \cup q$	r
q	$\bar{p}$	$q \cup \bar{r}$
r	0	p

   b. $\mathbb{B} = (\{a, b, c\}, \{p, q, r\}, \tau, p, \{p, q, r\})$, where the transition function is given by

	a	b	c
p	q	$p \cup q$	p
q	r	q	$q \cup \bar{r}$
r	p	1	r

3. For each of the systems of boolean language equations below, construct
   (α) All generalized derivatives for each of the variables
   (β) The boolean automaton for each of the variables and convert them into dfa

   a. $X = a \cdot a \cdot \overline{X}$, $X = a \cdot a \cdot a \cdot a \cdot \overline{\overline{X}}$, $X = a \cdot a \cdot a \cdot a \cdot a \cdot a \cdot \overline{X}$ over $A = \{a,b\}$.

   b. $X = a \cdot \overline{b \cdot \overline{X}}$, $X = a \cdot b \cdot a \cdot b \cdot \overline{\overline{X}}$, $X = a \cdot b \cdot a \cdot b \cdot a \cdot b \cdot \overline{X}$ over $A = \{a,b\}$.

   c. $X = a^* \cdot b^* \cdot \overline{a^* \cdot a \cdot \overline{X}}$ over the alphabet $A = \{a,b,c\}$.

   d. $X = a \cdot (\overline{Y} \cap (ab)^*) \cup b \cdot (Y \cap (aa \cup b)^*)$, $Y = a \cdot \overline{Y} \cup b \cdot (X \cap \overline{Y})$ over the alphabet $A = \{a,b\}$.

   e. $X = a \cdot \overline{X} \cap a(a \cdot \overline{X} \cup Y)$, $Y = aa \cdot \overline{X} \cup \lambda$ over the one-letter alphabet $A = \{a\}$.

   f. $X = a \cdot X \cup a \cdot \overline{Y}$, $Y = b \cdot Y \cup b \cdot \overline{Z}$, $Z = c \cdot Z \cup c \cdot \overline{X}$ over the alphabet $A = \{a,b,c\}$.

   g. Same as (e), but over the alphabet $A = \{a,b\}$.

   h. Same as (f), but over the alphabet $A = \{a,b,c,d\}$.

4. For the following systems of boolean language equations, determine whether they have (i) any solution, (ii) a unique solution, or (iii) multiple solutions. If a solution exists, determine at least one.

   a. $X = a^* \cdot (a^* X \cap b^* \cdot \overline{Y}$, $Y = b \cdot \overline{X}$.
      Hint: Substitute the expression for Y into that for X, so only one equation must be solved.

   b. $X = \overline{a^*} \cdot (a^* X \cup b^* \cdot \overline{Y}) \cap \overline{a} \cdot (a \cdot \overline{X} \cap b^* Y)$, $Y = \overline{a^* \cdot \breve{X} \cap \overline{b^*} \cdot Y}$.

5
More on Generalized Derivatives

About This Chapter: In Section 4.4, we defined generalized derivatives. This chapter attempts to take derivatives as far as we can. In particular, we define them for the most general expressions considered in this book, namely expressions with union, concatenation, star, and complementation. We formulate the corresponding version of the λ-property and derive several useful properties of these derivatives. Most significantly, it allows us to show that any explicit equation has a unique solution, provided its expression has this λ-property. We conclude the chapter with a discussion of techniques that permit us to determine whether a given word is in the solution, even though that solution may not be regular.

5.1 Derivatives and the λ-Property

Consider the set of expressions $\mathrm{EX}_A(\mathrm{CONST};\mathrm{OP};X_1,\ldots,X_n)$ where the class CONST denotes the constant languages over the alphabet A, $X_1,\ldots,X_n$ denote the variables, and OP contains the following operators:

- Union ($\cup$)
- Complementation ($^-$)
- Unrestricted concatenation ($\cdot$)
- Star ($\star$)

Assume we are given an expression $\alpha \in \mathrm{EX}_A(\mathrm{REG};\mathrm{OP};X_1,\ldots,X_n)$ and a word $w \in A^*$. As in the previous chapter, the generalized derivative of α with respect to w is written as α/w; it is defined below. Note that this definition is completely consistent with the one given in Section 4.4.

Definition.

A. For all $\alpha \in \text{EX}_A(\text{REG}; \text{OP}; X_1, \ldots, X_n)$, $\alpha/\lambda = \alpha$.

B. If $w = av$ with $a \in A$ and $v \in A^*$, then $\alpha/w = (\alpha/a)/v$.

C. For all $\alpha \in \text{EX}_A(\text{REG}; \text{OP}; X_1, \ldots, X_n)$ and all $a \in A$, α/a is defined inductively:

    a. *Basis*: If $\alpha = L \in \text{CONST}$, then $\alpha/a = L/a = \{u \in A^* \mid au \in L\}$.
       If $\alpha = X_i$ for some $i \in \{1, \ldots, n\}$, then $\alpha/a = X_{i,a}$.

    b. *Inductive step*: If $\alpha = \underline{\beta} \cup \gamma$, then $\alpha/a = \beta/a \cup \gamma/a$.
       If $\alpha = \overline{\beta}$, then $\alpha/a = \overline{\beta/a}$.
       If $\alpha = \beta \cdot \gamma$, then if $\lambda \notin \beta$, $\alpha/a = (\beta/a) \cdot \gamma$, and if $\lambda \in \beta$,
       $\alpha/a = (\beta/a) \cdot \gamma \cup \gamma/a$.
       If $\alpha = \beta^*$, then $\alpha/a = (\beta/a) \cdot \beta^*$.

The principal objective of derivatives is to formulate the question of whether a given word is contained in the expression in such a way that this question is reduced to several questions about the containment of other words (usually subwords, preferably proper subwords) in subexpressions, and ultimately the atoms, of the expression.[1] This informal observation is restated formally in Proposition 5.1 below.

Consider an expression α in the variable X; thus, $\alpha(X)$ can be viewed as a function mapping languages to languages. Specifically, $\alpha(L)$ is a language, not an expression; therefore, taking "derivatives" of $\alpha(L)$ is simply taking quotients of that language. However, we could first take derivatives of the *expression* $\alpha(X)$; these would simply be more expressions, except for the presence of the X_a terms mentioned in the basis case of the above definition. Ignoring these special terms for the moment, we could then view the derivative $\alpha(X)/w$ as a function of the variable X (and, of course, the special terms X_a) into which we can substitute specific languages L. Since these concepts are well understood, this leaves us to deal with the problem of the special terms X_a. We will assume the following: If we know that the variable X is eventually specified to be the language L, whenever, during the construction of a derivative, a term X_a occurs, we replace X_a by the quotient L/a. This process will be denoted by $[\alpha(X)/a]_L$ for the letter a. Extending this in the obvious way to words w yields $[\alpha(X)/w]_L$. Note that $[\alpha(X)/w]_L$ may still contain the variable X; thus, it does still make sense to replace all occurring variables in $[\alpha(X)/w]_L$ by L. The generalization of this process for more than one variable is obvious. Now we can state:

Proposition 5.1. *Let* $\alpha(X_1, \ldots, X_n) \in \text{EX}_A(\text{CONST}; \text{OP}; X_1, \ldots, X_n)$. *For any word* $w \in A^*$, *the following holds: For all languages* $L_1, \ldots, L_n$

---

[1]It is true that derivatives are traditionally defined only if no variables occur in the expression; however, Chapter 4 has indicated quite clearly that variables play an important role in our expressions.

over A,

$$w \in \alpha(L_1, \ldots, L_n) \quad \textit{iff } \lambda \in [\alpha(X_1, \ldots, X_n)/w]_{(L_1, \ldots, L_n)}(L_1, \ldots, L_n).$$

PROOF.   By induction on w. Clearly, the statement is true for $w = \lambda$. Hence, assume that it is true for words of length n; we show it is also true for words of length $n + 1$. This, however, is obvious by Part B of the definition of generalized derivatives.   □

We now come to a generalization of the λ-property for these expressions. Note that concatenation is now unrestricted. Recall that in Section 4.2, we observed that determining whether a word w is contained in $\alpha(L_1, \ldots, L_n)$ depends only on those words in the L_i that are no longer than w; moreover, if the expression has the λ-property, it depends only on strictly shorter words. We want the same to hold for the more general expressions studied in this chapter. The first part is quite obviously true:

Proposition 5.2. *Let $\alpha \in \mathrm{EX}_A(\mathrm{CONST}; \mathrm{OP}; X_1, \ldots, X_n)$. Then, for any languages $L_1, \ldots, L_n$ over A and any word $w \in A^*$,*

$$w \in \alpha(L_1, \ldots, L_n) \quad \textit{iff } w \in \alpha(L_1|_{\leq |w|}, \ldots, L_n|_{\leq |w|}).$$

PROOF.   By induction on the structure of the expression α. The basis is clearly satisfied, since for any variable X_i, the language L_i is substituted.

If $\alpha = \beta \cup \gamma$, then $w \in \alpha(L_1, \ldots, L_n)$ iff $w \in \beta(L_1, \ldots, L_n)$ or $w \in \gamma(L_1, \ldots, L_n)$, which, by inductive assumption, is true iff $w \in \beta(L_1|_{\leq |w|}, \ldots, L_n|_{\leq |w|})$ or $w \in \gamma(L_1|_{\leq |w|}, \ldots, L_n|_{\leq |w|})$.

If $\alpha = \overline{\beta}$, then $w \in \alpha(L_1, \ldots, L_n)$ iff $w \notin \beta(L_1, \ldots, L_n)$, which by inductive assumption is true iff $w \notin \beta(L_1|_{\leq |w|}, \ldots, L_n|_{\leq |w|})$.

If $\alpha = \beta \cdot \gamma$, then $w \in \alpha(L_1, \ldots, L_n)$ iff $u \in \beta(L_1, \ldots, L_n)$ and $v \in \gamma(L_1, \ldots, L_n)$ for some words u and v such that $w = uv$, which, by inductive assumption, is true iff $u \in \beta(L_1|_{\leq |w|}, \ldots, L_n|_{\leq |w|})$ and $v \in \gamma(L_1|_{\leq |w|}, \ldots, L_n|_{\leq |w|})$.

If $\alpha = \beta^*$, then $w \in \alpha(L_1, \ldots, L_n)$ iff there exists a nonnegative integer t such that $w = v_1 \cdots v_t$ and all $v_i \in \beta(L_1, \ldots, L_n)$, which, by inductive assumption, is true iff for all $i = 1, \ldots, n$, $v_i \in \beta(L_1|_{\leq |w|}, \ldots, L_n|_{\leq |w|})$.   □

Let us now define the λ-property in a way that the second part of Proposition 4.4 also holds. Consider an expression $\alpha \in \mathrm{EX}_A(\mathrm{CONST}; \mathrm{OP}; X_1, \ldots, X_n)$, where OP, as throughout this entire chapter, consists of

- Union
- Complementation
- Concatenation
- Star

The λ-property for such an expression α is defined below; note again that our definition is completely compatible with that given in Chapter 4. Before we do this, however, we need another definition: We say $\lambda \in \alpha(X_1, \ldots, X_n)$ (or $\lambda \in \alpha$, for short) iff there exist languages $L_1, \ldots, L_n$ such that $\lambda \in \alpha(L_1, \ldots, L_n)$. This definition is needed since we now have arbitrary concatenation, whereas before we only dealt with left-concatenation in which the left operand is always a constant language. Note that according to this definition,

$$\lambda \notin \overline{X} \cdot X,$$

since it is not possible to find a language L such that $\overline{L} \cdot L$ contains the empty word, but we have $\lambda \in \overline{X}$ and $\lambda \in X$ since for each of these two expressions we can find a language that satisfies the requirement (of course, this will not be the same language for both expressions).

For any expression $\alpha \in \text{EX}_A(\text{CONST}; \text{OP}; X_1, \ldots, X_n)$, it is possible to determine whether $\lambda \in \alpha$, since by Proposition 5.2, $\lambda \in \alpha(L_1, \ldots, L_n)$ iff $\lambda \in \alpha(L_1|_{\leq 0}, \ldots, L_n|_{\leq 0})$. Thus, in the worst case, one may have to test systematically for each variable X_i, the two possible languages $\{\lambda\}$ or $\emptyset$ which results in 2^n possible tests. If any one of them yields $\lambda \in \alpha(L_1|_{\leq 0}, \ldots, L_n|_{\leq 0})$, we know that $\lambda \in \alpha$; if none does, then $\lambda \notin \alpha$.

First, we define the λ-property of α with respect to the variable X_i by induction on the structure of α:

a. *Basis*: If $\alpha \in \text{CONST}$, then α has the λ-property with respect to X_i.

If $\alpha = X_j$ for $j \neq i$, then α has the λ-property with respect to X_i.

If $\alpha = X_i$, then α does not have the λ-property with respect to X_i.

b. *Inductive step*: Let $\alpha, \beta \in \text{EX}_A(\text{CONST}; \text{OP}; X_1, \ldots, X_n)$.

- $\alpha \cup \beta$ has the λ-property with respect to X_i iff both α and β have the λ-property with respect to X_i.
- $\overline{\alpha}$ has the λ-property with respect to X_i iff α has the λ-property with respect to X_i.
- $\alpha \cdot \beta$ has the λ-property with respect to X_i iff $\lambda \notin \alpha$ or $\lambda \notin \beta$ or at least one of α and β has the λ-property with respect to X_i.
- α^* has the λ-property with respect to X_i iff α has the λ-property with respect to X_i.

Then we say that $\alpha \in \text{EX}_A(\text{CONST}; \text{OP}; X_1, \ldots, X_n)$ has the λ-property iff α has the λ-property with respect to X_i for all $i = 1, \ldots, n$.

Proposition 5.3. *Let $\alpha \in \text{EX}_A(\text{CONST}; \text{OP}; X_1, \ldots, X_n)$. Then, for any languages $L_1, \ldots, L_n$ over A and any word $w \in A^*$,*

$$w \in \alpha(L_1, \ldots, L_n) \quad \textit{iff } w \in \alpha(L_1|_{< |w|}, \ldots, L_n|_{< |w|}).$$

if α has the λ-property.

In other words, if the expression has the λ-property, then determining whether a word w is contained in $\alpha(L_1, \ldots, L_n)$ depends only on those words in the L_i that are strictly shorter than w.

PROOF.   By induction on the structure of α. The basis reduces to the case $\alpha \in$ CONST which is trivially satisfied, since in the other case ($\alpha = X_i$), the expression does not have the λ-property.

If $\alpha = \beta \cup \gamma$, then both α and β must have the λ-property; therefore, $w \in \alpha(L_1, \ldots, L_n)$ iff $w \in \beta(L_1, \ldots, L_n)$ or $w \in \gamma(L_1, \ldots, L_n)$, which by inductive assumption is true iff $w \in \beta(L_1|_{<|w|}, \ldots, L_n|_{<|w|})$ or $w \in \gamma(L_1|_{<|w|}, \ldots, L_n|_{<|w|})$.

If $\alpha = \overline{\beta}$, then $w \in \alpha(L_1, \ldots, L_n)$ iff $w \notin \beta(L_1, \ldots, L_n)$, which by inductive assumption is true iff $w \notin \beta(L_1|_{<|w|}, \ldots, L_n|_{<|w|})$.

If $\alpha = \beta \cdot \gamma$, then, by assumption, $\alpha = \beta \cdot \gamma$ has the λ-property iff $\lambda \notin \beta$ or $\lambda \notin \gamma$ or at least one of β and γ has the λ-property. Consequently, $w \in \alpha(L_1, \ldots, L_n)$ iff $u \in \beta(L_1, \ldots, L_n)$ and $v \in \gamma(L_1, \ldots, L_n)$ for some words u and v such that $w = uv$ and either $|u| > 0$ or $|v| > 0$ or at least one of β and γ have the λ-property. Now, in the first two cases ($|u| > 0$ or $|v| > 0$), the claim follows since both u and v must be shorter than w. In the other cases, we first observe that by Proposition 5.1, we know that $u \in \beta(L_1|_{\leq|w|}, \ldots, L_n|_{\leq|w|})$ and $v \in \gamma(L_1|_{\leq|w|}, \ldots, L_n|_{\leq|w|})$; however, since at least one of β and γ has the λ-property, it follows by inductive hypothesis that $u \in \beta(L_1|_{<|w|}, \ldots, L_n|_{<|w|})$ or $v \in \gamma(L_1|_{<|w|}, \ldots, L_n|_{<|w|})$. However, since $w = uv$ must hold, the other of these two statements must also be true.

If $\alpha = \beta^*$, then $w \in \alpha(L_1, \ldots, L_n)$ iff there exists a nonnegative integer t such that $w = v_1 \cdots \cdot v_t$ and all $v_i \in \beta(L_1, \ldots, L_n)$, which, by inductive assumption, is true iff for all $i = 1, \ldots, n$, $v_i \in \beta(L_1|_{<|w|}, \ldots, L_n|_{<|w|})$. $\square$

Let us look at an example to illustrate this definition. Consider the expression over the alphabet $A = \{a, b\}$,

$$\alpha(X) = \overline{X} \cdot a \cdot \overline{X}.$$

This expression has the λ-property. It is intuitively clear that the question of whether a word w is in $\alpha(L)$ for any language L depends only those words in L that are shorter than w. However, one must be aware that the process of taking derivatives is no longer as easy as it was in Chapter 4. To explain why this is the case, consider α/a; by definition,

$$\alpha/a = \overline{X_a} \cdot a \cdot \overline{X} \cup \overline{X}$$

since $\lambda \in \overline{X}$ because $\lambda \notin X$. This suggests that even if the λ-property holds, a derivative with respect to a word of length 1 depends on X_a; this could never occur with the previous (more restrictive) definition of the λ-property. However, the important observation here is the following:

Because the λ-property holds for the expression, we can determine on the basis of derivatives with respect to strictly shorter words whether the empty word λ is contained in the derivative.

In our example, we know that the empty word is not in α [since it does possess the λ-property, we merely compute $\alpha(\emptyset)$ and determine whether λ is contained in it]; consequently, we can conclude that α/a does contain λ: λ is not contained in $\overline{X_a} \cdot a \cdot \overline{X}$ but it is in the second term, $\overline{X}$, because it is not in X. In fact, in this way, one can determine for all derivatives α/w, with respect to any word $w \in A^*$, whether λ is contained in it or not; this in spite of the fact that each α/w contains a term X_w [where X_w for words of length greater than 1 is defined by $(X_w)_a = X_{wa}$].

5.2 Existence and Uniqueness of Solutions

We will prove two major results in this section; the first (Theorem 5.4) establishes the existence of a solution, and the second (Theorem 5.5) the uniqueness of that solution. Note that nothing is said about what kind of constant languages may occur; therefore, the construction of the solutions will typically not be effective.

Theorem 5.4. *Consider the system of language equations*

$$X_i = \alpha_i \quad \text{with } \alpha_i \in \text{EX}_A(\text{CONST}; \text{OP}; X_1, \ldots, X_n), \; i = 1, \ldots, n.$$

If α_i has the λ-property for all $i = 1, \ldots, n$, then there always exists a solution of this system.

PROOF. If the α_i have the λ-property for all $i = 1, \ldots, n$, then we can determine whether λ must be contained in any solution by computing $\alpha_i(\emptyset, \ldots, \emptyset)$ and checking whether the empty word is contained in this language. (Note that this test may not be constructive since we did not specify what CONST is.) Because of the λ-property, we can successively determine whether α_i/w contains λ based on the information about whether α_i/v contains λ for all words v shorter than w. This uniquely determines whether α_i/w contains λ. Then, the solution of the system $X_i = \alpha_i$, $i = 1, \ldots, n$, is simply

$$(X_1, \ldots, X_n) = (S_1, \ldots, S_n),$$

where S_i is defined as

$$S_i = \{w \in A^* \mid \lambda \in \alpha_i/w\}. \qquad \square$$

The second major result of this chapter is stated in the next theorem.

Theorem 5.5. *Consider the system of language equations*

$$X_i = \alpha_i \quad \text{with } \alpha_i \in \text{EX}_A(\text{CONST}; \text{OP}; X_1, \ldots, X_n), \; i = 1, \ldots, n.$$

If α_i has the λ-property for all $i = 1, \ldots, n$, then there exists at most one solution of this system.

PROOF.   Assume there are two different solutions, namely

$$(X_1, \ldots, X_n) = (S_1, \ldots, S_n) \quad \text{and} \quad (X_1, \ldots, X_n) = (T_1, \ldots, T_n)$$

such that

$$S_i = \alpha_i(S_1, \ldots, S_n) \quad \text{and} \quad T_i = \alpha_i(T_1, \ldots, T_n)$$

and there exists a $j \in \{1, \ldots, n\}$ with $S_j \neq T_j$. Let v be a shortest word in the difference,

$$v \in \bigcup_{i=1,\ldots,n} (S_i - T_i) \cup (T_i - S_i).$$

Without loss of generality, $v \in S_t - T_t$ for some t. Thus,

$$v \in S_t = \alpha_t(S_1, \ldots, S_n), \quad \text{but } v \notin T_t = \alpha_t(T_1, \ldots, T_n).$$

However, since α_t has the λ-property, $v \in \alpha_t(S_1, \ldots, S_n)$ implies by Proposition 5.3 that $v \in \alpha_t(S_1, \ldots, S_n)$ iff $v \in \alpha_t(S_1|_{<|w|}, \ldots, S_n|_{<|w|})$. By the minimality of v, all these words must be also in the T_i's. Thus,

$$v \in \alpha_t(T_1, \ldots, T_n)$$

and since $T_t = \alpha_t(T_1, \ldots, T_n)$, $v \in T_t$, in contradiction to the assumption. Thus, two different solutions cannot exist.   □

It should be obvious that the determination of a solution in the proof of Theorem 5.4 is not constructive, since there is no assurance that the process of taking derivatives will terminate. In fact, we had this problem even in the much more restrictive setting of Chapter 4, where we had to resort to an argument that was outside of the realm of derivatives in order to prove that the process terminated. In our more general setting, it makes no sense to expect that the process would end in finitely many steps, as it is well known that the solutions of the equations we are dealing with are not necessarily regular (just consider the equation $X = aXb \cup \lambda$), but termination in finitely many steps necessarily implies the regularity of the solution.

The two theorems are important results. However, it is necessary to realize that they do not hold for equations other than explicit ones. In other words, if we are given explicit equations where the expressions on the right have the λ-property, Theorems 5.4 and 5.5 guarantee the existence of a unique solution of the system of equations; if the equations are not explicit (i.e., implicit or two-sided), then the fact that the expressions involved in the equations have the λ-property does not guarantee existence nor uniqueness of solutions.

To see that existence is not guaranteed, consider the following implicit equation in the variable X over the alphabet $A = \{a\}$:

$$a \cup aa = aa^*X.$$

Clearly, aa^*X has the λ-property; however, the equation does not have a solution. In a later chapter, we will give the complete theory on how to solve these equations. That this specific one has no solution follows directly if one observes that the left-hand side (the constant) is nonempty; thus, X must be nonempty as well. Now, however, the fact that for any nonempty X, the right-hand side is infinite while the left-hand side is finite yields a contradiction to the assumption that there exists a solution. For two-sided language equations, an analogous example is the equation

$$(aa \cup ab)X = aaX,$$

where both expressions have the λ-property but no solution exists.

To see that uniqueness of a solution is not guaranteed, consider the implicit equation

$$aa^* = aa^*X.$$

The expression has the λ-property, but there exist infinitely many solutions: For any language T over $\{a\}$, the language $\{\lambda\} \cup T$ is a solution. For a two-sided language equation, consider

$$aX \cup \lambda = aa^*X \cup \lambda,$$

where it is easily verified that a^ta^* is a solution for any $t \geq 0$, even though both expressions have the λ-property.

5.3   Examples

We show several examples to illustrate these concepts. In general, there will be infinitely many different derivatives. However, sometimes it is possible to guess from the first few (or not so few!) derivatives what the solution might be, as in the first example. In other cases, one might in fact be able to derive a representation of all derivatives from which one can then determine the solution.

1. Recall the expression over the alphabet $A = \{a, b\}$:

$$\alpha(X) = \overline{X} \cdot a \cdot \overline{X}.$$

This expression has the λ-property. We know already that

$$X_a = \overline{X_a} \cdot a \cdot \overline{X} \cup \overline{X} \quad \text{since } \lambda \in \overline{X} \text{ because } \lambda \notin X.$$

We can conclude the following: $:: \lambda \in X_a$

Let us determine the next few derivatives:

$$X_b = \overline{X_b} \cdot a \cdot \overline{X} \qquad\qquad\qquad :: \lambda \in X_b$$
$$X_{aa} = \overline{X_{aa}} \cdot a \cdot \overline{X} \cup \overline{X_a} \quad \text{since } \lambda \notin \overline{X_a} \qquad :: \lambda \notin X_{aa}$$
$$X_{ab} = \overline{X_{ab}} \cdot a \cdot \overline{X} \cup \overline{X_b} \qquad\qquad :: \lambda \notin X_{ab}$$
$$X_{ba} = \overline{X_{ba}} \cdot a \cdot \overline{X} \cup \overline{X} \quad \text{since } \lambda \in \overline{X_b} \qquad :: \lambda \in X_{ba}$$
$$X_{bb} = \overline{X_{bb}} \cdot a \cdot \overline{X} \qquad\qquad\qquad :: \lambda \notin X_{bb}$$
$$X_{aaa} = \overline{X_{aaa}} \cdot a \cdot \overline{X} \cup \overline{X_{aa}} \quad \text{since } \lambda \in \overline{X_{aa}} \qquad :: \lambda \in X_{aaa}$$
$$X_{aab} = \overline{X_{aab}} \cdot a \cdot \overline{X} \cup \overline{X_{ab}} \qquad\qquad :: \lambda \notin X_{aab}$$
$$X_{aba} = \overline{X_{aba}} \cdot a \cdot \overline{X} \cup \overline{X_{ba}} \quad \text{since } \lambda \notin \overline{X_{ab}} \qquad :: \lambda \notin X_{aba}$$
$$X_{abb} = \overline{X_{abb}} \cdot a \cdot \overline{X} \cup \overline{X_{bb}} \qquad\qquad :: \lambda \in X_{abb}$$
$$X_{baa} = \overline{X_{baa}} \cdot a \cdot \overline{X} \cup \overline{X_a} \quad \text{since } \lambda \notin \overline{X_{ba}} \qquad :: \lambda \notin X_{baa}$$
$$X_{bab} = \overline{X_{bab}} \cdot a \cdot \overline{X} \cup \overline{X_b} \qquad\qquad :: \lambda \in X_{bab}$$
$$X_{bba} = \overline{X_{bba}} \cdot a \cdot \overline{X} \cup \overline{X} \quad \text{since } \lambda \in \overline{X_{bb}} \qquad :: \lambda \in X_{bba}$$
$$X_{bbb} = \overline{X_{bbb}} \cdot a \cdot \overline{X} \qquad\qquad\qquad :: \lambda \notin X_{bbb}$$

It appears that the principle determining whether a derivative X_w contains the empty word is the number of a's in w. This suggests the following language as a possible solution:

$$b^*a(ab^*a \cup b)^*.$$

By direct substitution into the given equation, one can verify that this language is indeed a solution. Thus, by Theorem 5.5, it is the only one.

2. Consider the following equation in X over the one-letter alphabet $A = \{a\}$:

$$X = a(\overline{X})^* \qquad\qquad\qquad :: \lambda \notin X$$

We obtain

$$X_a = (\overline{X})^* \qquad\qquad\qquad :: \lambda \in X_a$$
$$X_{aa} = \overline{X_a} \cdot (\overline{X})^*, \qquad\qquad\qquad :: \lambda \notin X_{aa}$$
$$X_{aaa} = \overline{X_{aa}} \cdot (\overline{X})^* \quad \lambda \notin \overline{X_a} \qquad :: \lambda \in X_{aaa}$$
$$X_{aaaa} = \overline{X_{aaa}} \cdot (\overline{X})^* \quad \lambda \in \overline{X_{aa}} \qquad :: \lambda \notin X_{aaaa}$$

It follows by induction that the derivatives are defined as follows:

$$X_{a^{2i}} = \bigcup_{j=1,\dots,i} \overline{X_{a^{2j-1}}} \cdot (\overline{X})^* \quad \text{for } i \geq 1 \qquad :: \lambda \notin X_{a^{2i}}$$

$$X_{a^{2i+1}} = \bigcup_{j=1,\dots,i} \overline{X_{a^{2j}}} \cdot (\overline{X})^* \quad \text{for } i \geq 1 \qquad :: \lambda \in X_{a^{2i+1}}$$

and from this representation one concludes that

$$a(aa)^*$$

is the (unique) solution. This can also be verified though direct substitution into the equation.

Let us now consider the same equation, but over the alphabet $A = \{a, b\}$. In addition to the derivatives above, we obtain also the following:

$$X_b = \emptyset \qquad\qquad\qquad\qquad\qquad\qquad :: \lambda \notin X_b$$
$$X_{ab} = \overline{X}_b \cdot (\overline{X})^* = A^* \qquad\qquad\qquad :: \lambda \in X_{aa}$$

and in general

$$X_{a^{2i}b} = \emptyset \qquad \text{for all } i \geq 0 \qquad :: \lambda \notin X_{a^{2i}b}$$
$$X_{a^{2i+1}b} = A^* \qquad \text{for all } i \geq 0 \qquad :: \lambda \in X_{a^{2i+1}b}$$

It follows that the (unique) solution is given by

$$(aa)^*(\lambda \cup bA^*).$$

3. Consider the following equation in X over the one-letter alphabet $A = \{a\}$:

$$X = a(\overline{X} \cdot a)^* \qquad\qquad\qquad\qquad :: \lambda \notin X$$

We obtain:

$$X_a = (\overline{X} \cdot a)^* \qquad\qquad\qquad\qquad\qquad :: \lambda \in X_a$$
$$X_{aa} = \overline{X_a} \cdot a \cdot (\overline{X} \cdot a)^* \cup (\overline{X} \cdot a)^*, \lambda \in \overline{X} \qquad :: \lambda \in X_{aa}$$
$$X_{aaa} = \overline{X_{aa}} \cdot a \cdot (\overline{X} \cdot a)^* \cup \overline{X_a} \cdot a \cdot (\overline{X} \cdot a)^* \cup (\overline{X} \cdot a)^* \quad :: \lambda \in X_{aaa}$$
$$X_{aaaa} = \overline{X_{aaa}} \cdot a \cdot (\overline{X} \cdot a)^* \cup \overline{X_{aa}} \cdot a \cdot (\overline{X} \cdot a)^*$$
$$\cup \overline{X_a} \cdot a \cdot (\overline{X} \cdot a)^* \cup (\overline{X} \cdot a)^* \qquad\qquad :: \lambda \in X_{aaaa}$$

It follows by induction that the derivatives are defined

$$X_{a^i} = \bigcup_{j=1,\ldots,i-1} \overline{X_{a^j}} \cdot a \cdot (\overline{X} \cdot a)^* \cup (\overline{X} \cdot a)^* \quad \text{for } i \geq 1 \quad :: \lambda \in X_{a^i}$$

Thus, the (unique) solution is

$$aa^*.$$

This can also be verified though direct substitution into the equation. Let us now solve the given equation, but over the alphabet $A = \{a, b\}$:

$$X = a(\overline{X} \cdot a)^* \qquad\qquad\qquad\qquad :: \lambda \notin X$$

In addition to the derivatives listed above, we obtain the following:

$$X_b = \emptyset \qquad\qquad\qquad\qquad\qquad\qquad :: \lambda \notin X_b$$
$$X_{ab} = \overline{X_b} \cdot a \cdot (\overline{X} \cdot a)^* = A^* a \cdot (\overline{X} \cdot a)^* = A^* a \qquad :: \lambda \notin X_{ab}$$

since everything must end in a.

Furthermore, we get the general representation

$$X_{a^i b} = \bigcup_{j=1,\ldots,i-1} \overline{X_{a^j a}} \cdot a \cdot (\overline{X} \cdot a)^* \cup \overline{X_b} \cdot a \cdot (\overline{X} \cdot a)^*$$

$$= \left(\bigcup_{j=1,\ldots,i-1} \overline{X_{a^j a}} \cup \overline{X_b} \right) \cdot a \cdot (\overline{X} \cdot a)^*$$

$$= \left(\bigcup_{j=1,\ldots,i-1} \overline{X_{a^j a}} \cup A^* \right) \cdot a \cdot (\overline{X} \cdot a)^* = A^* a.$$

Thus, the unique solution of the equation over the alphabet $A = \{a, b\}$ is given by

$$a(a \cup bb^* a)^*.$$

We remark that a very small change in the equation, namely adding the empty word to this equation to yield

$$X = a(\overline{X} \cdot a)^* \cup \lambda \qquad\qquad :: \lambda \in X$$

gives us very different solutions from those for the equation studied above.

If we determine the unique solution of the present equation over the alphabet $A = \{a\}$, it turns out to be given by

$$\lambda \cup a \cup a^4 \cup a^5 \cup a^7 a^*.$$

Over the alphabet $A = \{a, b\}$, the solution is much more complicated; it is specified by the following dfa:

	a	b	
1	2	3	1
2	4	5	1
3	3	3	0
4	6	7	0
5	8	5	0
6	9	10	0
7	2	7	0
8	8	5	1
9	11	5	1
10	11	10	0
11	12	5	1
12	8	10	0

Constructing the derivatives for this equation for $A = \{a, b\}$ and deriving from them this automaton is a very involved process.

5.4 Techniques for Determining Whether a Word Is in a Solution

Techniques for Determining Whether a Word Is in a Solution We will discuss two different techniques that allow one to determine whether a given word is in the solution of a system of language equations. We will assume the system of language equations $X_i = \alpha_i$ with $\alpha_i \in \text{EX}_A(\text{CONST}; \text{OP}; X_1, \ldots, X_n)$, $i = 1, \ldots, n$, where OP contains union, complementation, (unrestricted) concatenation, and star. The class of constant languages is arbitrary; however, if it is too general, some of our ostensibly effective constructions may be no longer effective, as we will indicate below.

We will assume throughout this section that for all $i = 1, \ldots, n$, α_i has the λ-property. In particular, this guarantees us that there always exists a unique solution of the given system of equations (by Theorems 5.4 and 5.5).

The first technique is the derivative technique. It is clear that under the stated assumptions, for any given word $x \in A^*$, we can first determine the derivative α_i/w and then whether $\lambda \in \alpha_i/w$. Since the solution is unique, this will uniquely determine whether w is in the language that solves for X_i. It is important to note that the constant languages involved in the equations have some influence on the effectiveness of this process. Specifically, we must be able to take the quotient of these languages and test whether the languages that occur during this process contain the empty word. If these two operations are not effective, the overall construction is not effective.

The second technique does not have this defect. Its theoretical basis is provided by Proposition 5.3. It can be formulated as follows:

Suppose we are given a word w and want to determine whether w is contained in the unique solution of the system of equations $X_i = \alpha_i$ with $\alpha_i \in \text{EX}_A(\text{CONST}; \text{OP}; X_1, \ldots, X_n)$, $i = 1, \ldots, n$. Let $|w| = m$.

1. For $i = 1, \ldots, n$, define $S_{i,0} := \alpha_i(\emptyset, \ldots, \emptyset) \cup \{\lambda\}$.
2. For $j = 1, \ldots, m$ do
   for $i = 1, \ldots, n$ do
   $$S_{i,j} := \alpha_i(S_{1,j-1}, \ldots, S_{n,j-1}) \cap A* \big|_{\leq j}.$$
3. w is in the solution for X_i of the system iff $w \in \bar{S}_{i,m}$.

The correctness of this algorithm is fairly obvious. By Proposition 5.3, whether a word of length j is in α_i is exclusively determined by words of length $j-1$ or less (recall that the α_i have the λ-property). This, however, is carried out systematically by this technique. We note that all intermediate languages occurring in the evaluation of $\alpha_i(S_{1,j-1}, \ldots, S_{n,j-1}) \cap A^* \big|_{\leq j}$ can be restricted to that subset of their words that are no longer than j.

An interesting aspect of this second technique is that it is effective provided we can determine whether or not a given word is in a constant language. Thus, the recursive languages are fully acceptable in this technique. Since only words of length at most m in the constant languages may affect the question of whether w is in the solution, we can simply determine for each of the finitely many words in $A^*|_{\leq m}$, whether it is in each of the constant languages involved in the equations. Then, we may replace each constant language L by $L \cap A^*|_{\leq m}$ and proceed with our constructions which are now obviously effective since each of the new constants is finite and, therefore, regular.

We will illustrate this technique with the equation $X = \alpha(X)$ over the alphabet $A = \{a, b\}$, where α is given by

$$\alpha = \overline{X} \cdot a \cdot \overline{X} \cdot b \cdot \overline{X}.$$

We first determine S_0:

$$S_0 = \alpha(\emptyset|_{\leq 0})|_{\leq 0} = (\{\lambda\} \cdot a \cdot \{\lambda\} \cdot b \cdot \{\lambda\})|_{\leq 0} = \{ab\}|_{\leq 0} = \emptyset.$$

Now, we continue computing S_1, S_2, S_3, and S_4:

$$S_1 = \alpha(\emptyset|_{\leq 0})|_{\leq 1} = (\{\lambda\} \cdot a \cdot \{\lambda\} \cdot b \cdot \{\lambda\})|_{\leq 1} = \{ab\}|_{\leq 1} = \emptyset$$

$$S_2 = \alpha(\emptyset|_{\leq 1})|_{\leq 2} = (\{\lambda, a, b\} \cdot a \cdot \{\lambda, a, b\} \cdot b \cdot \{\lambda, a, b\})|_{\leq 2} = \{ab\}$$

$$S_3 = \alpha(\{ab\}|_{\leq 2})|_{\leq 3} = (\{\lambda, a, b, aa, ba, bb\} \cdot a \cdot \{\lambda, a, b, aa, ba, bb\}$$
$$\cdot b \cdot \{\lambda, a, b, aa, ba, bb\})|_{\leq 3}$$
$$= \{ab, aab, aba, abb, bab\},$$

$$S_4 = \alpha(\{ab, aab, aba, abb, bab\}|_{\leq 3})|_{\leq 4}$$
$$= \{ab, aab, aba, abb, bab, aaab, aaba, aabb, abaa, abab, abba, abbb,$$
$$baab, baba, babb, bbab\}.$$

Thus, we can conclude that neither the word $bbba$ nor the word aba are in the solution.

Often, one can speed up this process—for instance, if only certain lengths of the words are possible. To illustrate this, consider the equation $X = \alpha(X)$ over the alphabet $A = \{a, b\}$ with

$$\alpha = a \cdot \overline{X} \cdot b.$$

It should be clear that we can skip computing those S_i where i is odd. Thus, we get

$S_0 = \emptyset,$

$S_2 = \{ab\},$

$S_4 = \{ab, aab, abb, aaab, abab, abbb\},$

$S_6 = \{ab, aab, abb, aaab, abab, abbb, aaaab, aabab, abaab, ababb, abbab, abbbb,$

$aaaaab, aaabab, aaabbb, aabaab, aabbab, abaaab, abaabb, ababab,$

$ababbb, abbaab, abbabb, abbbab, abbbbb\}.$

It should be obvious that the second technique is unlikely to lead to any insight that might help one in finding a closed representation of the solution (see Section 5.3). In order to obtain such a representation of all words (which is, of course, typically a regular language), the derivative technique is more suitable; however, it is also much more complicated and time-consuming.

It is futile to hope for an algorithm that would determine whether a given equation has a regular solution, since already without complementation and without star, systems of the type of equations considered in this chapter naturally correspond to context-free grammars (see Section 3.5) and the question of whether a given context-free grammar generates a regular language is known to be undecidable. Since our equations yield solutions that are far more general than context-free languages (see Chapter 8 for a formal proof of this contention), whether the unique solution of a given system is regular is undecidable as well. Nevertheless, in the next chapter we briefly indicate that for a certain class of equations, namely star equations, relatively simple equations always have regular solutions if the constant languages are regular.

5.5   Bibliographical Notes

Derivatives of regular expressions were defined by Brzozowski in [Brzoz 63]. The present definition is based on work reported in [Leiss 81d].

5.6   Problems

1. Construct the first 40 or so derivatives for the equation

$$X = a(\overline{X} \cdot a)^* \cup \lambda$$

over the alphabet $A = \{a, b\}$. Determine which derivatives must be equated in order to arrive at the dfa given above.

2. Determine the solution of the equation

$$X = (\overline{X} \cdot a)^*$$

over the alphabet $A = \{a\}$. Determine which derivatives must be equated in order to arrive at the dfa given above.

3. Determine the solution of the equation

$$X = (\overline{X} \cdot a)^*$$

over the alphabet $A = \{a, b\}$. Determine which derivatives must be
equated in order to arrive at the dfa given above.

4. Determine the solution of the equation

$$X = a(a \cdot \overline{X} \cdot a)^*$$

over the alphabet $A = \{a\}$.

5. Determine the solution of the equation

$$X = a(a \cdot \overline{X} \cdot a)^*$$

over the alphabet $A = \{a, b\}$.

6. Determine the solution of the equation

$$X = a(a \cdot \overline{X} \cdot a)^* \cup \lambda$$

over the alphabet $A = \{a\}$.

7. Determine the solution of the equation

$$X = a(a \cdot \overline{X} \cdot a)^* \cup \lambda$$

over the alphabet $A = \{a, b\}$.

6

Star Equations

About This Chapter: Star equations are explicit language equations where the operators are union, left-concatenation, and star. If the constants are context-free, these equations always have a context-free solution. If the constants are regular, the solution is not guaranteed to be regular.

Consider the set of expressions $\text{EX}_A(\text{CONST}; \text{OP}; X_1, \ldots, X_n)$, where the class CONST denotes the constant languages over the alphabet A, $X_1, \ldots, X_n$ denote the variables and OP contains the following operators:

- Union ($\cup$)
- Left-concatenation ($\cdot$)
- Star ($\star$)

A system of star equations in the variables $X_1, \ldots, X_n$ is then defined by

$$X_i = \alpha_i \quad \text{where } \alpha_i \in \text{EX}_A(\text{CONST}; \text{OP}; X_1, \ldots, X_n).$$

The motivation for studying this type of equations is as follows. The star operation can be viewed as the closure of concatenation. Thus, we are interested in the question of whether allowing this closure of concatenation "adds less" than allowing unrestricted concatenation. Note that even in conjunction with left-concatenation, the star operator will result in concatenations that are not left-concatenations. For example, in the equation

$$X = a(aX)^*,$$

the star contains expressions such as $aXaX$. Here, "adding less" has the following meaning: We know that allowing arbitrary concatenation in our equations does not preserve regularity (i.e., even if all constants are regular), the solutions of the resulting equations are no longer guaranteed to be regular. We want to know whether adding the star operator (instead of unrestricted concatenation) does preserve regularity. First, however, we show that context-freeness is preserved.

Theorem 6.1. *Any system*

$$X_i = \alpha_i \quad for \ i = 1, \ldots, n$$

of star equations where $\alpha_i \in \mathrm{EX}_A(\mathrm{CFL}; \mathrm{OP}; X_1, \ldots, X_n)$ *always has a context-free solution.*

PROOF. Let us first assume that the α_i have the λ-property; we know therefore that there exists a unique solution. We will construct a context-free grammar G,

$$G = (N, A, P, S)$$

that generates a solution of the given system of star equations.

The set of grammar variables contains all the equation variables $X_1, \ldots, X_n$, a variable S_β for every proper subexpression β of the α_i, as well as additional variables as they may occur during the construction of G.

The starting symbol S is unspecified. It will usually be one of the variables X_i, in which case we will denote this specialization by the notation $G^{(S=X_i)}$.

The set P of productions will be constructed by induction on the structure of the α_i:

Basis: If $\alpha = L \in \mathrm{CFL}$, then there exists a context-free grammar $G_L = (N_L, A, P_L, S_L)$ such that $L(G_L) = L$ and S_L does not occur on the right-hand side of any production in P_L.

If $\alpha = X_i$, then no productions need be added.

Inductive step: Assume we have already context-free grammars for the expressions β and γ: $G_\beta = (N_\beta, A, P_\beta, S_\beta)$ and $G_\gamma = (N_\gamma, A, P_\gamma, S_\gamma)$ such that $N_\beta \cap N_\gamma = \emptyset$.

If $\alpha = \beta \cup \gamma$, then $G_\alpha = (N_\alpha, A, P_\alpha, S_\alpha)$, where

$$N_\alpha = N_\beta \cup N_\gamma \cup \{S_\alpha\},$$
$$P_\alpha = P_\beta \cup P_\gamma \cup \{S_\alpha \to S_\beta \mid S_\gamma\}.$$

If $\alpha = \beta \cdot \gamma$, then $G_\alpha = (N_\alpha, A, P_\alpha, S_\alpha)$, where

$$N_\alpha = N_\beta \cup N_\gamma \cup \{S_\alpha\},$$
$$P_\alpha = P_\beta \cup P_\gamma \cup \{S_\alpha \to S_\beta \cdot S_\gamma\}.$$

If $\alpha = \beta^*$, then $G_\alpha = (N_\alpha, A, P_\alpha, S_\alpha)$, where

$$N_\alpha = N_\beta \cup \{S_\alpha\},$$
$$P_\alpha = P_\beta \cup \{S_\alpha \to S_\beta \cdot S_\alpha \mid \lambda\}.$$

Finally, if $\alpha = \alpha_i$ for some $i \in \{1, \ldots, n\}$, then $S_\alpha = X_i$.

We now claim that

$$(G^{(S=X_1)}, \ldots, G^{(S=X_n)})$$

is the unique solution of the given system of star equations. The proof is analogous to that of Theorem 4.10 (with a similar series of lemmas) and is left to the reader.

It should now be clear that this construction works equally well if the expressions do not have the λ-property. In this case, we still get a solution in $(G^{(S=X_1)}, \ldots, G^{(S=X_n)})$, but it is no longer guaranteed to be unique.   □

We note that in this construction, we did not make use of the assumption that the concatenation was restricted to left-concatenation. Consequently, this construction applies to a more general class of equations:

Corollary 6.2. *Any system*

$$X_i = \alpha_i \quad for \; i = 1, \ldots, n$$

of equations where $\alpha_i \in \mathrm{EX}_A(\mathrm{CFL}; \mathrm{OP}; X_1, \ldots, X_n)$ *and* OP *contains precisely union, arbitrary concatenation, and star always has a context-free solution.*

Example: Consider the following system of star equations:

$$X = a(bX^* \cup aY)^*,$$
$$Y = (aX)^*.$$

We obtain the context-free grammar below where we simplified by eliminating variables whenever possible [if $V \to \sigma$ is the only V production, with $\sigma \in ((N - \{V\}) \cup T)^*$, V can be eliminated by substituting σ wherever V occurs, unless V is an equation variable; words w that are constant languages are written into the productions where the constants occur instead of having a grammar generate them separately]:

$$X \to a \cdot S_1,$$
$$Y \to S_2,$$
$$S_1 \to S_3 \cdot S_1 \mid \lambda,$$
$$S_2 \to a \cdot X \cdot S_2 \mid \lambda,$$
$$S_3 \to b \cdot S_4 \mid a \cdot Y,$$
$$S_4 \to X \cdot S_4 \mid \lambda.$$

If we systematically replace each constant language in a system of star equations by a letter so that any two constants are replaced by two different letters, we obtain special star equations, so-called *basic star equations*. For example, converting the above system into basic star equations would yield

$$X = a(bX^* \cup cY)^*,$$
$$Y = (dX)^*.$$

Recalling the definition of the λ-property, one concludes immediately that all basic star equations have the λ-property. Therefore, they always have unique solutions.

Proposition 6.3. *Let $X_i = \alpha_i$ be a system of basic star equations. Then, there always exists a unique solution of this system of explicit equations.*

It turns out that for each system of basic star equations, there exists a deterministic pushdown automaton (dpda) accepting the unique solution (where we vary, as always, only the initial state to obtain the languages corresponding to the different equation variables). A solution of a system of general star equations can be obtained by first deriving its corresponding basic star equations, constructing the dpda accepting the solution of these basic star equations, and then substituting the original constants for the corresponding letters in the solution. Since the substitution property holds (the operations are unions, concatenation, and star), all solutions can be obtained in this way, if the λ-property holds for the original system. If the λ-property does not hold for the original system, the observation in Section 3.5 provides a method for obtaining infinitely many solutions.

Since it is possible to decide for a dpda whether the language it accepts is regular, this gives us a test for regularity of basic star equations. Any star equation that corresponds to a basic star equation which has a regular solution therefore has a solution that can be represented as a regular expression in the constant languages only (the constants need not be regular for this to apply).

Unfortunately, the usefulness of this interesting result is limited since only rather simple basic star equations have regular solutions. Here are the two most complicated basic star equations that have regular solutions:

A.

$$X = a(bX \cup c)^* \cup dX \cup e.$$

Its solution is denoted by the following regular expression:

$$d^*[e \cup a(c \cup bd^*[a \cup e])^*].$$

B.

$$X = a(b(cX)^* \cup dX)^* \cup eX.$$

Its solution is denoted by the following regular expression:

$$e^*a(b^*de^*a)^*[\lambda \cup bb^*(\lambda \cup ce^*a[(c \cup d)e^*a \cup b]^*)].$$

This can be verified by (rather tedious) substitution of these regular expressions into the equations.

On the other hand, consider the following star equation:

$$X = 0(0X)^* \cup 1(1X)^*.$$

We claim that this equation does not have a regular solution. To this end, we construct the derivatives of X with respect to all words $w \in A^*$:

$$X_0 = (0X)^*,$$
$$X_1 = (1X)^*,$$
$$X_{00} = X(0X)^*,$$
$$X_{01} = \emptyset,$$
$$X_{10} = \emptyset,$$
$$X_{11} = X(1X)^*,$$
$$X_{000} = X_0,$$
$$X_{001} = (1X)^*(0X)^*,$$
$$X_{110} = (0X)^*(1X)^*,$$
$$X_{111} = X_1.$$

In general, we obtain

$$X_{(0011)^s0} = (0X)^*[(1X)^*(0X)^*]^s,$$
$$X_{(0011)^s1} = X_{(0011)^{s-1}001},$$
$$X_{(0011)^s00} = X(0X)^*[(1X)^*(0X)^*]^s,$$
$$X_{(0011)^s01} = X_{(0011)^s},$$
$$X_{(0011)^s000} = X_{(0011)^s0},$$
$$X_{(0011)^s001} = (1X)^*(0X)^*[(1X)^*(0X)^*]^s,$$
$$X_{(0011)^s0010} = X_{(0011)^s00},$$
$$X_{(0011)^s0011} = X[(1X)^*(0X)^*]^{s+1},$$

$$X_{(1100)^s0} = X_{(1100)^{s-1}110},$$
$$X_{(1100)^s1} = (1x)^*[(0X)^*(1X)^*]^s,$$
$$X_{(1100)^s10} = X_{(1100)^s},$$
$$X_{(1100)^s11} = X(1X)^*[(0X)^*(1X)^*]^s,$$
$$X_{(1100)^s110} = (0X)^*(1X)^*[(0X)^*(1X)^*]^s,$$
$$X_{(1100)^s111} = X_{(1100)^s1},$$
$$X_{(1100)^s1100} = X[(0X)^*(1X)^*]^{s+1},$$
$$X_{(1100)^s1101} = X_{(1100)^s11}.$$

In particular, one observes that for all $s \geq 2$,

$$X_{(1100)^s 1001} = X_{(1100)^{s-1}},$$

but

$$X_{(1100)^s (1001)^s} = \emptyset.$$

Since $\lambda \in X_{(0011)^s 0}$ for all $s \geq 1$, if follows that

$$(0011)^s (1001)^r O \in X \quad \text{iff } s \geq r.$$

Thus, the solution is not regular. Since the solution is unique, no regular solution of this (rather simple) star equation can exist.

It is an open problem whether one can determine if the solution of an arbitrary star equation is regular, assuming the λ-property holds. It may appear gratuitous to insist on the λ-property here. However, there is a good reason for this assumption: If the λ-property does not hold for a star equation, there is always the trivial solution A^*. This is easily verified if one observes that for star equations, if the λ-property does not hold for the star expression α, α can be equivalently rewritten in one of two forms:

$$\alpha = \beta \cup X \quad \text{or} \quad \alpha = \beta \cup X^*$$

with β an arbitrary star expression. This is the case because we have only union, left-concatenation, and star, and by the definition of the λ-property given in Chapter 5. Now, however, it is entirely trivial to see that A^* is always a solution of the equation.

6.1   Bibliographical Notes

Star equations were defined in [Leiss 85c]. Deterministic pushdown automata are standard devices that are discussed in most automata theory textbooks; we refer to [Hopcr/Ullma 79]. The result that one can test whether a dpda accepts a regular language was shown in [Stear 67]. Problem 7 (which is hard!) solves an open problem raised in [Leiss 85c].

6.2   Problems

1. Show that the unique solution of the basic star equation

$$X = a[b(cX)^* \cup dX]^* \cup e$$

over the alphabet $A = \{a, b, c, d, e\}$ is not regular.

2. Show how to derive a deterministic pushdown automaton for the unique solution of a basic star equation.

Hint: Construct the context-free grammar (cfg) as outlined above; then use this cfg to obtain the dpda.

3. Determine whether the unique solution of the star equation

$$X = a[b(cX)^* \cup cX]^* \cup e$$

over the alphabet $A = \{a, b, c, e\}$ is regular.

4. Determine whether the unique solution of the star equation

$$X = a[b(cX)^* \cup bX]^* \cup e$$

over the alphabet $A = \{a, b, c, e\}$ is regular.

5. Determine whether the unique solution of the star equation

$$X = a[b(cX)^* \cup aX]^* \cup e$$

over the alphabet $A = \{a, b, c, e\}$ is regular.

6. Determine whether the unique solution of the star equation

$$X = [b(cX)^* \cup dX]^* \cup e$$

over the alphabet $A = \{a, b, c, d, e\}$ is regular.

7. Show that the unique solution for X of the following system of star equations over the alphabet $A = \{0, 1, 2, 3\}$ is inherently ambiguous:

$$X = Y \cup Z,$$
$$Y = A_{2,3}0A_{2,3}[A_{2,3}0A_{2,3}YA_{2,3}]^* \cup A_{2,3}1A_{2,3}[A_{2,3}1A_{2,3}YA_{2,3}]^*,$$
$$Z = A_{0,1}2A_{0,1}[A_{0,1}2A_{0,1}ZA_{0,1}]^* \cup A_{0,1}3A_{0,1}[A_{0,1}3A_{0,1}ZA_{0,1}]^*,$$

where $A_{0,1} = (0 \cup 1)^*$ and $A_{2,3} = (2 \cup 3)^*$.

Hint: Show that the intersection of Y and Z is not context-free. Then, use this fact to show that infinitely many words in the intersection must have at least two different right-most derivations in any context-free grammar.

7

Explicit Equations over a One-Letter Alphabet

About This Chapter: We restrict the underlying alphabet to one letter, denoted by a. Languages over $\{a\}$ have interesting properties, some of which we derive. Then, we use them to show that any system of explicit equations over the alphabet $\{a\}$ where the operators are union, unrestricted concatenation, and star have solutions that are expressible as regular expressions in terms of the constant languages only. Most importantly, we provide a complete solution of the problem, including a parametric representation of all solutions if there is more than one. We also study the case (in Section 7.7) where complementation is added to this catalog of operators and show that such equations need not have context-free solutions even if the constants are single letters.

Throughout this chapter, the underlying alphabet A will contain one letter only. Usually, we will assume that this letter is a. In the first part of this chapter, we consider the set of expressions $\mathrm{EX}_{\{a\}}(\mathrm{CONST};\mathrm{OP};X_1,\ldots,X_n)$, where the class CONST denotes the constant languages over the one-letter alphabet $\{a\}$, $X_1,\ldots,X_n$ denote the variables, and OP contains the following operators:

- Union ($\cup$)
- Arbitrary concatenation ($\cdot$)
- Star ($\star$).

In the second part, we will add complementation to these operators.

The focus of our attention is on systems of explicit equations in the variables $X_1,\ldots,X_n$, defined by

$$X_i = \alpha_i \quad \text{where } \alpha_i \in \mathrm{EX}_A(\mathrm{CONST};\mathrm{OP};X_1,\ldots,X_n).$$

Again, we are probing the limits of concatenation. In the last chapter, we did this by introducing star equations, which incorporated a restricted closure of concatenation. In this chapter, we consider arbitrary concatenation but require the alphabet to contain just one letter. It is well known that languages over a one-letter alphabet have numerous special properties. Some of these will be derived in the first section. This is followed by sections describing how to solve arbitrary systems of explicit equations with union, concatenation, and star. Finally, the last section shows that adding complementation may result in solutions that are not context-free, even if the constant languages are just single letters.

7.1   Properties of Languages over a One-Letter Alphabet

Languages over $\{a\}$ have many properties that distinguish them from languages over larger alphabets. Some of these are summarized in this section. We begin with some useful identities.

Proposition 7.1. *Let B and C be arbitrary languages over the alphabet $\{a\}$. Then, the following identities hold:*

a. $B \cdot C = C \cdot B$ *(commutativity)*.
b. $(B \cup C)^* = B^* \cdot C^*$.
c. $(B \cdot C^*)^* = B \cdot B^* \cdot C^* \cup \lambda$.

PROOF.   The commutativity of languages follows from that of words, which, in turn, is implied by the fact that only the number of letters in a word is relevant, but not their order. This is also the main idea for the proof of (b): Any sequence of words from $B \cup C$ can be reorganized so that we have first all those from B, followed by all those from C. Clearly, the converse $((B \cup C)^* \supseteq B^* \cdot C^*)$ is true for any alphabet. Finally (c): Assume $u \in (B \cdot C^*)^*$. Either $u = \lambda$, or u is composed of one or more words from $B \cdot C^*$. However, this, because of (a), means that $u \in B \cdot B^* \cdot C^* \cup \lambda$. The converse holds for arbitrary alphabets.   □

Corollary 7.2.   *Any expression in* $\mathrm{EX}_{\{a\}}(\mathrm{CONST}; \mathrm{OP}; \emptyset)$ *can be equivalently written in a form that does not contain any nested stars.*

PROOF.   This is a direct consequence of (repeated applications) of Proposition 7.1(c).   □

This corollary is very important because it allows us to establish a very useful normal form for our expressions. One should note that this result does not hold for alphabets with more than one letter nor does it hold for the other unary operator of interest to us, complementation. We will return to this point in the last part of this chapter.

For example, the expression

$$[LL^*(M^*NP^* \cup Q^*)^*]^*$$

in the constant languages L, M, N, P, and Q can be written equivalently by repeated applications of the identities of Proposition 7.1 as

$$LNL^*M^*N^*P^*Q^* \cup LL^*Q^* \cup \lambda.$$

For any language L over $\{a\}$, we define $\text{GCD}(L)$ as follows. If L contains at least one word, then $\text{GCD}(L) = \gcd(\{|w| \mid w \in L\})$, otherwise $\text{GCD}(L) = 0$. Here, gcd denotes the greatest common divisor of integers. We first state two obvious observations:

Lemma 7.3.

a. For any language L over $\{a\}$, there exists a finite subset $L_f \subseteq L$ such that $\text{GCD}(L) = \text{GCD}(L_f)$.

b. If $n = \text{GCD}(L)$ for some language L over $\{a\}$, then $L \subseteq (a^n)^*$ and there does not exist any integer $r > n$ such that $L \subseteq (a^r)^*$.

Now we can formulate several properties that will be used later.

Lemma 7.4. Let L_1 and L_2 be arbitrary languages over $\{a\}$.

a. $\text{GCD}(L_1 \cdot L_2) = \gcd(\text{GCD}(L_1), \text{GCD}(L_2))$.

b. $\text{GCD}(L_1 \cup L_2) = \gcd(\text{GCD}(L_1), \text{GCD}(L_2))$.

c. $\text{GCD}(L^k) = \text{GCD}(L)$ for $k \geq 1$.

d. $\text{GCD}(L^*) = \text{GCD}(L)$.

PROOF.   Define $n_i = \text{GCD}(L_i)$, for $i = 1, 2$.

a. By Lemma 7.3(b), $L_1 \cdot L_2 \subseteq (a^{n_1})^* \cdot (a^{n_2})^*$. Since $(a^{n_1})^* \cdot (a^{n_2})^* \subseteq (a^{\gcd(n_1,n_2)})^*$ and $\gcd(n_1, n_2)$ is maximal [i.e., there does not exist an integer $r \geq \gcd(n_1, n_2)$ such that $(a^{n_1})^* \cdot (a^{n_2})^* \subseteq (a^r)^*$, we obtain

$$L_1 \cdot L_2 \subseteq (a^{\gcd(n_1,n_2)})^*$$

and consequently $\text{GCD}(L_1 \cdot L_2) = \gcd(n_1, n_2)$.

b. $L_1 \cup L_2 \subseteq (a^{n_1})^* \cdot (a^{n_2})^* \subseteq (a^{\gcd(n_1,n_2)})^*$ and $\gcd(n_1, n_2)$ is maximal, by the same argumentation. Therefore, $\text{GCD}(L_1 \cup L_2) = \gcd(n_1, n_2)$.

c. This follows from (a) by induction on k.

d. This follows from (b) and (c). $\square$

Proposition 7.5.

a. If L is an arbitrary language over $\{a\}$, then L^* is regular.

b. If $B \subseteq aa^*$, $B \neq \emptyset$, and $C \subseteq a^*$, then $B^* \cdot C$ is regular.

c. If $B, C \subseteq a^*$, $B \neq \emptyset$, then $B \cdot B^* \cdot C^* \cup C$ is regular.

d. If $B, C, D \subseteq a^*$, $B \neq \emptyset$, then $B \cdot [C \cdot (B \cup D)^k]^* \cup D$ is regular for all $k \geq 1$.

PROOF.

a. By Lemma 7.3(a), there exists a finite subset $L_f \subseteq L$ such that $\mathrm{GCD}(L) = \mathrm{GCD}(L_f) = n$. We claim that $L^* - (L_f)^*$ is finite. To see this, we observe that

$$(L_f)^* = F \cup a^N \cdot (a^n)^*,$$

where F is finite. Now, $L \subseteq L^* \subseteq (a^n)^*$ by Lemma 7.3(b), and since $(a^n)^* - a^N \cdot (a^n)^*$ is finite, the claim follows. Of course, $(L_f)^*$ is regular, and $(a^n)^* - a^N \cdot (a^n)^*$ is finite, therefore also regular; thus, L^* must be regular.

b. By assumption, B^* is infinite. Let $n = \mathrm{GCD}(B)$, then $B^* \subseteq (a^n)^*$ by Lemma 7.3(b). If $\mathrm{GCD}(B)$ divides $\mathrm{GCD}(C)$, the claim follows immediately. Otherwise, we have

$$\mathrm{GCD}(B^*C) = \gcd(\mathrm{GCD}(B), \mathrm{GCD}(C)).$$

Let B_f and C_f be the finite subsets of B and C such that $\mathrm{GCD}(B_f) = \mathrm{GCD}(B)$, $\mathrm{GCD}(C_f) = \mathrm{GCD}(C)$, respectively. Clearly,

$$B^* \cdot C = [(B_f)^* \cup (B^* - (B_f)^*)] \cdot C \supseteq (B_f)^* \cdot C_f \cup (B^* - (B_f)^*) \cdot C_f.$$

Now, $\mathrm{GCD}((B_f)^* \cdot C_f) = \mathrm{GCD}(B^*C)$, and therefore,

$$(B_f)^* \cdot C_f \subseteq B^*C \subseteq (a^{\mathrm{GCD}(B^*C)})^*.$$

However, $(B_f)^* \cdot C_f = (F \cup a^N \cdot (a^n)^*) \cdot C_f \subseteq (a^m)^*$ with $m = \mathrm{GCD}(B^*C)$, $n = \mathrm{GCD}(B)$, and N some multiple of n, according to Part (a) of Proposition 7.5. Thus,

$$(B_f)^* \cdot C_f = G \cup a^M \cdot (a^m)^*$$

for some integer M which is a multiple of m and some finite set G. This implies the claim.

c. BB^*C^* is regular by Part (b). Also, $\mathrm{GCD}(BB^*C^* \cup C) = \mathrm{GCD}(BB^*C^*)$. Therefore, $C - BB^*C^*$ must be finite; thus, the claim follows.

d. Obviously, $B \cdot [C \cdot (B \cup D)^k]^*$ is regular. Also, $\mathrm{GCD}(B \cdot [C \cdot (B \cup D)^k]^* \cup D) = \mathrm{GCD}(B \cdot [C \cdot (B \cup D)^k]^*)$. Thus, $D - B \cdot [C \cdot (B \cup D)^k]^*$ must be finite. Consequently, the claim follows. $\square$

7.2 Normal Forms of Expressions Without Complementation

In this section, we derive the normal form of expressions over the alphabet $\{a\}$ where the operations are union, concatenation, and star. We first formulate them for expressions in the single variable X; then, we generalize to n variables. We need two normal forms—one for expressions in which the star does not occur, the other where the star is permitted. Note that the substitution property holds.

Theorem 7.6. *Let $\alpha \in \mathrm{EX}_{\{a\}}(\mathrm{CONST}; \mathrm{OP}; X)$, where OP consists of union and concatenation. If α is not a constant, it can be equivalently written in the following form:*

$$\bigcup_{i=1}^{k} A_i X^i \cup B,$$

where $k \geq 1$ and $A_k \neq \emptyset$.

PROOF. By structural induction on α. The only interesting case is concatenation where commutativity implies the result.   □

Theorem 7.7. *Let $\alpha \in \mathrm{EX}_{\{a\}}(\mathrm{CONST}; \mathrm{OP}; X)$, where OP consists of union, concatenation, and star, $\alpha \neq \emptyset$. Then, α can be equivalently written in the following form:*

$$\bigcup_{i=0}^{k} A_i \cdot X^i \cdot \alpha_i \cup C,$$

where for $i = 0, \ldots, k$,

$$\alpha_i = \bigcup_j A_{i,j,0} \cdot (A_{i,j,1} \cdot X^{s_1})^* \cdot \ldots \cdot (A_{i,j,m_{i,j}} \cdot X^{s_{m_{i,j}}})^*$$

with $1 \leq s_1 < \cdots < s_{m_{i,j}}$ and all $A_{i,j,t}$ and C are nonempty expressions in terms of constant languages only, for all $m_i \geq 0$, $m \geq 0$.

PROOF. We show by structural induction that any regular expression in X over $\{a\}$ can be transformed into the given normal form, using only ordinary set identities plus the identities in Proposition 7.1.

If α is a constant language or the variable X, the claim follows trivially.

If $\alpha = \beta \cup \gamma$, then the union of two normal forms can be written in normal form.

If $\alpha = \beta \cdot \gamma$, then the concatenation of two normal forms can be written in normal form.

Finally, consider α^*. First, one sees that

$$\alpha^* = (A_0 \cdot X^0 \cdot \alpha_0)^* \cdot \ldots \cdot (A_m \cdot X^m \cdot \alpha_m)^* \cdot C^*,$$

then one has

$$(A_i \cdot X^i \cdot \alpha_i)^* = \left[\bigcup_j A_i \cdot X^i \cdot A_{i,j,0} \cdot (A_{i,j,1} \cdot X^{s_1})^* \right.$$
$$\left. \cdot \ldots \cdot (A_{i,j,m_{i,j}} \cdot X^{s_{m_{i,j}}})^* \right]^*$$

and each of the terms in this expression can be written in normal form, using the identities of Proposition 7.1. This reduces the problem to the already addressed problems of union and concatenation. □

We come now to the generalization to more than one variable. We assume that $\alpha(X_1, \ldots, X_n)$ is a regular expression in the variables $X_1, \ldots, X_n$, $\alpha \in \mathrm{EX}_{\{a\}}(\mathrm{CONST}; \mathrm{OP}; X_1, \ldots, X_n)$. Then, we have the following representation theorem:

Theorem 7.8. *Let $\alpha = \alpha(X_1, \ldots, X_n)$ be an expression in $\mathrm{EX}_{\{a\}}(\mathrm{CONST};$ $\mathrm{OP}; X_1, \ldots, X_n)$, where OP consists of union, concatenation, and star. Then, for any h, $h \in \{1, \ldots, n\}$, α can be equivalently written in the form:*

$$\alpha = \bigcup_{i=0}^{k} A_i X_h^i \alpha_i \cup C,$$

where for $i = 0, \ldots, k$,

$$\alpha_i = \bigcup_j A_{i,j,0} \cdot (A_{i,j,1} X_h^{s_1})^* \cdot \ldots \cdot (A_{i,j,m_{i,j}} X_h^{s_{m_{i,j}}})^*$$

with $1 \leq s_1 < \cdots < s_{m_{i,j}}$ and all $A_{i,j,t}$ are nonempty expressions in terms of constant languages and in terms of the variables $\{X_1, \ldots, X_n\} - \{X_h\}$, for all $m_i \geq 0$, $m \geq 0$.

PROOF. The proof is a direct consequence of Theorem 7.7, applied for the variable X_h. □

7.3   Two Key Theorems

We show two results each of which deals with a portion of the general problem. In the next section, we show how to use these two theorems in order to obtain a solution. The first result deals with equations in the variable X where no star operator is present. We will assume the normal form given in Theorem 7.6.

Theorem 7.9. *Consider the equation*

$$X = \bigcup_{i=1}^{k} A_i X^i \cup B$$

in the variable X over the one-letter alphabet $\{a\}$, where $k \geq 1$ and $A_k \neq \emptyset$.

a. *The language*

$$S = \left(\bigcup_{i=1}^{k} A_i B^{i-1} \right)^* B$$

is a solution of the equation.

b. If $\lambda \notin A_i$ for all $i = 1, \ldots, k$, then the solution given in (a) is unique.

c. If $\lambda \in A_i$ for some $i \in \{1, \ldots, k\}$, then any solution S of the equation is of the form

$$S = \left(\bigcup_{i=1}^{k} A_i (B \cup T)^{i-1} \right)^* (B \cup T)$$

where T is arbitrary if $\lambda \in B$ or $\lambda \in A_1$ or $T \subseteq B$, and $T = T' \cup \{\lambda\}$ with T' arbitrary otherwise.

d. Any solution of the equation is regular regardless of whether the A_i, B, or T are regular or not, provided $k \geq 2$ or (k = 1 and $A_1 \neq \{\lambda\}$).

PROOF.   First we show that $S = (B^0 A_1 \cup \cdots \cup B^{k-1} A_k)^* B$ is a solution of the given equation. Substitution of the language S on both sides of the equation yields

$$\left(\bigcup_{i=1}^{k} A_i B^{i-1} \right)^* B = \bigcup_{j=1}^{k} A_j \left[\left(\bigcup_{i=1}^{k} A_i B^{i-1} \right)^* B \right]^j \cup B,$$

and in order to show that S is a solution, we must verify that this is, in fact, an identity between languages. By Proposition 7.1, we have

$$A_j \left[\left(\bigcup_{i=1}^{k} A_i B^{i-1} \right)^* B \right]^j = A_j (A_1 B^0)^* \cdot \ldots \cdot (A_k B^{k-1})^* B^j.$$

Consequently,

$$\bigcup_{j=1}^{k} A_j \left[\left(\bigcup_{i=1}^{k} A_i B^{i-1} \right)^* B \right]^j \cup B$$

$$= (A_1 B^1 \cup \cdots \cup A_k B^k)(A_1 B^0)^* \cdot \ldots \cdot (A_k B^{k-1})^* \cup B$$
$$= (A_1 B^0 \cup \cdots \cup A_k B^{k-1})(A_1 B^0 \cup \cdots \cup A_k B^{k-1})^* B \cup B$$
$$= S.$$

Thus, S is a solution; Part (a) is proven.

Assume now that none of the A_i contains the empty word; we must show that S is the unique solution. We present two independent proofs of this fact. The first one is a simple appeal to Theorem 5.5 since it is easy to verify that in this case, the expression at hand has the λ-property. The second proof is a direct one. Let R be another solution and let w be the shortest word in the symmetric difference of R and S; without loss of generality, we assume $w \in R - S$ (the other case follows similarly). Clearly, w cannot be in B. Therefore, $w \in A_j R^j$ for some $j \in \{1, \ldots, k\}$. Since $\lambda \notin A_i$ for any i, $w = uv$ with $u \in A_j$ and $v \in R_j$ and $|v| < |w|$. It now follows that $v \in S^j$, since v consists of j words in R, $j \geq 1$, v is shorter than w, and w is shortest in $R - S$. Therefore, $w \in A_j S^j$ in contradiction to the assumption that $w \in R - S$. This proves Part (b).

Now assume that λ is in at least one of the A_i's. Consider

$$W = \left(\bigcup_{i=1}^{k} A_i (B \cup T)^{i-1} \right)^* (B \cup T)$$

with T as stated. We claim that W is a solution; that is,

$$W = \bigcup_{i=1}^{k} A_i W^i \cup B.$$

Let $\varphi = A_1 (B \cup T)^0 \cup \cdots \cup A_k (B \cup T)^{k-1}$; then,

$$W = \varphi^* (B \cup T) \quad \text{and} \quad W^i = \varphi^* (B \cup T)^i.$$

Therefore, our claim can be rewritten as

$$\varphi^* (B \cup T) = \varphi \varphi^* (B \cup T) \cup B.$$

To verify this, we distinguish three cases:

- If $T \subseteq B$, then the claim is obviously true [we can just take the proof of Part (a) of the theorem].
- If $\lambda \in B \cup T$, the claim is also true, since $\varphi \varphi^* (B \cup T) \cup B = \varphi \varphi^* (B \cup T) \cup (B \cup T) = \varphi^* (B \cup T)$.
- If $\lambda \in A_1$, then we also have $\varphi \varphi^* (B \cup T) \cup B = \varphi \varphi^* (B \cup T) \cup (B \cup T) = \varphi^* (B \cup T)$ by definition of φ.

Thus, in all three cases we have

$$\varphi \varphi^* (B \cup T) \cup B = \varphi^* (B \cup T) \cup B = \varphi^* (B \cup T) = W,$$

and, therefore, W is a solution.

So far, we have shown that any language W as defined above is a solution. Similarly, we show that for any solution V,

$$V = \left(\bigcup_{i=1}^{k} A_i (B \cup V)^{i-1} \right)^* (B \cup V).$$

Since V is a solution, we have

$$V = \bigcup_{i=1}^{k} A_i V^i \cup B;$$

it follows that V contains $B \cup V$. Also, since

$$V = \left(\bigcup_{i=1}^{k} A_i V^{i-1} \right) V \cup B \cup V,$$

by Proposition 3.1, V contains

$$\left(\bigcup_{i=1}^{k} A_i V^{i-1} \right)^* (B \cup V),$$

which, in turn, contains

$$\left(\bigcup_{i=1}^{k} A_i (B \cup V)^{i-1} \right)^* (B \cup V).$$

This proves the first inclusion. The converse is trivial since $B \cup V$ contains V. Therefore, the given representation is in fact the most general one. This concludes the proof of Part (c).

Finally, we come to Part (d). Part (c) gives the most general form of any solution. In order to use Proposition 7.5(b), we must show that φ^* contains a nonempty word, which is true if $k = 1$ and A_1 contains at least one nonempty word. If $k \geq 2$, two subcases must be distinguished. If at least one of the A_i's contains a nonempty word, then Proposition 7.5(b) applies. If no A_i contains a nonempty word, then φ^* is infinite iff $B \cup T$ contains a nonempty word. Finally, if neither any of the A_i nor $B \cup T$ contains a nonempty word, then the solution is either $\emptyset$ or $\{\lambda\}$, both of which are clearly regular. This concludes the proof of the last part and thereby of the entire theorem.   □

We note that in Part (d) of the proof, only two types of equations are excluded, namely the equations

$$X = B \quad \text{and} \quad X = X \cup B.$$

Both may have trivially nonregular solutions. In the first case, there is a unique solution, B, and if B is not regular, the solution is not regular. In the second case, even if B is regular, there may be a nonregular solution, as long as there exists a nonregular language which contains B. What Part (d) states is that in all cases except those two trivial ones, all solutions are regular! This includes even equations of the form $X = X^k$ or $X = X^k \cup B$.

Examples:

1. Consider the equation $X = a^5 X^3 \cup a^4 X^4 \cup a^3$. According to Part (a) of Theorem 7.9, this equation has a unique solution, given by $(a^{13} \cup a^{11})^* a^3$. This can be shown to be equal to $F \cup a^{123} a^*$, where F is given by

$$F = \{a^i \mid i = 3, 14, 16, 25, 27, 29, 36, 38, 40, 42, 47, 49, 51, 53, 55, 58,$$
$$60, 62, 64, 66, 68 : 69, 71, 73, 75, 77, 79 : 82, 84, 86, 88,$$
$$90 : 95, 97, 99, 101 : 108, 110, 112 : 121\}.$$

($i : j$ for $i < j$ denotes $i, i+1, i+2, \ldots, j$.)

2. The equation $X = aX \cup aX^3 \cup aX^5 \cup a^2$ has, by Theorem 7.9, the unique solution $(a^9 \cup a^5 \cup a)^* a^2 = a^2 a^*$. The same equation, but without the aX term, $X = aX^3 \cup aX^5 \cup a^2$, has the solution $(a^5 \cup a^9)^* a^2$ which is equal to

$$a^{2,7,11:12,16:17,20:22,25:27,29:32} \cup a^{34} a^*.$$

(We use $a^{i,j}$ to stand for $a^i \cup a^j$ and $a^{i:j}$ for $a^i \cup a^{i+1} \cup \cdots \cup a^j$ for $i < j$.)

3. The equation $X = (a^2 \cup a^3)X^2 \cup (a^4 \cup a^6)X^4 \cup a^3 \cup a^5$ has the unique solution

$$[a^{2,3}(a^{3,5})a^{4,6}(a^{3,5})^3]^*a^{3,5},$$

which can be rewritten as $a^{3,5} \cup a^8 a^*$.

4. The equation $X = (a^3)^*X^4 \cup aX^3 \cup a^2$ has, according Theorem 7.9(c), the following general representation of a solution:

$$[(a^3)^*(a^2 \cup T)^3 a^8 a^* \cup a(a^2 \cup T)^2]^*(a^2 \cup T).$$

Since the empty word must be in T, and thus $\lambda \in a^2 \cup T$, it follows that $a(a^2 \cup T)^2$ contains a; therefore,

$$[(a^3)^*(a^2 \cup T)^3 \cup a(a^2 \cup T)^2] = [(a^3)^*(a^2 \cup T)^3 \cup a(a^2 \cup T)^2 \cup a]$$

and, hence,

$$\begin{aligned}
[(a^3)^*(a^2 \cup T)^3 &\cup a(a^2 \cup T)^2 \cup a]^*(a^2 \cup T) \\
&= [(a^3)^*(a^2 \cup T)^3 \cup a(a^2 \cup T)^2]^*a^*(a^2 \cup T) \\
&= a^*(a^2 \cup T) \\
&= a^*.
\end{aligned}$$

Consequently, this equation has a unique solution, namely a^*, independent of the choice of T.

5. Consider the equation $X = (a^3)^*X^4 \cup a^2$. We obtain the general solution from Theorem 7.9(c) which can be rewritten as

$$\varphi = (\lambda \cup a^2 a^*)(a^4 T)^*(a^2 T^2)^*(T^3)^*(a^8 \cup a^6 T \cup a^4 T^2 \cup a^2 T^3 \cup T^4) \cup a^2 \cup T.$$

Since we must have $\lambda \in T$, it follows that $(a^8 \cup a^6 T \cup a^4 T^2 \cup a^2 T^3 \cup T^4)$ contains λ, and therefore $\lambda \cup a^2 a^*$ is contained in the expression φ. Thus, if $a \in T$, then a^* is the corresponding solution; otherwise, the solution is $\lambda \cup a^2 a^*$. Hence, there are exactly two solutions.

6. Consider the equation $X = (a^3)^*X^4 \cup (a^3)^*$ (compare with the last one). After simplification, one obtains the following general representation of a solution:

$$(a^3)^*T^*.$$

In this case, there are infinitely many different solutions (e.g., for $T = \{a^{3t+1}\}$ for fixed $t \geq 0$). In general, any choice of T will give a solution, including nonregular languages T, even though the solutions themselves will, of course, be regular. In fact, there are uncountably many languages T, but only countably many solutions (since there are only countably many regular languages altogether).

7. Consider the equation $X = X^4 \cup a^4$. After simplification, one obtains the following general representation of a solution:

$$(a^4)^*T^*.$$

Theorem 7.10. *Consider the equation* $X = B(CX^k)^* \cup D$ *over* $\{a\}$. *Then, the expression* $B(C(B \cup D)^k)^* \cup D$ *represents a solution for* $k \geq 1$. *Furthermore, if* $\lambda \notin B$ *or* $\lambda \notin C$, *then this solution is unique.*

PROOF.   That the given language is a solution is again verified by tedious substitution. The uniqueness follows again either appealing to Theorem 5.5 after having verified that the expression involved in the equation has the λ-property or directly as follows. Assume that R is a solution different from the solution S given in the theorem. Let w be a shortest word in $R - S$ (the other case follows similarly). Clearly, w is not in D. Since $w \in R - D$, $w \in B(CR^k)^*$. It now follows that w cannot be in B, for otherwise it would obviously be in S. Thus, $w = bv$ with $b \in B$ and $v \in (CR^k)^i$ for some $i \geq 1$. Therefore, $v = v_1, \ldots, v_i$ and $v_j \in CR^k$ for $j = 1, \ldots, i$, and hence $v_j = c_j u_j$ with $c_j \in C$ and $u_j \in R^k$. By assumption, either the empty word is not in B, then $|v| < |w|$, or the empty word is not in C, then $|u_j| < |v_j|$ for all $j = 1, \ldots, i$. In every case, it follows that $u_j \in S^k$ and, therefore, $w \in S$, in contradiction to the assumption that w was a shortest word in $R - S$. Therefore, S is the unique solution.   □

Examples:

1. Consider the equation

$$X = a^3(X^3)^* \cup a^3.$$

According to Theorem 7.10, this equation has a unique solution, given by

$$a^3(a^{18})^*.$$

2. The equation

$$X = a^3(a^6 X^3)^* \cup a$$

has according to Theorem 7.10 the unique solution $a^3[a^6(a^3 \cup a)^3]^* \cup a$, which is equal to

$$a^{1,3,12,14,17,18,21,23,25,27} \cup a^{29}a^*.$$

3. The equation

$$X = a^2(a^2 X^2)^* \cup \{a^p \mid p \text{ is a prime}\}$$

has the unique solution

$$a^2[a^2(a^2 \cup \{a^p \mid p \text{ is a prime}\})^2]^* \cup \{a^p \mid p \text{ is a prime}\},$$

which can be simplified to $a^{2,3,5} \cup a^7 a^*$.

We now address the question of uniqueness. The proof of Theorem 7.10 indicates that the solution specified there could be nonunique only if $\lambda \in B \cap C$. In this case, we claim the following:

Proposition 7.11. *Any equation of the form*

$$X = B(C \cdot X^k)^* \cup D$$

with $\lambda \in B$ and $\lambda \in C$ can be transformed into an equation of the form

$$X = E(X^k)^* \cup D$$

with $\lambda \in E$ such that S is a solution of the first equation iff S is a solution of the second equation.

PROOF. We first rewrite the given equation as

$$X = B(C' \cdot X^k \cup X^k)^* \cup D$$
$$= B(C' \cdot X^k)^*(X^k)^* \cup D,$$

where $C' = C - \{\lambda\}$. We apply Theorem 7.10 to this equation with the following correspondence:

$$B \leftrightarrow B(X^k)^*, \qquad C \leftrightarrow C', \qquad D \leftrightarrow D.$$

Then the theorem gives us the following solution which is unique since the condition for uniqueness stated in that theorem is satisfied:

$$X = B(X^k)^*[C' \cdot (B(X^k)^* \cup D)^k]^* \cup D$$

$$= B(X^k)^*[C' \cdot \left(\bigcup_{1 \le i \le k} B^i(X^k)^* \cup D^{k-i} \right) \cup C' \cdot D^k]^* \cup D$$

$$= B[(C' \cdot B^1)^* \cdot (C' \cdot B^2)^* \cdot \ldots \cdot (C' \cdot B^k)^* \cdot (C')^* \cdot (C' \cdot D^1)^*$$
$$\cdot \ldots \cdot (C' \cdot D^k)^*]^*(X^k)^* \cup D$$

or $X = E(X^k)^* \cup D$

with $E = B[(C' \cdot B^1)^* \cdot (C' \cdot B^2)^* \cdot \ldots \cdot (C' \cdot B^k)^* \cdot (C')^* \cdot (C' \cdot D^1)^* \cdot \ldots \cdot (C' \cdot D^k)^*]^*$ and, clearly, E is a constant language and contains the empty word λ. By construction, it is now obvious that S is a solution of $X = B(C \cdot X^k)^* \cup D$ iff S is a solution of $X = E(X^k)^* \cup D$.   □

We now come to our second observation:

Proposition 7.12. *Consider the equation $X = E(X^k)^* \cup D$, where $\lambda \in E$. Then, S is a solution of this equation iff $S = E^* D^* T^*$ for some language T over $\{a\}$.*

PROOF. We first show that for any language T over $\{a\}$, $E^* D^* T^*$ is a solution:

$$E[(E^* D^* T^*)^k]^* \cup D = EE^* D^* T^* \cup D = E^* D^* T^* \cup D = E^* D^* T^*$$

since $\lambda \in E$. Then, we have to show the converse. Let S be a solution of $X = E(X^k)^* \cup D$:

$$S = E(S^k)^* \cup D.$$

Since $\lambda \in E$, $\lambda \in S$, and, therefore, $(S^k)^* = S^*$. Thus, $S = ES^* \cup D$, and, hence, $S \supseteq S^*$ and $S \supseteq E \cup D$, which, in turn, implies

$$S \supseteq S^* = S^* S \cup \lambda \supseteq S^*(E \cup D) \cup \lambda \supseteq S^*(E \cup D)^* \cup \lambda$$
$$= S^* E^* D^* \cup \lambda = E^* D^* S^*.$$

Since the other inclusion holds trivially, we know that

$$S = E^* D^* S^*.$$

Thus, by choosing $T = S$, we have shown that any solution can be written as $E^* D^* T^*$ for some language T over the alphabet $\{a\}$. $\square$

We can now give the complete characterization of the solutions of our equation.

Theorem 7.13. *Given an equation* $X = B(C \cdot X^k)^* \cup D$ *with* $\lambda \in B$ *and* $\lambda \in C$, *there exists a parametric representation of all solutions of this equation.*

PROOF.   We first apply Proposition 7.11 to transform the given equation equivalently and uniquely into an equation of the form

$$X = E(X^k)^* \cup D$$

with $\lambda \in E$. Then, we apply Proposition 7.12 to get a parametric representation of all solutions of the second equation. Since a language S is a solution of the first equation iff it is a solution of the second, the claim of the theorem follows. $\square$

Example: Consider the equation

$$X = (a^2)^*[(a^3)^* X^4]^* \cup a^5.$$

We first transform it into

$$X = (a^2)^*[X^4]^* \cdot [a^3(a^3)^* X^4]^* \cup a^5.$$

Simplifying it yields

$$\begin{aligned}
X &= (a^2)^*[X^4]^* \cdot [a^3(a^3)^*((a^2)^*(X^4)^* \cup a^5)^4]^* \cup a^5 \\
&= (a^2)^*[X^4]^* \cdot [a^3(a^3)^*((a^2)^*(X^4)^* \cup a^5(a^2)^*(X^4)^* \\
&\quad \cup a^{15}(a^2)^*(X^4)^* \cup a^{10}(a^2)^*(X^4)^* \cup a^{20})]^* \cup a^5 \\
&= (a^2)^*[X^4]^* \cdot [a^3(a^3)^*((a^2)^* \cup a^5(a^2)^*)(X^4)^*]^* \cup a^5 \\
&= (a^2)^*[X^4]^* \cdot [(a^3(a^2)^* \cup a^6(a^2)^*)(X^4)^*]^* \cup a^5 \\
&= (a^2)^*[X^4]^* \cdot [(a^3 \cup a^5 a^*)(X^4)^*]^* \cup a^5 \\
&= (a^2)^*[X^4]^* \cdot [a^3 \cup a^5 a^*]^*[X^4]^* \cup a^5 \\
&= (a^2)^*[a^3 \cup a^5 a^*]^*[X^4]^* \cup a^5 \\
&= (a^{0,3} \cup a^5 a^*)[X^4]^*.
\end{aligned}$$

Therefore, by Proposition 7.12, we obtain

$$X = (a^{0,3} \cup a^5 a^*)^* T^*$$

since $D = \emptyset$, or

$$X = (a^{0,3} \cup a^5 a^*) T^*.$$

This represents all solutions as any choice of T will yield a solution. It turns out that there are only three different solutions:

If $a \in T$, then the solution is a^*.
If $a \notin T$ and $aa \in T$, then the solution is $a^0 \cup a^2 a^*$.
If $a \notin T$ and $aa \notin T$, the solution is $a^{0,3} \cup a^5 a^*$.

7.4   Solving General Equations in One Variable

In this section, we consider the single equation

$$X = \alpha(X),$$

where $\alpha \in \text{EX}_{\{a\}}(\text{CONST}; \text{OP}; X)$ is an expression over $\{a\}$ with the operators union, concatenation, and star, in the single variable X. Furthermore, we assume that α is in the normal form specified by Theorem 7.7. Here is the procedure for solving this equation.

Procedure $P(X)$:

1. If α contains any occurrences of X outside of the scope of a star, apply Theorem 7.9 once to eliminate all such occurrences of X. This yields an expression β in X. β has the property that it contains no X unless it is within the scope of a star.
2. Choose a term $(CX^k)^*$ occurring in β. Apply Theorem 7.10 to this term and denote the resulting expression again by β.
3. Repeat Step 2 until no term of the form $(CX^k)^*$ occurs in β.

Here is an example. Consider the equation

$$X = LX^2 \cup M(X^3)^* X^4 \cup N(PX)^*,$$

where L, M, N, and P are constant languages over the alphabet $\{a\}$, with the empty word not contained in $L \cup M \cup (N \cap P)$. Step 1 of Procedure $P(X)$ applies Theorem 7.9 with $k = 4$ and

$$A_1 = \emptyset,$$
$$A_2 = L,$$
$$A_3 = \emptyset,$$
$$A_4 = M(X^3)^*,$$
$$B = N(PX)^*.$$

This yields the equation

$$X = \{[N(PX)^*]L \cup [N(PX)^*]^3 M(X^3)^*\}^* N(PX)^*,$$

which can be simplified to

$$X = [MN^4(LN)^*(MN^3)^*(PX)^*](X^3)^* \cup N(LN)^*(PX)^*.$$

This equation contains the variable X in two star terms, namely $(PX)^*$ and $(X^3)^*$. We first concentrate on the term $(X^3)^*$; applying Theorem 7.10 with

$$B = MN^4(LN)^*(MN^3)^*(PX)^*,$$
$$C = \{\lambda\},$$
$$D = N(LN)^*(PX)^*$$

yields, after simplification, the following equation for X:

$$X = N(LN)^*[MN^3(MN^3)^*(N^3)^* \cup \lambda](PX)^*.$$

In this equation, X occurs only in $(PX)^*$. Applying Theorem 7.10 one last time yields the desired regular expression in the constant languages L, M, N, and P:

$$X = N(LN)^*[\lambda \cup MN^3(MN^3)^*(N^3)^*](NP)^*.$$

Since the conditions for uniqueness in Theorems 7.9 and 7.10 hold [as $\lambda \notin L \cup M \cup (N \cap P)$ by assumption], this solution expression is unique. If one substitutes languages over $\{a\}$ for L, M, N, and P in this expression, the resulting language is the solution of the corresponding equation, since the substitution property holds. For example, if $L = a^2$, $M = a^3$, $N = a^4$, and $P = a^5$, then the solution evaluates to $a^4 \cup a^{10}(a^3)^*$.

At this point, $P(X)$ is a procedure. In order to demonstrate that $P(X)$ will actually give a solution, it is necessary to show that it will terminate in finitely many steps. This is contained in the following:

Theorem 7.14. *Applying the Procedure $P(X)$ to the equation $X = \alpha$, where $\alpha \in \mathrm{EX}_{\{a\}}(\mathrm{CONST};\ OP;\ X)$, results within finitely many steps in an expression in the constant languages which represents a solution of the given equation.*

PROOF.   Since Theorems 7.9 and 7.10 preserve language identities, the successively resulting equations must have the same solutions as the original one. Thus, all that remains to be shown is that $P(X)$ terminates. To this end, we observe that after applying Theorem 7.9 (at most) once, any occurrences of X will be within the scope of some star. Inspection of the solution given by Theorem 7.10 then shows that each application will effectively eliminate one term of the form $(CX^k)^*$ without introducing another term $(C'X^{k'})^*$ for a pair (C', k') which had not been present before (after putting the resulting expression in normal form). Since the number of such terms is finite for any given expression, the process must terminate.   □

It is interesting that the order in which the two theorems are applied is crucial. Even though both theorems correspond to independent fix-point operations, it is generally impossible to eliminate all starred terms first, and only then all unstarred variables. This is because an application of Theorem 7.10 in the presence of unstarred variables may very well introduce starred terms $(C'X^{k'})^*$ for pairs (C', k') which had not been present before. This is easily verified using the equation

$$X = (L \cup MX^2)X^* \cup N,$$

where each application of Theorem 7.10 (without having first eliminated the X^2 term) will introduce a term previously not present. Thus, the procedure does not terminate; no solution is obtained.

7.5   Solving Systems of Equations

We come now to the final generalization of our solution technique, namely to a system of n equations in n variables,

$$X_i = \alpha_i(X_1, \ldots, X_n), \quad i = 1, \ldots, n.$$

where for $i = 1, \ldots, n$, $\alpha_i \in \mathrm{EX}_{\{a\}}(\mathrm{CONST}; \mathrm{OP}; X_1, \ldots, X_n)$, with OP consisting of union, unrestricted concatenation, and star. The solution of such a system of equations can be obtained by using the following procedure:

Procedure $PP(X_1, \ldots, X_n)$:

1. for $i := 1, \ldots, n$ do
   (**1.1**) Apply Procedure $P(X_i)$ to the equation for X_i so that the variable X_i occurs nowhere in the expression for that equation. Let γ_i be the resulting expression.
   (**1.2**) Substitute the expression γ_i for X_i (this is an expression in terms of constant languages and in terms of the variables X_{i+1} through X_n) wherever X_i occurs in the equations for $X_{i+1}, \ldots, X_n$.

2. The expression γ_n is in terms of constant languages only; let L_n be the constant language denoted by this expression.

3. for $i := n - 1, \ldots, 1$ do
   (**3.1**) Substitute the language L_{i+1} into all expressions $\gamma_i, \gamma_{i-1}, \ldots, \gamma_1$.
   (**3.2**) The expression γ_i is now in terms of constant languages only; let L_i be the constant language denoted by this expression.

It remains to be shown that $PP(X_1, \ldots, X_n)$ does, in fact, terminate.

Theorem 7.15. *Applying Procedure $PP(X_1, \ldots, X_n)$ to a system of equations $X_i = \alpha_i$, where $\alpha_i \in \mathrm{EX}_{\{a\}}(\mathrm{CONST}; OP; X_1, \ldots, X_n)$ for $i = 1, \ldots, n$, with OP consisting of union, unrestricted concatenation, and* *star, results within finitely many steps in an expression in the constant languages which represents a solution of the system of equations.*

PROOF.   The proof consists of repeated applications of Theorem 7.14.   □

Let us look at a simple example; a more complicated one is worked out in the next section. Consider the following system of three equations in the variables X, Y, and Z:

$$X = (a^2 X^3)^* \cup aX^2 \cup aY,$$
$$Y = (a^2 Z^2)^*,$$
$$Z = a(a^2 X^3)^* Z^2 \cup a.$$

Instead of going through the tedious derivations, we give just the results:

$$X = a^*,$$
$$Y = \lambda \cup a^{4,6} \cup a^8 a^*,$$
$$Z = a^{1,3} \cup a^5 a^*.$$

It can be verified that these are indeed solutions. Since the solutions for these equations are unique, they must be the only ones.

7.6   Uniqueness and Regularity of Solutions

We restate and amplify our results concerning uniqueness and regularity of solutions of systems of equations over the one-letter alphabet $\{a\}$ where the operations are union, concatenation, and star. We also briefly deal with the question of how to construct the regular language $L(G)$, where G is a context-free grammar with a one-letter alphabet of input symbols.

7.6.1   Uniqueness

Both Theorems 7.9 and 7.10 state conditions which assure the uniqueness of the (expressions for the) solutions. If these conditions are satisfied in each step in Procedure $P(X)$ or $PP(X_1, \ldots, X_n)$, the resulting solution (for specific languages) is necessarily unique. Consider the system of equations

$$X = YZ^* \cup Z,$$
$$Y = aX^*Z,$$
$$Z = (XY)^*Y \cup a.$$

One can easily verify that neither Y, nor Z, nor X can contain λ. Therefore, for $i = 1$ (we number X, Y, and Z as variables 1, 2, and 3), there is no Step (1.1) in $PP(X, Y, Z)$; Step (1.2) results in

$$Y = aZZ^*Y^*Y \cup aZZ^*,$$
$$Z = ((YZ^* \cup Z)Y)^*Y \cup a.$$

For $i = 2$, Step (1.1) will solve the equation for Y by one application of Theorem 7.9 and one of Theorem 7.10 for Y^*. The result is

$$Y = a^2 Z^2 (aZ)^* Z^* \cup aZZ^*$$

and the substitution into Z [Step (1.2)] yields (after considerable work)

$$Z = aZZ^*(aZ)^* \cup a.$$

Then, one solves the equation for Z [$i = 3$, Step (1.1)] and obtains

$$Z = aa^*$$

and from this

$$Y = a^2 a^* \quad \text{and} \quad X = aa^*.$$

Finally, one can verify directly that these three languages are indeed a solution of the given system, and since all uniqueness conditions are satisfied, it is in fact the only one.

If the uniqueness criteria of Theorems 7.9 and 7.10 are not satisfied, then Theorem 7.9(c) and Theorem 7.13 yield parametric representations of all solutions of the equations. Consider the equation

$$X = (a^{0,3} X^2)^* X^3 \cup (a^5)^*.$$

Applying Theorem 7.9 once yields the following equation after considerable work:

$$X = (a^5)^* T^* (a^{0,3} X^2)^* \quad \text{for } T \text{ an arbitrary language over } \{a\}.$$

From this, by applying Theorem 7.13 we obtain the following parametric representation of all solutions:

$$X = (a^3)^* (a^5)^* T^* S^* \quad \text{for } S \text{ and } T \text{ arbitrary languages over } \{a\}.$$

Since $(a^3)^*(a^5)^* = a^{0,3,5,6} \cup a^8 a^*$, it follows that there are only finitely many different solutions since $a^* - (a^3)^*(a^5)^* = a^{1,2,4,7}$.

7.6.2 Regularity

The regularity of solutions follows essentially analogously to their uniqueness. Applying Theorems 7.9 and 7.10, the regularity of the solutions is established. The conditions for regularity in Theorem 7.9 are very mild; essentially, all nontrivial equations (i.e., all equations other than $X = B$ and $X = X \cup B$) are guaranteed to have regular solutions. The solutions given in Proposition 7.12 are always regular [by Propositions 7.1(b) and 7.5(a)] and the solution of Theorem 7.10 is also regular (for $B \neq \emptyset$), by Proposition 7.5(d). Thus, for all but the most degenerate equations, the solutions are regular, even if the constant languages are nonrecursively enumerable languages!

7.6.3   CFL over $\{a\}$

We conclude with the construction of a regular expression for the language generated by a context-free grammar over a one-letter alphabet. It is well known that such a language is always regular, but explicitly constructing a regular language is a very nontrivial task when using the traditional approach. The techniques developed in this chapter make this task easy.

Let $G = (N, T, P, S)$ be a context-free grammar with $T = \{a\}$. Define a system of equations as follows:

The set of variables of the equations is N.

For each grammar variable $A \in N$ construct one equation, as follows: Let all A productions in P be $A \to \alpha_1|\cdots|\alpha_n$. Then the equation corresponding to the equation variable A is given by

$$A = \alpha_1 \cup \cdots \cup \alpha_n.$$

These equations clearly satisfy the assumptions stated in the previous sections. Thus, the resulting system can be solved; the regular solution expression corresponding to the starting symbol S denotes exactly the language $L(G)$. Even though the initial equations involve only union and concatenation, intermediate equations will also contain stars. Therefore, it is not sufficient to apply only Theorem 7.9; the technique described in Section 7.5 is necessary for producing the solution.

Consider the grammar $G = (\{A, B, C\}, \{a\}, P, A)$ with P given by

$$A \to BaB \mid ACACA \mid \lambda,$$
$$B \to CCC,$$
$$C \to AA \mid \lambda.$$

The resulting system of equations is

$$A = BaB \cup ACACA \cup \lambda,$$
$$B = CCC,$$
$$C = AA \cup \lambda$$

or, in normal form,

$$A = C^2 A^3 \cup aB^2 \cup \lambda,$$
$$B = C^3,$$
$$C = A^2 \cup \lambda.$$

Solving these equations yields $A = B = C = a^*$. With the traditional methods, it is unlikely that this result could be obtained as directly and systematically as it is obtained using language equations.

The whole construction is very straightforward. However, we must note that the presence of productions of the form $A \to A$ might render solutions nonunique. For example, if our set of productions were given by $P = \{S \to$

$S \mid SaSaS \mid a\}$, the resulting single equation would be $S = a^2S^3 \cup S \cup a$, and this equation does not satisfy the uniqueness condition of Theorem 7.9. The general solution of this equation is

$$(a^4)^*(a^3T)^*(a^2T^2)^*(a \cup T)$$

for T any arbitrary language. Choosing $T = \emptyset$, this expression gives $a(a^4)^*$, which is equal to $L(G)$. However, for other values of T, other valid solutions of the equation can be obtained. For example, $T = a^2$ gives the solution $a^{1,2} \cup a^5a^*$. Problems due to useless productions can be avoided in two ways:

- by removing them from the given grammar; this does not affect the language generated [note that $L(G)$ denotes the least fix point, whereas through language equations, one can obtain any fix point].
- by choosing $T = \emptyset$ in Theorem 7.9(c).

Both approaches are equivalent and yield $L(G)$.

7.7 Explicit Equations over $\{a\}$ with Complementation

In Chapter 4 on boolean equations, we demonstrated that even expressions with arbitrarily nested complementation operators have effectively constructible regular solutions (for CONST = REG) provided concatenation was restricted to left-concatenation. In the preceding sections of this chapter, we have shown that in the case of a one-letter alphabet, arbitrary concatenation can be dealt with, in the sense that any system of equations with regular constants has a regular solution, too. In this section, we attempt to marry complementation and arbitrary concatenation, provided the alphabet contains only one letter. It turns out that this does not work; more specifically, if we have equations over $\{a\}$ where complementation and unrestricted concatenation occur, then it is possible that only nonregular (which, in view of the last section, means non-context-free) solutions exist even though all constant languages occurring in the equations are regular.

In order to simplify our notation, we abbreviate, as before, $a^{m,\ldots,n} = \{a^m, a^{m+1}, \ldots, a^n\}$, and write $\alpha^2 = \alpha\alpha$ for any expression α.

Theorem 7.16. *There exist explicit equations in a single variable over the alphabet $A = \{a\}$ using concatenation and complementation only whose constant languages are regular and whose only solutions are non-context-free.*

PROOF.   Consider the equation

$$X = a\overline{\overline{\overline{X}^2}^2}^2 \ .$$

First, we note that, by Theorem 5.5, this equation has a unique solution, because the expression on the right has the λ-property. Then, we observe that the following language is a solution

$$S = \bigcup_{i \geq 0} a^{2^{3i}..2^{3i+2}} - 1.$$

This can be verified by direct substitution of S into the equation:

$$\overline{S} = \lambda \cup \bigcup_{i \geq 0} a^{2^{3i+2}..2^{3i+3}-1},$$

$$\overline{S}^2 = \lambda \cup \bigcup_{i \geq 0} a^{2^{3i+2}..2^{3i+4}-2},$$

$$\overline{\overline{S}^2} = \bigcup_{i \geq 0} a^{2^{3i+1}..2^{3i+2}-1},$$

$$\overline{\overline{S}^2}^2 = \bigcup_{i \geq 0} a^{2^{3i+1}..2^{3i+3}-2},$$

$$\overline{\overline{\overline{S}^2}^2} = \bigcup_{i \geq 0} a^{2^{3i}-1..2^{3i+1}-1},$$

$$\overline{\overline{\overline{S}^2}^2}^2 = \bigcup_{i \geq 0} a^{2^{3i}-1..2^{3i+2}-2},$$

and from this, the claim follows.

We now show that S is not regular; more specifically, we claim that for any integer $M \geq 1$, there exists an integer M_0 such that

$$a^{M_0..M_0+M-1} \cap S = \emptyset.$$

Indeed, there are arbitrarily large gaps between successive powers of 2. In our case, the gap between $a^{2^{3i+2}}$ and $a^{2^{3i+3}}$ is of size 2^{3i+2}. Thus, for any given M, M_0 is equal to the smallest number of the form 2^{3i+2} not less than M:

$$M_0 = 2^{3\lceil (\log_2 M - 2)/3 \rceil + 2}.$$

Therefore, S cannot be regular, and thus S cannot be context-free either. In fact, S cannot even lie in the closure of CFL under all boolean operations, concatenation, and star. $\square$

Observation: The equation given in Theorem 7.16 is the simplest with a nonregular solution, in the following sense: Dropping one or more complementation or squaring operations in the regular expression on the right yields an equation whose (unique) solution is regular.

This can be verified directly.

Theorem 7.17. *Consider an explicit language equation $X = \alpha$ over the alphabet $\{a\}$ with regular constant languages, where the operations are* *union, concatenation, star, and complementation. If this equation has any solution, then there always exists a context-sensitive one.*

For the proof, we refer to [Leiss, 94b].

Corollary 7.18. *There exist regular language equations over an arbitrary alphabet using only concatenation and complementation which have solutions that are not contained in the closure of CFL under boolean operations, concatenation, and star.*

PROOF.   Consider the same equation as in the proof of Theorem 7.16, except that the alphabet is now arbitrary, say $\{a, b, \ldots\}$. Let S and T be the solutions of this equation for the alphabets $\{a\}$, $\{a, b, \ldots\}$, respectively. It follows that $S = T \cap a^*$, and this implies the statement of the corollary.   □

7.8 Conclusion and Open Problems

Certain language equations have always provided a means to start with one class of languages and get solutions in a more general class. Usually, concatenation is implicated in such situations. Examples are given by the equations derived from context-free grammars (e.g., $X = aXb \cup \lambda$ derived from the context-free productions $X \to aXb \mid \lambda$) and the star equations studied in Chapter 6. However, in this way, one could never get more than CFL when starting from regular languages. In Section 7.7, we have shown that even for a one-letter alphabet, adding complementation to the canon of permitted operations will result in equations whose solutions are no longer even context-free, nor do they lie in the closure of CFL under the standard operations. This appears to be the first demonstration that the notion of language equations with the standard operations can be used to generate non-context-free languages.

We raise the following fundamental question: Given a system of equations over a one-letter alphabet with regular constants whose operators are union, concatenation, and complementation, is it decidable whether the system has a regular solution? In [Leiss 94b], it was shown that the problem is recursively enumerable. However, it is not known whether the problem is decidable.

7.9 Bibliographical Notes

It has long been known that languages over a one-letter alphabet behave differently from those over alphabets with more letters. In particular, all languages over $\{a\}$ are commutative and all context-free languages over $\{a\}$ are regular [Ginzb/Rice 62]. Most of the properties of languages over $\{a\}$ that are summarized in Section 7.1 are well known; they are taken from

[Leiss 94a]. The two key results allowing us to solve arbitrary language equations over $\{a\}$ with union, concatenation, and star are also adapted from that paper, as is the general construction of solutions for systems of equations. The parametric representation of all solutions was hinted at in [Leiss 94a] but is formally carried out only here. The major results of Section 7.7, in particular the fact that adding complementation yields equations whose solutions need not be regular even though all constants are, were first shown in [Leiss 94b].

7.10   Problems

1. Assume you are given a system of explicit language equations over $\{a\}$ with the operators union, concatenation, and star. Show that the (uniquely determined) solution obtained by using Theorem 7.9(a) and Theorem 7.10 yields the minimal solution (i.e., where all parameters are equal to the empty language) if there are multiple solutions.
2. For the following systems of equations over $\{a\}$:

   i. Determine the minimal solution.
   ii. Determine whether there is a unique solution.
   iii. Determine a parametric representation of all solutions.
   iv. Determine whether there are finitely many solutions.
   v. Determine whether there are infinitely many solutions.

   a. $X = a^2(X^2)^*(aX^3)^*X^4 \cup \lambda$;
   b. $X = a^2X^4 \cup a^3Y^5 \cup a(a^6X^2)^*$,
      $Y = aX^3Y^5 \cup a(aX)^*(aY)^*$;
   c. $X = (a^4)^*((a^3)^*X^3)^*((a^6)^*X^6)^*$;
   d. $X = a^2(a^3X^2)^*Y^2 \cup \lambda$,
      $Y = a^3XY \cup a^2XY^2 \cup aXY^3 \cup a$.

3. For the context-free grammars G given below, determine the regular language $L(G)$.

   a. $G = (\{S, A, B\}, \{a\}, P, S)$ with P as follows:
   $$S \rightarrow a^3AS \mid a^5BS \mid a,$$
   $$A \rightarrow a^4S \mid aS,$$
   $$B \rightarrow a^4S \mid a^2S^2.$$

   b. $G = (\{S, A, B, C\}, \{a\}, P, S)$ with P as follows:
   $$S \rightarrow a^4A^2S \mid a^5BS^3 \mid a^3,$$
   $$A \rightarrow a^4S \mid aSC^4,$$
   $$B \rightarrow a^4S \mid a^2S^2,$$
   $$C \rightarrow aS^4 \mid a^2CS^2.$$

8

Implicit Equations with Union and Left-Concatenation

About This Chapter: We begin our coverage of implicit equations by considering the exact analogue to the classical (explicit) equations solved in Chapter 3. Specifically, the operations are union and left-concatenation and the constants are over an arbitrary alphabet. We first establish that, in contrast to explicit equations, implicit ones need not have any solutions. Furthermore, there exist implicit equations with context-free constants whose only solutions are non-context-free. Then we show a general criterion for the existence of a solution. This criterion is constructive if the constants are regular. Furthermore, the criterion gives rise to a test whether there exist finitely or infinitely many solutions. If the constants are regular, solutions can be constructed effectively; moreover, if there are finitely many solutions, all solutions can be constructed, and if there are infinitely many, an arbitrarily large number of them can be constructed.

Let $\alpha_1, \ldots, \alpha_m$ be expressions in $\mathrm{EX}_A(\mathrm{CONST};\ \mathrm{OP};\ X_1, \ldots, X_n)$ where CONST is arbitrary and OP consists of union and left-concatenation. Let $L_1, \ldots, L_m$ be languages in CONST. Then,

$$L_i = \alpha_i \quad \text{for } i = 1, \ldots, m$$

is a system of m implicit language equations in the n variables $X_1, \ldots, X_n$. Thus, these equations are exact analogues of the (explicit) classical equations studied in Chapter 3, except that they are implicit. In the present chapter, we will develop a theory of implicit language equations. In contrast to the classical language equation where the number m of equations is equal to the number n of variables (i.e., each variable has exactly one equation representing it), for implicit equations, the numbers m and n are entirely unrelated. We first establish a normal form result.

Theorem 8.1. *Let $L_i = \alpha_i$ for $i = 1, \ldots, m$ be a system of implicit equations where the α_i are expressions in $\mathrm{EX}_A(\mathrm{CONST}; \mathrm{OP}; X_1, \ldots, X_n)$ with OP consisting of union and left-concatenation. Then there exists a system*

$$L = S \cdot X,$$

where $L = (L_1, \ldots, L_{m'})$, $X = (X_1, \ldots, X_{n'})$, and $S = (S_{ij})_{1 \leq i \leq m, 1 \leq j \leq n}$ is an (m, n) matrix consisting of elements of CONST such that

$$L = S \cdot X \text{ has a solution } \quad \text{iff } L_i = \alpha_i \text{ for } i = 1, \ldots, m \text{ has one.}$$

PROOF.   We know from Section 3.1 that each α_i can be written in the form

$$\alpha_i = \bigcup_{j=1,\ldots,n} S_{i,j} \cdot X_j \cup S_{i,0},$$

where all the $S_{i,t}$ are elements of CONST. Thus, what remains to be shown is that the terms $S_{i,0}$ can be eliminated in our implicit equations. This, however, follows immediately from the observation that for each $i = 1, \ldots, m$, we can add a new variable Y_i together with the implicit equation $S_{i,0} = Y_i$. Then, the resulting system of equation is in the stipulated normal form and, moreover, $(X_1, \ldots, X_n) = (M_1, \ldots, M_n)$ is a solution of the original system iff $(X_1, \ldots, X_n, Y_1, \ldots, Y_n) = (M_1, \ldots, M_n, S_{1,0}, \ldots, S_{m,0})$ is a solution of the new system of equations.   □

We define restricted implicit language equations by stipulating that all elements of the matrix S be either the empty language $\emptyset$ or the language $\{\lambda\}$ consisting only of the empty word. Whereas for explicit equations, this restriction would render the resulting equations trivial, restricted implicit language equations may have rather nonobvious solutions, or none at all, as the next section demonstrates.

Note that in view of Theorem 8.1, an alternative way of looking at systems of restricted implicit language equations is the following: They are precisely the systems of equations

$$Li = \alpha_i, \quad i = 1, \ldots, m,$$

where for all i, L_i is a constant language and $\alpha_i \in \mathrm{EX}_A(\mathrm{CONST}; \mathrm{OP}'; X_1, \ldots, X_n)$ with OP' consisting only of the operation union.

8.1 Basic Properties of Implicit Language Equations

8.1.1 Existence of Solutions

Our systems of implicit language equations appear to be natural analogues of systems of classical equations. However, their behavior is very different, as the following proposition shows.

Proposition 8.2. *There exist single implicit language equations in one variable that do not have a solution.*

PROOF. Consider the equation $M \cdot X = L$ in the variable X where the constant language L is finite and nonempty and the constant language M is infinite. Clearly, if there existed a solution X, it must be either empty or nonempty. In both cases, one obtains a contradiction; therefore, no solution can exist. □

Consider the following system of four restricted implicit language equations in four variables:

$$L = S \cdot X,$$

where $L = ((aa)^*, (aaa)^*, (aa)^*, (aa)^*)$ and S is given by

$$\begin{vmatrix} \emptyset & \{\lambda\} & \{\lambda\} & \{\lambda\} \\ \{\lambda\} & \emptyset & \{\lambda\} & \emptyset \\ \{\lambda\} & \{\lambda\} & \emptyset & \{\lambda\} \\ \emptyset & \emptyset & \emptyset & \{\lambda\} \end{vmatrix}.$$

Assume that there exists a solution of this system. From the fourth equation, one concludes that $X_4 = (aa)^*$. Then, both $X_2 \cup X_3$ (by the first equation) and $X_1 \cup X_2$ (by the third equation) must be contained in $(aa)^*$, thus $X_1 \cup X_2 \cup X_3 \subseteq (aa)^*$, whereas by the second equation, $X_1 \cup X_3$ must be equal to $(aaa)^*$. This, however, is impossible. Thus, no solution exists. Consequently, we can state the following:

Corollary 8.3. *There exist systems of restricted implicit language equations (over any alphabet) that do not have a solution.*

Before we show other basic properties, let us look at some examples. Specifically, we examine three restricted systems of implicit language equations. General systems will be discussed in the next section.

Examples:

1. Two restricted implicit language equations in three variables, with finitely many solutions:

$$X_1 \cup X_2 = a^*,$$
$$X_1 \cup X_3 = b^*.$$

There are exactly five different solutions, namely

$$(X_1, X_2, X_3) = (\emptyset, a^*, b^*), (\{\lambda\}, a^*, b^*), (\{\lambda\}, aa^*, b^*),$$
$$(\{\lambda\}, a^*, bb^*), (\{\lambda\}, aa^*, bb^*).$$

This can be seen as follows: $(X_1 \cup X_2) \cap (X_1 \cup X_3) = a^* \cap b^* = \{\lambda\}$; thus, there are two possibilities for X_1, namely $\emptyset$ and $\{\lambda\}$. Having fixed X_1, the possible solutions for the other two variables are determined similarly.

2. Six restricted implicit language equations in four variables, with infinitely many solutions:

$$X_1 \cup X_2 = a^*,$$
$$X_1 \cup X_3 = a^*,$$
$$X_1 \cup X_4 = a^*,$$
$$X_2 \cup X_3 = (aa)^*,$$
$$X_2 \cup X_4 = (aa)^*,$$
$$X_3 \cup X_4 = (aaaa)^*.$$

It is easy to verify by direct substitution that there are infinitely many different solutions; for example, $(X_1, X_2, X_3, X_4) = (a^*, (aa)^*, (aaaa)^*, L)$ for any language L contained in $(aaaa)^*$ or $((a, aa, aaa)(aaaa)^*, (aa)^*, (aaaa)^*, (aaaa)^*)$.

3. Three restricted implicit language equations in four variables, with no solution:

$$X_1 \cup X_2 \cup X_3 = a^*,$$
$$X_1 \cup X_2 \cup X_4 = b^*,$$
$$X_2 \cup X_3 \cup X_4 = a^*.$$

One derives from the first two equations that $X_1 \cup X_2$ must be contained in $\{\lambda\}$ (the intersection of a^* and b^*), and therefore (by the second equation) bb^* must be contained in X_4 which gives a contradiction to the third equation. Thus, no solution exists.

Note that for the explicit language equations involving only union and left-concatenation, it is not possible to have an analogous situation: Explicit systems of classical language equations where there are fewer equations than variables would almost always have infinitely many solutions. We will take this issue up in more detail in Chapter 10.

8.1.2 Nonclosure of CFL Under Implicit Language Equations

Let $L = S \cdot X$ be a system of implicit language equations with union and left-concatenation, $L = (L_1, \ldots, L_n)$ and $X = (X_1, \ldots, X_n)$. We will call a solution of such a system regular (context-free, recursive, r.e.), if all the languages of the solution are regular (context-free, recursive, r.e.). In another indication that implicit language equations behave substantially differently from explicit equations, we show that there exist systems of implicit language equations with CONST = CFL that have only non-context-free solutions. Moreover, this surprising result holds even for restricted implicit language equations.

Theorem 8.4. *Let $L = S \cdot X$ be a system of implicit language equations with union and left-concatenation where all constant languages are context-free. Then, no solution of this system need be context-free.*

PROOF. Consider the following system of seven restricted implicit language equations in nine variables:

$$
\begin{vmatrix}
\{\lambda\} & \{\lambda\} & \emptyset & \emptyset & \emptyset & \emptyset & \emptyset & \emptyset & \emptyset \\
\{\lambda\} & \emptyset & \{\lambda\} & \emptyset & \emptyset & \emptyset & \emptyset & \emptyset & \emptyset \\
\emptyset & \emptyset & \emptyset & \{\lambda\} & \{\lambda\} & \emptyset & \emptyset & \emptyset & \emptyset \\
\emptyset & \emptyset & \emptyset & \{\lambda\} & \emptyset & \{\lambda\} & \emptyset & \emptyset & \emptyset \\
\emptyset & \emptyset & \emptyset & \emptyset & \emptyset & \emptyset & \{\lambda\} & \{\lambda\} & \emptyset \\
\emptyset & \emptyset & \emptyset & \emptyset & \emptyset & \emptyset & \{\lambda\} & \emptyset & \{\lambda\} \\
\{\lambda\} & \emptyset & \emptyset & \{\lambda\} & \emptyset & \emptyset & \{\lambda\} & \emptyset & \emptyset
\end{vmatrix}
\cdot
\begin{vmatrix}
X_1 \\ X_2 \\ X_3 \\ X_4 \\ X_5 \\ X_6 \\ X_7 \\ X_8 \\ X_9
\end{vmatrix}
=
\begin{vmatrix}
\{a^m b^m c^* \mid m \geq 1\} \\
\{a^m b^* c^m \mid m \geq 1\} \\
\{a^m b^m c^* \mid m \geq 1\} \\
\{a^m b^* c^* c^{m+1} \mid m \geq 1\} \\
\{a^m b^m c^* \mid m \geq 1\} \\
\{a^m b^* c^n \mid n < m\} \\
\{a^m b^m c^* \mid m \geq 1\}
\end{vmatrix}.
$$

By the first and second equations, the solution for X_1 must be contained in the intersection of $\{a^m b^m c^* \mid m \geq 1\}$ and $\{a^m b^* c^m \mid m \geq 1\}$, which is the non-context-free language $\{a^m b^m c^m \mid m \geq 1\}$. From the third and fourth equations, we see that X_4 must be contained in the language $\{a^m b^m c^m cc^* \mid m \geq 1\}$, and by the next two equations, X_7 must be contained in $\{a^m b^m c^n \mid 0 \leq n < m \text{ and } m \geq 1\}$. It is easily verified that for all $i \neq j$, $i, j \in \{1, 4, 7\}$, X_i and X_j are pairwise disjoint. Therefore, the last equation implies that for these three languages, equality must hold in the above inclusions; i.e.,

$$X_1 = \{a^m b^m c^m \mid m \geq 1\},$$
$$X_4 = \{a^m b^m c^m cc^* \mid m \geq 1\},$$
$$X_7 = \{a^m b^m c^n \mid 0 \leq n < m \text{ and } m \geq 1\}.$$

However, these three languages are clearly non-context-free, which proves the theorem. Note that the other six solution languages (X_j for $j =$

2, 3, 5, 6, 8, 9) may be context-free, but since they are not uniquely determined, they could also not be context-free.   □

Corollary 8.5. *Theorem 8.4 holds even in the case of restricted implicit language equations.*

8.2   A Procedure for Determining That No Solution Exists

In this section, we derive a condition that allows us to determine that no solution exists; by itself, it only gives us a procedure for determining the converse. Thus, the resulting method for determining a solution is a procedure that is not guaranteed to terminate and, therefore, not an algorithm.

Assume a system $L = S \cdot X$ of implicit language equations with CONST arbitrary and OP consisting of union and left-concatenation. Consider its ith equation,

$$S_{i,1} \cdot X_1 \cup \cdots \cup S_{i,n} \cdot X_n = L_i.$$

It follows that for any word w in L_i, if there is a solution in X, we must have

$$w \in S_{i,1} \cdot X_1 \cup \cdots \cup S_{i,n} \cdot X_n.$$

This, however, is true if and only if

$$\exists j \in \{1, \ldots, n\}\colon \exists u \in S_{i,j} \text{ and } u \text{ a prefix of } w, w/u \in X_j.$$

Similarly, for any word w not in L_i, if there is a solution in X, w necessarily must not be in $S_{i,1} \cdot X_1 \cup \cdots \cup S_{i,n} \cdot X_n$. This is true if and only if

$$\forall j \in \{1, \ldots, n\}\colon \forall u \in S_{i,j} \text{ and } u \text{ a prefix of } w, w/u \notin X_j.$$

We recall that x/y denotes the quotient of the word x with respect to its prefix y, which is defined as z if $x = yz$. Furthermore, if L and M are languages over the alphabet A, the quotient of L with respect to M is defined by

$$L/M = \{z \in A^* \mid z = x/y \text{ for some } x \in L \text{ and some } y \in M$$
$$\text{such that } y \in \mathrm{PREF}(L)\}.$$

PREF(L) for any language L denotes the set of all prefixes (not necessarily proper) of L:

$$\mathrm{PREF}(L) = \{x \in A^* \mid w = xy \text{ and } w \in L, y \in A^*\}.$$

The statement "$\exists j \in \{1, \ldots, n\}$: $\exists u \in S_{i,j}$ and u a prefix of w, $w/u \in X_j$" can be reformulated as the following boolean expression $\pi(i, w)$:

$$\pi(i, w) = \underset{j=1,\ldots,n}{\text{or}} \quad \underset{u \in S_{i,j} \text{ and } u \in \text{PREF}(w)}{\text{or}} \quad w/u \in X_j \equiv \textbf{true}.$$

It is clear that this is a boolean expression of finite length since the length of w is finite.

Similarly, the statement "$\forall j \in \{1, \ldots, n\}$: $\forall u \in S_{i,j}$ and u a prefix of w, $w/u \notin X_j$" can be written as the boolean expression $\nu(i, w)$:

$$\nu(i, w) = \underset{j=1,\ldots,n}{\text{and}} \quad \underset{u \in S_{i,j} \text{ and } u \in \text{PREF}(w)}{\text{and}} \quad \text{not}(w/u \in X_j) \equiv \textbf{true}.$$

Again, this is a boolean expression of finite length.

From these observations, it follows that we can construct a boolean expression $F_i(K)$ consisting of atoms of the form $x \in X_j$ or $\text{not}(x \in X_j)$ for x a word over the underlying alphabet A, combined by logical **and** and **or** operators; this boolean expression can be stated as follows:

$F_i(K) := \textbf{true};$
for $k := 0..K$ **do**
    for every w of length k **do**
        if $w \in L_i$ **then** $F_i(K) := F_i(K)$ **and** $\pi(i, w)$
                               else $F_i(K) := F_i(K)$ **and** $\nu(i, w)$

The boolean expression $F(K)$ is then defined as

$$F(K) = F_1(K) \text{ \textbf{and} } F_2(K) \text{ \textbf{and} } \ldots \text{ \textbf{and} } F_m(K).$$

Lemma 8.6. *If there exists a K such that $F(K) \equiv \textbf{false}$, then no solution exists.*

PROOF. $F(K) \equiv \textbf{false}$ if and only if there exists i such that $F_i(K) \equiv \textbf{false}$, and this, in turn, is the case iff there exists a word w such that $|w| \leq K$ and either $w \in L_i$ and $\pi(i, w) \equiv \textbf{false}$ or else $w \notin L_i$ and $\nu(i, w) \equiv \textbf{false}$. This, however, amounts to contradicting requirements for the existence of a solution; therefore, no solution can exist. $\square$

Clearly, for any fixed K, $F(K)$ is a boolean expression of finite length. Furthermore, by construction of $F(K)$, if $F(K) \equiv \textbf{false}$ for some value of K, then $F(K') \equiv \textbf{false}$ for any $K' > K$.

The construction of the boolean expression $F(K)$ started as an attempt at determining a necessary and sufficient condition for the existence of a solution. However, Lemma 8.6 is only a sufficient condition for the nonexistence of a solution. Thus, we have a procedure that will terminate if no solution exists, since for any given K, constructing $F(K)$ and testing whether $F(K)$ is identically **false** can be done effectively, provided we have effective methods for testing for membership in the constant languages S_{ij} and L_i, $i = 1, \ldots, m$ and $j = 1, \ldots, n$. However, we do not have an algorithm since this procedure will continue with ever-increasing K without yielding $F(K) \equiv$ **false** if there does exist a solution. We summarize:

Theorem 8.7. *Consider a system in normal form of implicit language equations with union and left-concatenation. If all constant languages occurring in the system are recursive, nonexistence of a solution of the system of implicit language equations is recursively enumerable.*

8.3 Solving Implicit Language Equations

This section reformulates the conditions $\pi(i, w)$ and $\nu(i, w)$ and derives an algorithm for determining the existence of a solution and, if one exists, a solution itself. Again, we assume we are given a system of implicit language equations in normal form,

$$L = S \cdot X,$$

with $S = (S_{ij})_{1 \leq i \leq m, 1 \leq j \leq n}$, $X = (X_1, \ldots, X_n)$, and $L = (L_1, \ldots, L_n)$ with all $S_{ij}, L_i \in \text{CONST}$. From $\nu(i, w)$ we obtain

for all $w \notin L_i$ [for $j = 1, \ldots, n$ [for all prefixes u
of w with $u \in S_{ij}$: **not**$(w/u \in X_j)]]$.

By interchanging the two quantifiers and reformulating the condition, this can be restated as

$$\bigcup_{j=1,\ldots,n} \bigcup_{w \notin L_i} [w/[\text{PREF}(w) \cap S_{ij}] \cap X_j] = \emptyset,$$

and this, in turn, is equivalent to

$$\bigcup_{j=1,\ldots,n} [\overline{L_i}/\text{PREF}(\overline{L_i}) \cap S_{ij}] \cap X_j] = \emptyset$$

since $y/[\text{PREF}(y) \cap M] \cap L \cup z/[\text{PREF}(z) \cap M] \cap L = (y \cup z)/[\text{PREF}(y \cup z) \cap M] \cap L$, for any words y and z and any languages M and L. Furthermore, since $M/\text{PREF}(M) \cap L = M/L$ for any languages M and L, this is further simplified to

$$\bigcup_{j=1,\ldots,n} [\overline{L_i}/S_{ij} \cap X_j] = \emptyset.$$

Therefore, we must have

$$\bigcup_{i=1,\ldots,m} \bigcup_{j=1,\ldots,n} [\overline{L_i}/S_{ij} \cap X_j] = \emptyset. \tag{8.1}$$

We now define

$$X_j = \overline{\overline{L_1}/S_{1j} \cup \overline{L_2}/S_{2j} \cup \cdots \cup \overline{L_m}/S_{mj}} \quad \text{for } j = 1, \ldots, n. \tag{8.2}$$

It should be obvious that (8.1) is satisfied by (8.2); furthermore, there do not exist any languages Y_j properly containing X_j for any $j \in \{1, \ldots, n\}$ that satisfy (8.1). Thus, the X_j defined in (8.2) are maximal; any languages for X_j satisfying (8.1) must be contained in the languages defined in (8.2).

For the following, we recall that the existence of a solution of the given system of implicit language equations is equivalent to $\pi(i, w)$ holding for all $w \in L_i$ and $\nu(i, w)$ holding for all $w \notin L_i$, for $i = 1, \ldots, m$. We have equivalently transformed the second of these requirements into (8.1) and determined the maximal solution (8.2) of (8.1). We must now return to the condition $\pi(i, w)$; using the same process by which we obtained (8.1) from $\nu(i, w)$, we derive

$$\forall_{i=1,\ldots,m} \; \forall_{w \in L_i} \left[\bigcup_{j=1,\ldots,n} (w/S_{ij} \cap X_j) \right] \neq \emptyset. \tag{8.3}$$

Therefore, the existence of a solution is equivalent to (8.1) and (8.3). Recall that (8.2) is a maximal solution of (8.1). Thus, we claim:

Lemma 8.8. *The system $L = S \cdot X$ has a solution iff the languages X_j defined in (8.2) satisfy (8.3).*

PROOF. Since (8.1) and (8.3) are equivalent to the existence of a solution and (8.2) satisfies (8.1), (8.2) is a solution of $L = S \cdot X$ if it satisfies (8.3). Assume now that there exists a solution $X' = (X_1', \ldots, X_n')$, different from X. Clearly, X' must satisfy (8.1), and since (8.2) is maximal, X_j contains X_j' for all j. Now, since X' must satisfy (8.3), as it is a solution, and since enlarging X_j' to X_j will maintain the nonemptiness of the intersections in (8.3), (8.2) must also satisfy (8.3). $\square$

Note that (8.3) does not provide an effective method. However, effectiveness is not necessary; (8.3) was only needed to establish that the maximal solution (8.2) of (8.1) must be a solution of the given system, if one exists at all. Conversely, if no solution exists, (8.2) must fail to satisfy (8.3). In practice, we will take the languages defined by (8.2) and substitute them directly into the given system of implicit language equations. By Lemma 8.8, we then know that a solution exists if and only if (8.2) is a solution of the system of implicit language equations. Therefore, we can summarize:

Theorem 8.9. *Consider the system $L = S \cdot X$ of m implicit language equations in n variables. If all constant languages S_{ij} and L_i are regular, there exists an algorithm to determine whether a solution exists. Furthermore, if a solution exists, the maximal solution is given by (8.2) and consists exclusively of regular languages.*

PROOF. We have already established that (8.2) is a solution if any solution exists and that this is the maximal solution. What remains to show is that (8.2) can be constructed effectively and that it gives rise to regular languages. Since all the constant languages are regular and since there are well-known algorithms to construct the quotient, the union, and the complement of regular languages effectively, which are all regular again, the claim follows.   □

Note that it is only the maximal solution that is guaranteed to be regular. If there are other solutions, it is quite possible that these are nonregular [see the Example 2 in Section 8.1 where $(a^*, (aa)^*, (aaaa)^*, L)$ was a solution for any $L \subseteq (aaaa)^*$, and clearly, L need not be regular].

Corollary 8.10. *Consider a system of implicit language equations with arbitrary constants (not necessarily regular). If the system has any solution, it must have one that is maximal, i.e., for any other solution X', the maximal solution must contain the solution X' componentwise.*

PROOF. The derivations of (8.1) and (8.3) did not depend on any property of regular languages. Regularity of the constant languages came only into play when effectiveness (such as testing for emptiness) and closure of language classes (such as closure of regular languages under quotient, union, and complementation) were at issue.   □

It should be clear that the construction in (8.2) is valid regardless of the choice of CONST. However, it is equally obvious that not every choice of CONST renders the construction (8.2) effective. Thus, in the remainder of this section, we work out several systems of implicit language equations where CONST = REG. We begin with the three numbered examples at the end of Section 8.1. All three were restricted systems (i.e., all S_{ij} are either $\{\lambda\}$ or $\emptyset$. In this case (8.2) can be simplified to

$$X_j = \bigcap_{\substack{j \in \{1,...,m\} \\ \text{such that } S_{ij} = \{\lambda\}}} L_i.$$

The first of the three examples was $X_1 \cup X_2 = a^*$, $X_1 \cup X_3 = b^*$. Applying (8.2), we obtain $X_1 = L_1 \cap L_2 = \{\lambda\}$, $X_2 = L_1 = a^*$, and $X_3 = b^*$. Since this is, indeed, the maximal of the five solutions listed there, we do not have to verify that these languages are in fact a solution.

The second example was $X_1 \cup X_2 = a^*$, $X_1 \cup X_3 = a^*$, $X_1 \cup X_4 = a^*$, $X_2 \cup X_3 = (aa)^*$, $X_2 \cup X_4 = (aa)^*$, $X_3 \cup X_4 = (aaaa)^*$. We obtain from (8.2) $X_1 = a^*$, $X_2 = (aa)^*$, $X_3 = (aaaa)^*$, and $X_4 = (aaaa)^*$. Again, we know this is the maximal solution and need not verify it separately.

The third example was $X_1 \cup X_2 \cup X_3 = a^*$, $X_1 \cup X_2 \cup X_4 = b^*$, $X_2 \cup X_3 \cup X_4 = a^*$. We obtain from (8.2), $X_1 = \{\lambda\}$, $X_2 = \{\lambda\}$, $X_3 = a^*$, and $X_4 = \{\lambda\}$, and now the verification that these languages are a solution fails. Therefore, no solution can exist, in concordance with the derivation in Section 8.2.

Let us consider one more restricted system, namely the one given by

$$S = \begin{vmatrix} \{\lambda\} & \{\lambda\} & \emptyset \\ \{\lambda\} & \emptyset & \{\lambda\} \\ \emptyset & \{\lambda\} & \{\lambda\} \end{vmatrix}, \qquad L = \begin{vmatrix} aa(aa)^* \\ aaa(aa)^* \\ aaa^* \end{vmatrix}.$$

It follows from applying (8.2) that $X_1 = \emptyset$, $X_2 = aa(aa)^*$, and $X_3 = aaa(aa)^*$. Substituting these languages into the equations yields identities and, therefore, they are a solution (indeed the only one).

Consider the following system of two implicit language equations in three variables:

$$a(ab)^* X_1 \cup a(b^*a)^* X_2 = a(a \cup b)^* \qquad (= L_1),$$

$$X_1 \cup aX_3 = aa(a \cup b)^* \qquad (= L_2).$$

We obtain from (8.2)

$$\begin{aligned}
X_1 &= \overline{\overline{L_1}/S_{11} \cup \overline{L_2}/S_{21}} \\
&= \overline{[b(a \cup b)^* \cup \lambda]/a(ab)^* \cup [\lambda \cup a \cup (ab \cup b)(a \cup b)^*]/\lambda} \\
&= \overline{\emptyset \cup \overline{L_2}} \\
&= L_2 = aa(a \cup b)^*, \\
X_2 &= \overline{\overline{L_1}/S_{12} \cup \overline{L_2}/S_{22}} \\
&= \overline{[b(a \cup b)^* \cup \lambda]/a(b^*a)^*} \\
&= \overline{\emptyset} \\
&= (a \cup b)^*, \\
X_3 &= \overline{\overline{L_1}/S_{13} \cup \overline{L_2}/S_{23}} \\
&= \overline{[\lambda \cup a \cup (ab \cup b)(a \cup b)^*]/a} \\
&= a(a \cup b)^*.
\end{aligned}$$

We now have to substitute these three languages into the given system:

$$a(ab)^* aa(a \cup b)^* \cup a(b^*a)^*(a \cup b)^* = a(a \cup b)^*$$

since $\lambda \notin (b^*a)^*$. This is equal to L_1.

$$aa(a \cup b)^* \cup aa(a \cup b)^* = aa(a \cup b)^*.$$

This is equal to L_2. Therefore, this system has a solution and the above languages are the maximal solution.

Consider another system of two implicit language equations in three variables:

$$a^* X_1 \cup b(bb)^* X_2 \cup bX_3 = (a \cup b)^* \qquad (= L_1),$$

$$aX_1 \cup aX_2 = ab^*a(a \cup b)^* \qquad (= L_2).$$

From (8.2), we obtain

$$
\begin{aligned}
X_1 &= \overline{\overline{L_1}/S_{11} \cup \overline{L_2}/S_{21}} \\
&= \overline{\overline{(a \cup b)^*/a^*} \cup \overline{a(a^* \cup b^*)a(a \cup b)^*/a}} \\
&= \overline{\overline{\emptyset/a^*} \cup [\lambda \cup ab^* \cup b(a \cup b)^*]/a} \\
&= \overline{\overline{b^*}} \\
&= b^*a(a \cup b)^*, \\
X_2 &= \overline{\overline{L_1}/S_{12} \cup \overline{L_2}/S_{22}} \\
&= \overline{\overline{\emptyset/b(bb)^*} \cup [\lambda \cup ab^* \cup b(a \cup b)^*]/a} \\
&= b^*a(a \cup b)^*, \\
X_3 &= \overline{\overline{L_1}/S_{13}} \\
&= \overline{\overline{\emptyset/b}} \\
&= (a \cup b)^*.
\end{aligned}
$$

One must now verify that these three languages satisfy the two equations:

First equation:

$$
\begin{aligned}
a^*b^*a(a \cup b)^* \cup b(bb)^*b^*a(a \cup b)^* \cup b(a \cup b)^* & \\
= [a^*b^*a \cup bb^*a \cup b](a \cup b)^* = (a \cup b)(a \cup b)^* &\neq L_1.
\end{aligned}
$$

Second equation:

$$
ab^*a(a \cup b)^* \cup ab^*a(a \cup b)^* = ab^*a(a \cup b)^* = L_2.
$$

It is clear that the left-hand side does not equal the right-hand side of the system; therefore, no solution exists.

As a final example, consider the following system of three implicit language equations in two variables:

$$
\begin{aligned}
aaX_1 \cup X_2 &= a \cup aa(a \cup b)^* \cup aba(aa \cup ba)^* &(= L_1), \\
b(bb)^*X_1 \cup ba^*X_2 &= b(a \cup b)^* &(= L_2), \\
(ab)^*X_1 \cup (ba)^*X_2 &= (a \cup b)^* &(= L_3).
\end{aligned}
$$

From (8.2), we obtain

$$
\begin{aligned}
X_1 &= \overline{\overline{L_1}/aa \cup \overline{L_2}/b(bb)^* \cup \overline{L_3}/(ab)^*} \\
&= \overline{\overline{(\lambda \cup ab(aa \cup ab)^*(\lambda \cup b(a \cup b)^*)}/aa \cup \overline{(\lambda \cup a(a \cup b)^*)}/b(bb)^* \cup \overline{\emptyset}/(ab)*} \\
&= \overline{\overline{\emptyset} \cup \overline{\emptyset} \cup \overline{\emptyset}} \\
&= (a \cup b)^*, \\
X_2 &= \overline{\overline{L_1}/\lambda \cup \overline{L_2}/ba^* \cup \overline{L_3}/(ba)^*} \\
&= \overline{\overline{L_1}/\lambda \cup \overline{(\lambda \cup a(a \cup b)^*)}/ba^* \cup \overline{\emptyset}/(ba)^*} \\
&= \overline{\overline{L_1} \cup \overline{\emptyset} \cup \overline{\emptyset}}
\end{aligned}
$$

$$= L_1$$
$$= a \cup aa(a \cup b)^* \cup aba(aa \cup ba)^*.$$

One must now verify that these two languages satisfy the three equations:

First:

$$aa(a \cup b)^* \cup L_1 = L_1$$

since L_1 contains $aa(a \cup b)^*$.

Second:

$$b(bb)^*(a \cup b)^* \cup ba^* L_1 = b(a \cup b)^*$$
$$= L_2$$

since the first term is equal to $b(a \cup b)^*$ and the second contains only words starting with b.

Third:

$$(ab)^*(a \cup b)^* \cup (ba)^* L1 = (a \cup b)^*$$
$$= L_3$$

as the first term equals $(a \cup b)^*$.

Thus, $((a \cup b)^*, a \cup aa(a \cup b)^* \cup aba(aa \cup ba)^*)$ is the maximal solution of the system.

In this example, it is interesting how we determined the languages L_1, L_2, and L_3: We first fixed the six languages in S, then chose X_1 to be the star of the union of them,

$$[aa \cup \lambda \cup b(bb)^* \cup ba^* \cup (ab)^* \cup (ba)^*]^*,$$

which can be simplified to

$$(aa \cup ab)^*(\lambda \cup b(a \cup b)^*),$$

and X_2 to be the complement of X_1,

$$a(aa \cup ba)^*.$$

Then we determined the resulting languages L_1, L_2, and L_3. It is clear that the obtained solution is not equal to these languages, the reason being that they were not the maximal solution!

8.4 Characterizing Uniqueness in Implicit Language Equations

We derive a criterion for uniqueness of a solution of systems of implicit language equations. Again, the criterion is valid for all choices of CONST but effective only for some choices of CONST, in particular if all constant languages are regular. It can be used to determine whether there exists a finite or an infinite number of solutions. If there are finitely many, all solutions can be determined; if there are infinitely many, an infinite number of them can be constructed.

Theorem 8.11. *Consider a system of m implicit language equations $L = S \cdot X$ using union and left-concatenation, where $L = (L_1, \ldots, L_n)$, $S = (S_{ij})_{1 \le i \le m, 1 \le j \le n}$ with all S_{ij} and L_i arbitrary languages in CONST. Assume that $X = (X_1, \ldots, X_n)$ is its maximal solution. This maximal solution is unique if and only if*

> *For all $j = 1, \ldots, n$, there does not exist a word $w \in X_j$ such that $S_{ij} \cdot \{w\}$ is contained in*

$$S_{i,1}X_1 \cup \cdots \cup S_{i,j-1}X_{j-1} \cup S_{i,j+1}X_{j+1}$$
$$\cup \cdots \cup S_{i,n}X_n \quad \textit{for all } i = 1, \ldots, m.$$

PROOF.

A. Assume there exists a word $w \in X_j$ violating the condition of the theorem. We claim that $Y = (Y_1, \ldots, Y_n)$ with $Y_s = X_s$ for $s \in \{1, \ldots, n\} - \{j\}$ and $Y_j = X_j - \{w\}$ is a solution (which is clearly different from X). Now, Y is a solution if for all i such that $S_{ij} \ne \emptyset$, $S_{ij}\{w\}$ is contained in $S_{i1}X_1 \cup \cdots \cup S_{ij-1}X_{j-1} \cup S_{ij+1}X_{j+1} \cup \cdots \cup S_{in}X_n$. This, however, is precisely the condition of the theorem since for $S_{ij} = \emptyset$, $S_{ij} \cdot \{w\} = \emptyset$, which is trivially contained in any set.

B. For the converse, we observe that X is maximal by construction; therefore, if there exists a different solution $Y = (Y_1, \ldots, Y_n)$, there exists an $s \in \{1, \ldots, n\}$ such that $X_s - Y_s \ne \emptyset$. Let $w \in X_s - Y_s$. We claim that for this s and this w, $S_{ij} \cdot \{w\}$ is contained in $S_{i1}Y_1 \cup \cdots \cup S_{ij-1}Y_{j-1} \cup S_{ij+1}Y_{j+1} \cup \cdots \cup S_{in}Y_n$ for all $i = 1, \ldots, m$. This, however, follows immediately, since, by assumption, Y is a solution. Therefore, the claim of the theorem follows. □

Theorem 8.11 holds for arbitrary constant languages. However, since the constructions required in this theorem are not effective for classes of languages such as CFL or RE, we assume from now on that all constants occurring in the definition of these systems are regular. Under this assumption, we can show that the necessary and sufficient condition in Theorem 8.11 can be tested for effectively.

For each $j = 1, \ldots, m$ and for each $i = 1, \ldots, m$, we determine the largest subset Z_{ij} of X_j such that

$$S_{ij} \cdot Z_{ij} \text{ is contained in } S_{i,1}X_1 \cup \cdots \cup S_{i,j-1}X_{j-1}$$
$$\cup S_{i,j+1}X_{j+1} \cup \cdots \cup S_{i,n}X_n.$$

The union on the right is a regular language; let us denote it by M_{ij}. Then,

$$Z_{ij} = M_{ij}/S_{ij}.$$

Taking the quotient of a regular language with respect to another regular language is an effective operation, yielding another regular language. Therefore, if we define

$$Z_j = \bigcap_{\substack{i \in \{1,\dots,m\} \\ \text{such that } S_{ij} \neq \emptyset}} Z_{ij},$$

it follows that Z_j is regular, can be effectively constructed, and has the property that it contains precisely all those words w for which the language $S_{ij} \cdot \{w\}$ is contained in $S_{i1} X_1 \cup \cdots \cup S_{ij-1} X_{j-1} \cup S_{ij+1} X_{j+1} \cup \cdots \cup S_{in} X_n$ for all $i = 1, \dots, m$. Thus, the test for uniqueness is equivalent to the effective test whether

$$Z_j \neq \emptyset.$$

Theorem 8.12. *Given a system of implicit language equations with union and left-concatenation where* CONST = REG. *There exists an effective test whether any solution of the system is unique.*

PROOF.   First, we construct the maximal solution. If it is different from the given solution, we have two solution and, therefore, nonuniqueness. If it is equal, apply the test outlined above. If $Z_j \neq \emptyset$ for some j, then we can conclude nonuniqueness; otherwise, the maximal solution is the only one.   □

This test will be called the Z-test in the following. It should be clear that the maximality of the X_i's does not come into play in this discussion. Therefore, the Z-test can be applied to any given solution; if it succeeds (i.e., if there exists a j such that $Z_j \neq \emptyset$), then this given solution is not unique.

The last question we address in this section is how to determine whether there are infinitely many solutions. It is clear that any subset of words in Z_j can be removed from the maximal solution X_j so that one still obtains a solution. Therefore, we construct Z_j for all $j = 1, \dots, n$ and determine whether any one of them is infinite. Again, this is effective since testing a regular language for infiniteness is effective. If all of them are finite, then there exist exactly finitely many solutions; otherwise, there exist infinitely many solutions. We summarize:

Theorem 8.13. *Given a system of implicit language equations with union and left-concatenation where* CONST = REG. *There exists an effective test whether this system has finitely many solutions.*

It follows from the above that every solution can be constructed if there are only finitely many solutions. This is a consequence of the fact that in this case, all solutions must be regular (every subset of any of the Z_j's is finite and, therefore, regular). Care must be taken with the iterative selection of subsets of Z_j since choosing a specific subset for one j may restrict the possible choices of subsets for other indices. This will be illustrated by the examples below. It also follows that in the case of infinitely many solutions, we can construct an infinite number of them, but not all since not all are regular.

Examples:

1. Consider Example 1 in Section 8.1,

$$X_1 \cup X_2 = a^*,$$
$$X_1 \cup X_3 = b^*.$$

The maximal solution is $(\{\lambda\}, a^*, b^*)$. Let us construct the sets Z_{ij}, for $i = 1, 2$ and $j = 1, 2, 3$, as required:

$$
\begin{aligned}
(i,j) = (1,1): \quad & Z_{11} = a^*, \\
(1,2): \quad & Z_{12} = \{\lambda\}, \\
(1,3): \quad & \text{not applicable since } S_{12} = \emptyset, \\
(2,1): \quad & Z_{21} = b^*, \\
(2,2): \quad & \text{not applicable since } S_{22} = \emptyset, \\
(2,3): \quad & Z_{23} = \{\lambda\}.
\end{aligned}
$$

Then we get

$$Z_1 = Z_{11} \cup Z_{21} = a^* \cap b^* = \{\lambda\},$$
$$Z_2 = Z_{12} = \{\lambda\},$$
$$Z_3 = Z_{23} = \{\lambda\}.$$

We therefore conclude that there are finitely many solutions.

It follows that any one of the maximal X_j could have the empty word λ removed; thus, there are three additional solutions of the system, namely

$$
\begin{aligned}
(\emptyset, a^*, b^*) \quad & \text{for } X_1 - \{\lambda\}, \\
(\{\lambda\}, aa^*, b^*) \quad & \text{for } X_2 - \{\lambda\}, \\
(\{\lambda\}, a^*, bb^*) \quad & \text{for } X_3 - \{\lambda\}.
\end{aligned}
$$

Every one of these three new solutions must now be subjected to the Z-test. For the first one, $(\emptyset, a^*, b^*)$, the Z-test fails; thus, it will not yield any solutions by removing words from any of its languages. Applying the Z-test to the solution $(\{\lambda\}, aa^*, b^*)$ indicates that λ can be removed from b^*, yielding the new solution $(\{\lambda\}, aa^*, bb^*)$. Applying this procedure to the solution $(\{\lambda\}, a^*, bb^*)$ and consequently removing λ from a^* yields exactly the same solution. Applying the Z-test to the solution not yet tested [namely $(\{\lambda\}, aa^*, bb^*)$] fails. Therefore, there are precisely five solutions which are obtained as follows:

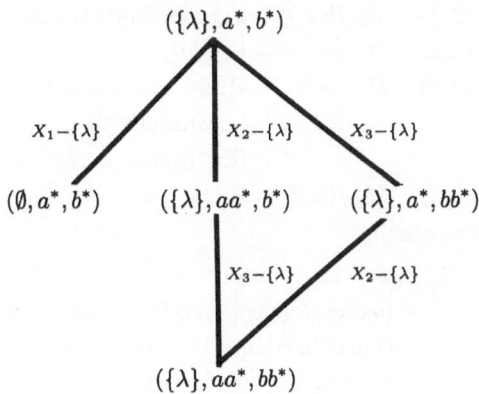

2. Consider the last example of Section 8.2:

$$aaX_1 \cup X_2 = a \cup aa(a \cup b)^* \cup aba(aa \cup ba)^* \qquad (= L_1),$$

$$b(bb)^* X_1 \cup ba^* X_2 = b(a \cup b)^* \qquad (= L_2),$$

$$(ab)^* X_1 \cup (ba)^* X_2 = (a \cup b)^* \qquad (= L_3).$$

The maximal solution had been determined as

$$((a \cup b)^*, a \cup aa(a \cup b)^* \cup aba(aa \cup ba)^*).$$

We now apply Theorem 8.11. Let us first determine all M_{ij}:

$$
\begin{aligned}
(i,j) = (1,1) \quad & S_{12}X_2 = a \cup aa(a \cup b)^* \cup aba(aa \cup ba)^* \\
(1,2) \quad & S_{11}X_1 = aa(a \cup b)^*, \\
(2,1) \quad & S_{22}X_2 = ba^*(a \cup aa(a \cup b)^* \cup aba(aa \cup ba)^*) \\
& \qquad = ba \cup baa(a \cup b)^* \cup baba(aa \cup ba)^*, \\
(2,2) \quad & S_{21}X_1 = b(bb)^*(a \cup b)^* \\
& \qquad = b(a \cup b)^*, \\
(3,1) \quad & S_{32}X_2 = (ba)^*(a \cup aa(a \cup b)^* \cup aba(aa \cup ba)^*), \\
(3,2) \quad & S_{31}X_1 = (ab)^*(a \cup b)^* \\
& \qquad = (a \cup b)^*.
\end{aligned}
$$

Then we determine all $Z_{ij} = M_{ij}/S_{ij}$:

$$(i,j) = (1,1) \quad M_{11}/aa \quad = (a \cup b)^*,$$
$$(1,2) \quad M_{12}/\{\lambda\} \quad = aa(a \cup b)^*,$$
$$(2,1) \quad M_{21}/b(bb)^* = a \cup aa(a \cup b)^* \cup aba(aa \cup ba)^*,$$
$$(2,2) \quad M_{22}/ba^* \quad = (a \cup b)^*,$$
$$(3,1) \quad M_{31}/(ab)^* \quad = a(aa \cup ba)^* \cup (ba)^*(a \cup aa(a \cup b)^*$$
$$\cup aba(aa \cup ba)^*)$$
$$= (ba)^*(a \cup aa(a \cup b)^* \cup aba(aa \cup ba)^*),$$
$$(3,2) \quad M_{32}/(ba)^* \quad = (a \cup b)^*.$$

Therefore we obtain

$$Z_1 = Z_{11} \cap Z_{21} \cap Z_{31}$$
$$= (a \cup b)^* \cap (a \cup aa(a \cup b)^* \cup aba(aa \cup ba)^*)$$
$$\cap (ba)^*(a \cup aa(a \cup b)^* \cup aba(aa \cup ba)^*)$$
$$= a \cup aa(a \cup b)^* \cup aba(aa \cup ba)^*$$
$$Z_2 = Z_{12} \cap Z_{22} \cap Z_{32}$$
$$= aa(a \cup b)^* \cap (a \cup b)^* \cap (a \cup b)^*$$
$$= aa(a \cup b)^*.$$

It follows, therefore, that there are infinitely many solutions since any nonempty subset of the language denoted by $a \cup aa(a \cup b)^* \cup aba(aa \cup ba)^*$ can be removed from the solution $X_1 = (a \cup b)^*$ or alternatively, any nonempty subset of $aa(a \cup b)^*$ can be removed from $X_2 = a \cup aa(a \cup b)^* \cup aba(aa \cup ba)^*$, and in each of these cases, a different solution is obtained. Furthermore, once one has chosen an index j (1 or 2) and a specific subset to be subtracted from X_j, one can repeat the Z-test for this new solution; if the condition is again satisfied, words may be removed from $X_{j'}$ for $j' \neq j$. Since an infinite regular language has infinitely many regular subsets, this process allows one to determine arbitrarily many regular solutions.

8.5   Conclusion

We have defined the implicit analogue of classical language equations and illustrated how significantly they differ from the explicit classical equations, as far as existence and uniqueness of solutions are concerned. We have derived an approach to determining whether a solution exists and constructing the maximal solution if this is so. Furthermore, we have shown how to determine whether a given system has zero, finitely many, or infinitely many solutions. In the case of finitely many solutions, all solutions can be constructed. All these tests and constructions are effective if CONST = REG. For more general language classes, the problem of determining a solution in a constructive way is likely to be intractable, as the operations involved in the tests are not effective for many of these classes; this is also illustrated by the fact that there are implicit language equations defined exclusively with context-free constants that have only non-context-free solutions.

For explicit equations, it is often possible to obtain a parameterization of all solutions if they are not unique (see, for example, [Salom 69] and [Leiss 86]). It appears exceedingly difficult to obtain similar representations for the solutions of implicit language equations even if all constants are regular.

8.6 Bibliographical Notes

For classical language equations, we refer to [Salom 69] as well as to Chapter 3. Implicit language equations were introduced and discussed in [Leiss 95]. The results presented in this chapter are taken from that paper. Somewhat related results, for a single equation in a single variable, were reported in [Kari 94]; however, this paper restricts the class $EX_A(CONST; OP; X_1, \ldots, X_n)$ in our terminology to one where only a single operator occurs, which, moreover, is assumed invertible with respect to words (not languages). Effectively, this excludes the standard language equations; the equations considered in [Kari 94] are essentially word equations. Even more damaging for the generality of these results, only a single equation can be treated at a time, since in order to be able to talk about (nontrivial) systems of equations, it is necessary to have at least two variables present in at least one equation. Therefore, this paper does not contribute significantly toward our goal of establishing a theory of language equations.

8.7 Problems

1. For the following systems of implicit language equations over the alphabet indicated, with union and left-concatenation, and with CONST = REG:

    i. Determine whether there is a solution.
    ii. If a solution exists, determine the maximal solution.
    iii. If a solution exists, determine whether the maximal solution is unique.
    iv. If the maximal solution is not unique, determine whether there are finitely many solutions.
    v. If there are finitely many solutions, determine all of them.

a. Two equations over $A = \{a, b\}$ in three variables:
$$aA^* = aaX \cup a^*Y,$$
$$A^*a = aY \cup bZ \cup a.$$

b. Two equations over $A = \{a, b\}$ in three variables:
$$aA^* = aX \cup a^*Y,$$
$$A^*a = aY \cup bZ \cup a.$$

c. Two equations over $A = \{a, b\}$ in three variables:
$$aA^* = aX \cup a^*Y,$$
$$A^*a = aY \cup b^*Z \cup a.$$

d. One equation over $A = \{a, b\}$ in two variables:
$$a^*bA^* = aX \cup bY.$$

e. Two equations over $A = \{a, b, c\}$ in three variables:
$$aa^*X \cup bY \cup cZ = AaA^*,$$
$$b^*c^*(X \cup Y) \cup Z = AA^*.$$

f. Two equations over $A = \{a, b, c\}$ in three variables:
$$aa^*X \cup bY \cup cZ = AaA^*,$$
$$b^*c^*(X \cup Y) \cup Z = A^*aA^*.$$

g. Three equations over $A = \{a, b\}$ in three variables:
$$a^*X \cup b^*Y \cup aZ = aA^*b,$$
$$b^*X \cup a^*Y \cup bZ = bA^*b,$$
$$X \cup Y \cup Z = A^*b.$$

h. Three equations over $A = \{a, b\}$ in three variables:
$$a^*X \cup ab^*Y \cup aZ = aA^*b,$$
$$b^*X \cup ba^*Y \cup bZ = bA^*b,$$
$$X \cup Y \cup Z = A^*b.$$

i. Three equations over $A = \{a, b\}$ in three variables:
$$a^*X \cup ab^*Y \cup aZ = aA^*b,$$
$$bb^*X \cup ba^*Y \cup bZ = bA^*b,$$
$$X \cup Y \cup Z = A^*b.$$

9

Regular Implicit Equations over a One-Letter Alphabet with Union, Concatenation, and Star

About This Chapter: We continue our coverage of implicit equations by considering the regular analogue of the explicit equations we studied in the first part of Chapter 7. Specifically, the operations involved in the expressions are union, unrestricted concatenation, and star, and the constants are regular languages over a one-letter alphabet. The main result is a constructive approach to finding a regular solution of a given system of implicit equations over $\{a\}$. Questions of maximality and uniqueness of solutions are also addressed.

Throughout this chapter, let $\alpha_1, \ldots, a_m$ be expressions in $\text{EX}_A(\text{CONST}; \text{OP}; X_1, \ldots, X_n)$, where the alphabet A is $\{a\}$ and OP consists of union, unrestricted concatenation, and star. In many cases, CONST consists of all regular languages REG over $\{a\}$, but several results hold for arbitrary languages. Let $L_1, \ldots, L_m$ be regular languages in CONST. Then the object of our attention in this chapter is the system

$$L_i = \alpha_i \quad \text{for } i = 1, \ldots, m,$$

a system of m implicit language equations in the n variables $X_1, \ldots, X_n$. Note that these equations are the analogues of the (explicit) equations studied in the first part of Chapter 7.

9.1 Properties of Expressions over a One-Letter Alphabet

In this section, we prove several properties of expressions over the alphabet $\{a\}$ where the operations consist of union, arbitrary concatenation, and star. These lay the foundation on which we will base an algorithm for solving implicit equations with regular constants over the alphabet $\{a\}$.

Throughout this chapter, we will make use of the properties of languages over $\{a\}$ that we derived in Section 7.1. In particular, we recall that these languages are commutative. Furthermore, we will employ the following observations about regular languages over the alphabet $\{a\}$. Let L be an arbitrary regular language over $\{a\}$; we consider the reduced automaton $\mathbb{R} = (\{a\}, Q, \tau, 0, W)$ for L. This reduced automaton $\mathbb{R}$ can be represented as follows:

- $Q = \{0, 1, \ldots, n\}$ for $n \geq 0$.
- W is a subset of Q.
- The transition function τ is defined by

$$\tau(i, a) = i + 1 \text{ for } i = 0, \ldots, n - 1 \text{ and } \tau(n, a) = r \text{ for some } r \in Q.$$

Furthermore, L can be uniquely represented as

$$L = F \cup G(a^s)^*$$

where the finite languages F and G and the period s (≥ 1) are derived directly from $\mathbb{R}$, specifically

$$F = \{a^t \mid t \in \{0, \ldots, r - 1\} \cap W\},$$
$$G = \{a^t \mid t \in \{r, \ldots, n\} \cap W\},$$
$$s = n - r + 1.$$

In the following, we will call this representation $L = F \cup G(a^s)^*$ of the regular language L over the alphabet $\{a\}$ its canonical representation. Furthermore, if $L = F \cup G(a^s)^*$ is the canonical representation of the regular language L over $\{a\}$, we will use $\text{Per}(L)$ to denote its period s.

Lemma 9.1. Let $\alpha(X_1, \ldots, X_n)$ be an expression in $\text{EX}_{\{a\}}(\text{REG}; \text{OP}; X_1, \ldots, X_n)$, where OP consists of union, concatenation, and star, and let M and N be arbitrary languages over the alphabet $\{a\}$. Then, for all $i \in \{1, \ldots, n\}$

$$\alpha(X_1, \ldots, X_{i-1}, M \cdot N^*, X_{i+1}, \ldots, X_n)$$
$$\subseteq \alpha(X_1, \ldots, X_{i-1}, M, X_{i+1}, \ldots, X_n) \cdot N^*.$$

PROOF. The claim follows by structural induction on $\alpha(X_1, \ldots, X_n)$. In the following, we will write $\alpha(L)$ instead of $\alpha(X_1, \ldots, X_{i-1}, L, X_{i+1}, \ldots, X_n)$.

Basis: If $\alpha = L$ for L a constant language, or if $\alpha = X_j$ for $j \in \{1, \ldots, n\}$, the claim follows trivially.

Inductive step: Assume that the claim holds for the expressions $\beta(X_1, \ldots, X_n)$ and $\gamma(X_1, \ldots, X_n)$.

If $\alpha = \beta \cup \gamma$, then we have

$$\alpha(M \cdot N^*) = \beta(M \cdot N^*) \cup \gamma(M \cdot N^*)$$
$$\subseteq \beta(M) \cdot N^* \cup \gamma(M) \cdot N^* = \alpha(M) \cdot N^*.$$

If $\alpha = \beta \cdot \gamma$, then we have (by Proposition 7.1)

$$\alpha(M \cdot N^*) = \beta(M \cdot N^*) \cdot \gamma(M \cdot N^*)$$
$$\subseteq \beta(M) \cdot N^* \cdot \gamma(M) \cdot N^* = \beta(M) \cdot \gamma(M) \cdot N^* = \alpha(M) \cdot N^*.$$

If $\alpha = \beta^*$, then we have

$$\alpha(M \cdot N^*) = [\beta(M \cdot N^*)]^* \subseteq [\beta(M) \cdot N^*]^* = \lambda \cup \beta(M) \cdot [\beta(M)]^* \cdot N^*$$
$$\subseteq N^* \cup \beta(M) \cdot [\beta(M)]^* \cdot N^* = [\beta(M)]^* \cdot N^* = \alpha(M) \cdot N^*.$$

Consequently the claim of the lemma follows.   □

For any finite language M, we define $\max(M)$ to be $\max\{|x| \mid x \in M\}$ if $M \neq \emptyset$ and $\max(\emptyset) = -1$.

Lemma 9.2. *Let $\alpha(X_1, \ldots, X_n)$ be an expression in $\mathrm{EX}_{\{a\}}(\mathrm{CONST}; \mathrm{OP}; X_1, \ldots, X_n)$ with OP consisting of union, concatenation, and star, and CONST arbitrary. Let L be a regular language over the alphabet $\{a\}$ with the canonical representation $L = F \cup G(a^s)^*$. Let $S_1, \ldots, S_n$ be arbitrary languages over $\{a\}$ such that*

$$\alpha(S_1, \ldots, S_n) \subseteq L.$$

Let $w \in S_j$ for some $j \in \{1, \ldots, n\}$ such that $|w| > \max(F)$. Define $T_i = S_i$ for all $i \neq j$ and $T_j = S_j \cup w \cdot (as)^*$. Then,

$$\alpha(T_1, \ldots, T_n) \subseteq L.$$

PROOF.   First, we observe that by the choice of w [$|w| > \max(F)$],

$$\alpha(S_1, \ldots, S_n) \cap F = \alpha(T_1, \ldots, T_n) \cap F.$$

Then, we note that $F \cup [G(a^s)^*](a^s)^* = L$; this holds even if L is finite. Now, the claim is a direct consequence of the previous lemma since for "long enough" words w, we can replace w by $w(a^s)^*$, and then (by the previous lemma) we can "pull to the end of the expression" the term $(a^s)^*$ and by definition of w, the additional words [i.e., the words in $\alpha(T_1, \ldots, T_n) - \alpha(S_1, \ldots, S_n)$] must then all be contained in $[G(a^s)^*](a^s)^* = G(a^s)^*$.   □

Corollary 9.3. *Let $\alpha(X_1, \ldots, X_n)$ be an expression in $\mathrm{EX}_{\{a\}}(\mathrm{CONST}; \mathrm{OP}; X_1, \ldots, X_n)$ with OP and CONST as in Lemma 9.2. Let L be a regular* *language over the alphabet $\{a\}$ with the canonical representation $L = F \cup G(a^s)^*$. Let $S_1, \ldots, S_n$ be arbitrary languages over $\{a\}$ such that*

$$\alpha(S_1, \ldots, S_n) = L.$$

Let $w \in S_j$ for some $j \in \{1, \ldots, n\}$ such that $|w| > \max(F)$. Define $T_i = S_i$ for all $i \neq j$ and $T_j = S_j \cup w \cdot (a^s)^*$. Then,

$$\alpha(T_1, \ldots, T_n) = L.$$

PROOF. The proof of Lemma 9.2 for containment applies essentially verbatim for the equality postulated in the corollary.   □

Corollary 9.4. *Consider the equation $L = \alpha(X_1, \ldots, X_n)$, where α is an expression in $\mathrm{EX}_{\{a\}}(\mathrm{REG}; \mathrm{OP}; X_1, \ldots, X_n)$ with OP consisting of union, concatenation, and star, and L is a regular language. If there exists any solution of this equation, then there also exists a regular solution.*

PROOF. Let $(S_1, \ldots, S_n)$ be a solution, and assume that one of the S_i's, say S, is not regular. (If there are several such nonregular S_i's, then we repeat the following argument for each of them.) Then, in particular, S must be infinite, and, therefore, there are words w in S that are "long enough" to satisfy the assumption of Corollary 9.3. Let S' be the set of all words in S that are longer than the longest word in F. Then, by Corollary 9.3, $\alpha(S \cup S'(a^s)^*) = L$; thus, $S \cup S'(a^s)^*$ is a solution which is regular since $S - S'$ is finite and $S'(a^s)^*$ is regular by Proposition 7.5.   □

In the next section, we require the definition of *strict dependence*. An expression α in $\mathrm{EX}_{\{a\}}(\mathrm{REG}; \mathrm{OP}; X_1, \ldots, X_n)$ is defined to be strictly dependent on the variable X_i by structural induction:

a. If $\alpha = L$ for L a constant language, then α is strictly independent of X_i. If $\alpha = X_j$ for $j \neq i$, then α is strictly independent of X_i. If $\alpha = X_i$, then α is strictly dependent on X_i.
b. If $\alpha = \beta \cup \gamma$, then α is strictly dependent on X_i if and only if both β and α are strictly dependent on X_i. If $\alpha = \beta \cdot \gamma$, then α is strictly dependent on X_i if and only if at least one of β and γ is strictly dependent on X_i. If $\alpha = \beta^*$, then α is strictly independent of X_i.

Lemma 9.5. *Any expression α in $\mathrm{EX}_{\{a\}}(\mathrm{REG}; \mathrm{OP}; X_1, \ldots, X_n)$, with OP consisting of union, concatenation, and star, can be written as*

$$\alpha = \alpha^{(0)} \cup \alpha^{(1)} \cup \cdots \cup \alpha^{(n)},$$

where $\alpha^{(i)}$ is strictly dependent on X_i for $i = 1, \ldots, n$ and $\alpha^{(0)}$ is strictly independent of any variable.

PROOF. By structural induction on α.

Basis: If $\alpha = L$ for L a constant language, then $\alpha^{(0)} = L$ and $\alpha^{(i)} = \emptyset$ for all $i = 1, \ldots, n$. If $\alpha = X_j$ for $1 \leq j \leq n$, then $\alpha^{(j)} = X_j$ and $\alpha^{(i)} = \emptyset$ for all $i = 0, 1, \ldots, n$ with $i \neq j$.

Inductive step: Let β and γ be expressions in $\text{EX}_{\{a\}}(\text{REG}; \text{OP};$ $X_1, \ldots, X_n)$ and inductively assume their representations according to the lemma are

$$\beta = \beta^{(0)} \cup \beta^{(1)} \cup \cdots \cup \beta^{(n)}$$

and

$$\gamma = \gamma^{(0)} \cup \gamma^{(1)} \cup \cdots \cup \gamma^{(n)}.$$

If $\alpha = \beta \cup \gamma$, then $\alpha^{(i)} = \beta^{(i)} \cup \gamma^{(i)}$ for all $i = 0, 1, \ldots, n$.
If $\alpha = \beta \cdot \gamma$, then $\alpha^{(0)} = \beta^{(0)} \cdot \gamma^{(0)}$ and $\alpha^{(i)} = \beta^{(i)} \cdot \gamma$ for $i = 1, \ldots, n$.
If $\alpha = \beta^*$, then $\alpha^{(0)} = \beta^{(0)} \cup \{\lambda\}$ and $\alpha^{(i)} = \beta^{(i)} \cdot \beta^*$ for $i = 1, \ldots, n$.

$\square$

Corollary 9.6. *If $\alpha \in \text{EX}_{\{a\}}(\text{REG}; \text{OP}; X_1, \ldots, X_n)$ with OP consisting of union, concatenation, and star is written as*

$$\alpha = \alpha^{(0)} \cup \alpha^{(1)} \cup \cdots \cup \alpha^{(n)},$$

where $\alpha^{(i)}$ is strictly dependent on X_i for $i = 1, \ldots, n$ and $\alpha^{(0)}$ is strictly independent of any variable, then for all $i = 1, \ldots, n$,

$$\alpha^{(i)} = \alpha'^{(i)} \cdot X_i \quad \text{for some } \alpha'^{(i)} \in \text{EX}_{\{a\}}(\text{REG}; \text{OP}; X_1, \ldots, X_n).$$

9.2   Solving One Equation in One Variable

Let L be a regular language over the one-letter alphabet $\{a\}$ with the canonical representation $L = F \cup G(a^s)^*$. Let α be an expression in $\text{EX}_{\{a\}}(\text{REG};$ OP; X) with OP consisting of union, concatenation, and star. We want to determine a solution of the equation $L = \alpha(X)$ if one exists. Consider the following (greedy) algorithm:

Algorithm to solve one implicit language equation in one variable

$S := \emptyset$; length := $\max(F)$;
for $i := 0$ to length do
   if $\alpha(S \cup \{a^i\}) \subseteq L$ then $S := S \cup \{a^i\}$;
if not $(\alpha(S) \supseteq F)$ then stop: no solution exists;
while $\alpha(S) \neq L$ do
   begin
      let y be the shortest word in $L - \alpha(S)$;
      for $i := $ length $+ 1$ to $|y|$ do
         if $\alpha(S \cup a^i) \subseteq L$ then $S := S \cup \{a^i(a^s)^*\}$;
      if $y \notin \alpha(S)$ then stop: no solution exists
         else length:= $|y|$;
   end;
stop: S is a solution

Proposition 9.7. *The algorithm to solve one implicit language equation in one variable is correct.*

PROOF. We claim that this algorithm correctly determines whether a solution exists and, furthermore, if one exists, that S is a solution. First, we show that the algorithm terminates. We claim that the while-loop will be executed fewer than s times. To see this, observe that there are fewer than s elements in G; consequently, at most $s - 1$ words y will occur because in the for-loop inside the while-loop, all words u that can be put in S will be put there, and, in fact, not just u but $u(a^s)^*$ which is valid according to Corollary 9.3. To see now that S as a solution is trivial, because this is the termination condition of the while-loop. Thus, it remains to show that the algorithm gives the correct answer if there is no solution. However, this again is quite trivial, since in the algorithm every word u that can be placed in S will be; furthermore, we note that for any word x and any language Z,

$$x \in \alpha(Z) \quad \text{if and only if } x \in \alpha(Z \cap \{a^k \mid k = 0, 1, \ldots, |x|\}).$$

Consequently, there is no solution iff there does not exist a language Z such that $\alpha(Z) \subseteq L$ or there exists a word $y \in L$ such that $y \notin \alpha(Z \cap \{a^k \mid k = 0, 1, \ldots, |y|\})$. This, however, is exactly what the algorithms determines in the tests $\alpha(S) \supseteq F$ and $y \notin \alpha(S)$. Consequently, the algorithm correctly determines whether there exists a solution, and if a solution exists, it determines one correctly. $\square$

In formulating the while-loop of the algorithm, we used as a loop termination criterion the condition $\alpha(S) = L$. For technical reasons, let us now replace the corresponding (continuation) condition

$$\alpha(S) \neq L$$

by

$$\alpha(S) \neq L \quad \text{or} \quad \text{length} < \max(G) + s.$$

It is obvious that this does not affect in any way the correctness of the algorithm; the only difference is that in the modified algorithm, we continue iterating the while-loop until at least length $\geq \max(G) + s$.

With this modification, we now show that the solution S determined in the algorithm is maximal (i.e., any solution T is contained in S):

Lemma 9.8. *If the given equation has a solution, the modified algorithm will determine the unique maximal solution.*

PROOF. Assume the contrary (i.e., there exists a solution T such that $T - S \neq \emptyset$. Let u be the shortest word in $T - S$. Because of the construction of S, the length of u must be at least $\max(G) + s$. Thus, by Corollary 9.3, $T' = T \cup u(a^s)^*$ is also a solution such that $T' - S \neq \emptyset$. Define $u' = a^{|u|-s}$.

Clearly, $|u'| = \max(G)$. Let

$$\alpha = \alpha^{(0)} \cup \alpha^{(1)}$$

be the decomposition of α into the expression $\alpha^{(0)}$ which is strictly independent of X and the expression $\alpha^{(1)}$ which is strictly dependent on X; then, it is clear because of the length of u that

$$\alpha^{(1)}(\{u\}) \subseteq G(a^s)(a^s)^*.$$

We claim that

$$\alpha^{(1)}(\{u'\}) \subseteq \alpha^{(1)}(\{u\})/(a^s)(a^s)^*.$$

where M/N denotes the (right) quotient of M with respect to N defined by

$$M/N = \{x \in \{a\}^* \mid w = x \cdot u, \text{ where } w \in M \text{ and } u \in N\}.$$

Note that we are dealing with languages over $\{a\}$; therefore, the right quotient is the same as the left quotient. Let v be a word in $\alpha^{(1)}(\{u'\})$. Since $\alpha^{(1)}(X)$ is strictly dependent on X and is over the alphabet $\{a\}$, it can be written as $\beta \cdot X$ with $\beta \in \mathrm{EX}_{\{a\}}(\mathrm{REG}; \mathrm{OP}; X)$ by Corollary 9.6; therefore, when writing v as concatenation of words from the constant languages of $\alpha^{(1)}$ and of u', we can add to any occurrence of u the word a^s (note that there will be at least one). This shows that u' must also be in $\alpha^{(1)}(\{u\})/(a^s)(a^s)^*$. It now follows that

$$\alpha^{(1)}(\{u'\}) \subseteq G(a^s)^*.$$

This, however, means that any word u that is "too long" can be replaced by a word u' that is shorter than u by s so that the resulting language is still a solution. It should be clear that this process can be repeated until the word u is no longer "too long," i.e., $|u| < \max(G) + s$. However, in this case, u must be placed into the language S by construction of S. Thus, we conclude that the solution T as postulated cannot exist; consequently, the solution S as constructed by the algorithm is maximal. $\qquad \square$

Since the solution S as constructed by the algorithm is obviously regular (it is a finite union of regular languages), it follows that the maximal solution is also regular. Thus, any solution T of the equation $L = \alpha(X)$ must be contained in the regular solution S. We summarize:

Theorem 9.9. *Let α be an expression in $\mathrm{EX}_{\{a\}}(\mathrm{REG}; \mathrm{OP}; X)$ with OP consisting of union, concatenation, and star. Let L be a regular language over $\{a\}$ with the canonical representation $L = F \cup G(a^s)^*$. There exists an effective algorithm to determine whether the implicit equation $L = \alpha$ has a solution. Furthermore, if a solution exists, the algorithm determines the maximal solution of the equation. This maximal solution is regular.*

9.3 Solving Systems of Equations

We now address the question of how to solve a system of m implicit language equations in n variables,

$$L_i = \alpha_i(X_1, \ldots, X_n), \quad i = 1, \ldots, m,$$

where for all $i = 1, \ldots, m$, $\alpha_i(X_1, \ldots, X_n) \in \mathrm{EX}_{\{a\}}(\mathrm{REG}; \mathrm{OP}; X_1, \ldots, X_n)$ with OP consisting of union, concatenation, and star, and let the L_i be regular languages over $\{a\}$. Starting from the canonical representation of the L_i's as $L_i = F_i \cup G_i(a^{s_i})^*$, we obtain the following representation of the constant languages L_i,

$$L_i = F_i \cup H_i(a^s)^* \quad \text{for all } i = 1, \ldots, m,$$

where s is the least common multiple of all the s_i's, and H_i is a finite language for all i,

$$s = \mathrm{LCM}(s_1, \ldots, s_m) \quad \text{and} \quad H_i \subseteq G_i[a^{s_i} \cup \lambda]^s \text{ for all } i = 1, \ldots, m.$$

Furthermore, we define

$$M = \max_{i=1,\ldots,m} \{\max(H_i)\}.$$

It turns out that the general situation (two or more equations in two or more variables) differs considerably from the case of one equation in one variable. Most importantly, whereas in the one-variable case, there exists a maximal solution, this is no longer the case for equations in two or more variables. To see this, consider the single equation in the two variables X and Y:

$$aa = aX \cup aY \cup aXY.$$

It is obvious that $(X, Y) = (\{a\}, \emptyset)$ is a solution, as is $(X, Y) = (\emptyset, \{a\})$; however, there is no solution that contains both of these solutions. That this has nothing to do with the fact that the solutions consist of finite languages is shown in the following example. It is easy to verify that the single equation in the two variables X and Y,

$$aa \cup a^5 \cdot (a^5)^* = aX \cup aY \cup aXY,$$

has two solutions [set one of X and Y to $\emptyset$ and the other to $a \cup a^4 \cdot (a^5)^*$), but it does not have a solution that contains both, or, in fact, a solution (X, Y) in which both languages are nonempty. One can verify that these two solutions are the only solutions of this equation.

Another difference between equations in one variable and equations in several variables is somewhat more technical. Our greedy algorithm essentially will add a word to a potential solution whenever it is possible to add it, not just when it is necessary. This is, of course, essential in order to obtain maximality. However, as the following example shows, when we have to deal with several variables, it is possible that at some point in the algorithm, we may add words that should never be added. Consider the equation

$$aX^3 \cup aX(aY)^* = a^2 \cdot (a^2)^*.$$

If we start by testing whether λ can be added to the initially empty X, the answer is obviously no. Thus, X remains empty. However, when we use $X = \emptyset$ to determine whether λ can be put into Y, the fact that X is empty yields the answer that λ can be put into Y, even though this is obviously wrong! In fact, $X = Y = a(a^2)^*$ happens to be the maximal solution of this equation (see the examples in Section 9.4). On the other hand, we note that it is not possible to require that all languages involved in a solution must be nonempty, as the previous example demonstrated.

For these reasons, we have to modify our approach somewhat. Instead of starting the algorithm with the initialization $(\emptyset, \ldots, \emptyset)$, we assume that an n-tuple $(T_1, \ldots, T_n)$ of languages is given with the property that

$$L_{k,0} \subseteq \alpha_k(T_1, \ldots, T_n) \subseteq L_k \quad \text{for all } k = 1, \ldots, m,$$

where the finite language $L_{k,0}$ is defined as follows: Let $\alpha_k = \alpha_k^{(0)} \cup \alpha_k^{(1)} \cup \cdots \cup \alpha_k^{(n)}$ be the representation given in Lemma 9.5. Consider $L_k - \alpha_k^{(0)}$; if this language is nonempty, let z be its shortest word and define $L_{k,0} = [L_k \cap a^{\leq |z|}] \cup F_k \cup H_k$. If $L_k - \alpha_k^{(0)}$ is empty, define $L_{k,0} = F_k \cup H_k$ [it is true that in this case, $(\emptyset, ..., \emptyset)$ is a solution, but since it need not be maximal in the sense soon to be defined, we have to continue]. Then, all further "intermediate" or "approximate solutions" $(S_1, \ldots, S_n)$ are obtained by adding all words to $(T_1, \ldots, T_n)$ that can be added [i.e., we are still using a greedy approach, but now it is primed, with the initialization $(T_1, \ldots, T_n)$]. For technical reasons, we assume that all T_i consist of words of length at most N, where $N = \max\{\max(L_{k,0}) \mid k = 1, \ldots, m\}$; this is no restriction since we can always replace a given T_i that violates this condition with $T_i \cap a^{\leq N}$ (where $a^{\leq s}$ denotes the set of all words in a^* of length s or less). Note that $N \geq M$.

Algorithm to solve m implicit language equations in n variables
ILE($\{\alpha_i(X_1, \ldots, X_n), L_i \mid i = 1, \ldots, m\}; (T_1, \ldots, T_n)$)

if $\exists k \in \{1, \ldots, m\}$, $L_{k,0} \subseteq \alpha_k(T_1, \ldots, T_n) \subseteq L_k$ is violated
   then stop: input does not satisfy initialization requirement;
$(S_1, \ldots, S_n) := (T_1, \ldots, T_n)$; length := N;
for $i := 0$ to length do
   for $j := 1$ to m do
      if $\exists k \in \{1, \ldots, m\}$, $\alpha_k(S_1, \ldots, S_{j-1}, S_j \cup \{a^i\}, S_{j+1}, \ldots, S_n) \subseteq L_k$
         then if $i < \max\{\min(H_h) \mid h = 1, \ldots, m\}$ then $S_j := Sj \cup \{a^i\}$
                                 else $S_j := S_j \cup \{a^i(a^s)^*\}$;
while $\exists k \in \{1, \ldots, m\}$ such that $\alpha_k(S_1, \ldots, S_n) \neq L_k$ or length $< M$ do
   begin

if $\bigcup_{k=1,\ldots,m} [L_k - \alpha_k(S_1,\ldots,S_n)] \neq \emptyset$

 then begin let y be its shortest word; set $K := |y|$;

       $J := \{h \in \{1,\ldots,m\} \mid y \in L_h - \alpha_h(S_1,\ldots,S_n)\}$

    end

 else begin $K := M + s$; $J := \emptyset$ end;

for $i :=$ length $+ 1$ to K do

for $j := 1$ to m do

  if $\forall k \in \{1,\ldots,m\}$, $\alpha_k(S_1,\ldots,S_{j-1},S_j \cup \{a^i\},S_{j+1},\ldots,S_n) \subseteq L_k$

  then if $i < \max\{\min(H_h) \mid h = 1,\ldots,m\}$ then $S_j := S_j \cup \{a^i\}$

                   else $S_j := S_j \cup \{a^i(a^s)^*\}$

 if $\exists j \in J$, $y \notin \alpha_j(S_1,\ldots,S_n)$ then stop: no solution exists

               else length $:= K$;

 end;

stop: $(S_1,\ldots,S_n)$ is a solution

We now claim that this algorithm determines whether a solution exists, that the algorithm will determine one if a solution does exist, that the solution $(S_1,\ldots,S_n)$ determined by the algorithm is maximal among all that contain $(T_1,\ldots,T_n)$, and that all languages in $(S_1,\ldots,S_n)$ are regular. We first show:

Lemma 9.10. *Given a system of m implicit language equations in n variables,*

$$L_i = \alpha_i(X_1,\ldots,X_n), \quad i = 1,\ldots,m,$$

where for all $i = 1,\ldots,m$, $\alpha_i(X_1,\ldots,X_n) \in \mathrm{EX}_{\{a\}}(\mathrm{REG}; \mathrm{OP}; X_1,\ldots,X_n)$ with OP consisting of union, concatenation, and star, and let the $L_i = F_i \cup H_i(a^s)^*$ be regular languages over $\{a\}$ in canonical form, then the following holds:

There exists a solution $(Q_1,\ldots,Q_n)$ iff there exists an n-tuple $(T_1,\ldots,T_n)$ such that

$$L_{k,0} \subseteq \alpha_k(T_1,\ldots,T_n) \subseteq L_k \quad \text{for all } k = 1,\ldots,m$$

and $\mathrm{ILE}(\{\alpha_i(X_1,\ldots,X_n), L_i \mid i = 1,\ldots,m\}; (T_1,\ldots,T_n))$ produces $(S_1,\ldots,S_n)$ as a solution with $Q_i \subseteq S_i$ for all $i = 1,\ldots,n$.

PROOF. If the condition of the theorem holds, then obviously $(Q_1,\ldots,Q_n)$ is a solution with $Q_i = S_i$ for all $i = 1,\ldots,n$.

For the converse, let us assume that $(Q_1,\ldots,Q_n)$ is a solution. Define

$$T_i := Q_i \cap a^{\leq N} \quad \text{for all } i = 1,\ldots,n.$$

Clearly $L_{k,0} \subseteq \alpha_k(T_1,\ldots,T_n) \subseteq L_k$ for all $k = 1,\ldots,m$ since $(Q_1,\ldots,Q_n)$ is a solution. By definition of N, Lemma 9.2 applies and, therefore, whenever ILE adds in the while-loop a word u to S_j for some j, it adds $u(a^s)^*$.

Thus, there are two possibilities how the claim of the lemma may fail to hold:

a. The algorithm ILE determines there is no solution for the given system of implicit equations; this would occur iff $y \notin \alpha_j(S_1, \ldots, S_n)$ for some y and j as determined in ILE. However, since $(Q_1, \ldots, Q_n)$ is a solution, $y \in \alpha_j(Q_1, \ldots, Q_n)$. Moreover, at this point in the algorithm,

$$S_i \cap a^{\leq |y|} \supseteq Q_i \cap a^{\leq |y|} \quad \text{for all } i = 1, \ldots, n$$

since ILE is a greedy algorithm; consequently, it will add a word whenever it is possible, even if it is not required. Thus, it is impossible that $y \notin \alpha_j(S_1, \ldots, S_n)$ for some y and j.

b. ILE produces a solution $(S_1, \ldots, S_n)$, but this solution does not satisfy $Q_i \subseteq S_i$ for all $i = 1, \ldots, n$. Again, this situation is impossible since

$$S_i \cap a^{\leq |y|} \supseteq Q_i \cap a^{\leq |y|} \quad \text{for all } i = 1, \ldots, n$$

as long as there is a word $y \in L_k - \alpha_k(S_1, \ldots, S_n)$ for some $k \in \{1, \ldots, m\}$.

It follows that the claim must hold. Thus the lemma is proven. $\square$

Using the result of Lemma 9.10, we can now show that the algorithm ILE, when started with an appropriate initialization, will effectively construct a regular solution that, moreover, is maximal with respect to all solutions that contain the assumed initialization. Specifically, we state:

Theorem 9.11. *Assume we are given a system of m implicit language equations in n variables,*

$$L_i = \alpha_i(X_1, \ldots, X_n), \quad i = 1, \ldots, m,$$

where for all $i = 1, \ldots, m$, $\alpha_i(X_1, \ldots, X_n) \in \mathrm{EX}_{\{a\}}(\mathrm{REG}; \mathrm{OP}; X_1, \ldots, X_n)$ with OP consisting of union, concatenation, and star, and let the $L_i = F_i \cup H_i(a^s)^*$ be regular languages over $\{a\}$ in canonical form. Let $(T_1, \ldots, T_n)$ be an n-tuple of languages satisfying $L_{k,0} \subseteq \alpha_k(T_1, \ldots, T_n) \subseteq L_k$ for all $k = 1, \ldots, m$.

Then $\mathrm{ILE}(\{\alpha_i(X_1, \ldots, X_n), L_i \mid i = 1, \ldots, m\}; (T_1, \ldots, T_n))$ correctly determines whether there exists a solution $(S_1, \ldots, S_n)$ such that $T_i \subseteq S_i$ for all $i = 1, \ldots, n$, and if one exists, that solution will contain all solutions $(Q_1, \ldots, Q_n)$ satisfying $T_i \subseteq Q_i$ for all $i = 1, \ldots, n$.

PROOF. The only claim that remains to be shown is that the solution $(S_1, \ldots, S_n)$ determined by ILE is maximal with respect to the property of containing $(T_1, \ldots, T_n)$. This, however, follows from the observation that $(S_1, \ldots, S_n)$ is obtained from $(T_1, \ldots, T_n)$ by adding all words that can possibly be added. $\square$

Corollary 9.12. *There exists an effective algorithm to determine whether a solution exists for a given system of m implicit language equations in n variables,*

$$L_i = \alpha_i(X_1, \ldots, X_n), \quad i = 1, \ldots, m,$$

where for all $i = 1, \ldots, m$, $\alpha_i(X_1, \ldots, X_n) \in \mathrm{EX}_{\{a\}}(\mathrm{REG}; \mathrm{OP}; X_1, \ldots, X_n)$ with OP *consisting of union, concatenation, and star, and $L_i = F_i \cup H_i(a^s)^*$ is a regular language over $\{a\}$ in its canonical form. Furthermore, if a solution exists, there also exists a regular one, and it can be constructed effectively.*

PROOF. It is obvious that the algorithm ILE is effective. The only thing that remains to be shown is that the determination of the n-tuple $(T_1, \ldots, T_n)$ satisfying

$$L_{k,0} \subseteq \alpha_k(T_1, \ldots, T_n) \subseteq L_k \quad \text{for all } k = 1, \ldots, m$$

is also effective. Since we can restrict our attention to languages T_i with words of length at most N, all such n-tuples $(T_1, \ldots, T_n)$ can be effectively determined. Thus, we can effectively determine whether a solution of a given system of m implicit equations in n variables exists; furthermore, if a solution exists, we can construct one effectively. Finally, the solution determined by ILE is clearly regular.   □

9.4   Uniqueness of Solutions

The question of uniqueness of a solution of a system of implicit equations is nontrivial. In the case of explicit equations in $\mathrm{EX}_{\{a\}}(\mathrm{REG}; \mathrm{OP}; X)$ with OP consisting of union, concatenation, and star, it was relatively easily answered because we gave parameterized representations for all solutions (see Chapter 3). In the case of implicit equations over an arbitrary alphabet where the operations were just union and left-concatenation, we gave a test to determine whether or not there were one, finitely many, or infinitely many solutions (see Chapter 8). For the equations studied in the present paper, the question of providing a necessary and sufficient condition for uniqueness is still open. However, we can make the following observations.

It should be clear that ILE, in an effort to construct a maximal solution, may add words to S_j that are not needed; this may occur in the first i-loop in ILE or in the i-loop that is contained in the while-loop. More specifically, completely eliminate the first i-loop and change the condition for adding a^i to S_j in the second i-loop by adding the requirement that for some $p \in J$,

$$y \in \alpha_p(S_1, \ldots, S_{j-1}, S_j \cup \{a^i\}, S_{j+1}, \ldots, S_n);$$

then the algorithm (suitably modified to assure that these words y are dealt with appropriately) will still produce a solution [if one exists for the given initialization $(T_1, \ldots, T_n)$], but it may be no longer maximal [for $(T_1, \ldots, T_n)$]. Clearly, if this produces a different solution, we have established that the original solution was not unique. Similarly, since there are possibly many different initializations $(T_1, \ldots, T_n)$, if two yield different solutions, the nonuniqueness of any solution is also established. However, as the following example shows, this is a sufficient but not a necessary condition. Consider the equation

$$a^* = XX;$$

all processes described in this chapter yield exactly one solution, namely $X = a^*$. However, one can verify that there are infinitely many solutions; for example, for any $p \geq 2$, $a^* - \{a^p\}$ is a solution which is different from all other solutions (for different values of p). Thus, a different approach is needed.

Lemma 9.13. *Let $(S_1, \ldots, S_n)$ be a solution of a system of m implicit language equations in n variables,*

$$L_i = \alpha_i(X_1, \ldots, X_n), \quad i = 1, \ldots, m,$$

where for all $i = 1, \ldots, m$, $\alpha_i(X_1, \ldots, X_n) \in \mathrm{EX}_{\{a\}}(\mathrm{REG};\ OP;\ X)$ with OP consisting of union, concatenation, and star, and let the $L_i = F_i \cup H_i(a^s)^*$ be regular languages over $\{a\}$ in canonical form.

There exists a solution $(Q_1, \ldots, Q_n) \neq (S_1, \ldots, S_n)$ such that $Q_i \subseteq S_i$ for $i = 1, \ldots, n$ iff there exists a $j \in \{1, \ldots, n\}$ and there exists a word $z \in S_j$ such that for all $k = 1, \ldots, m$,

$$\alpha_k(S_1, \ldots, S_{j-1}, \{z\}, S_{j+1}, \ldots, S_n)$$
$$\subseteq \alpha_k(S_1, \ldots, S_{j-1}, S_j - \{z\}, S_{j+1}, \ldots, S_n).$$

PROOF.   If there exists a solution $(Q_1, \ldots, Q_n) \neq (S_1, \ldots, S_n)$ such that $Q_i \subseteq S_i$ for $i = 1, \ldots, n$, let j be an index such that $Q_j \neq S_j$ and let z be a word in $S_j - Q_j$. Then, the condition must hold. Conversely, if there exist an index j and a word z so that the condition holds, then $(S_1, \ldots, S_{j-1}, S_j - \{z\}, S_{j+1}, \ldots, S_n)$ is a solution different from $(S_1, \ldots, S_n)$.   □

Now, if $(S_1, \ldots, S_n)$ is the result of ILE, then every S_j has a canonical representation

$$S_j = B_j \cup D_j(a^s)^*,$$

where D_j is empty if S_j is finite. Since B_j is finite, it is easy to test the condition of Lemma 9.13 for each word in B_j, for every $j = 1, \ldots, n$. However, how to test (in general) the condition of Lemma 9.13 for words z in $D_j(a^s)^*$ is an open problem.

9.5   Examples

We give several examples worked out in considerable detail to illustrate the constructions presented in the previous sections of this chapter.

1. Consider the following single equation in the two variables X and Y:

$$a^{1,3} \cup a^5(a^3)^* = aX^2 \cup a(aY)^*.$$

It follows that $L_0 = a^{1,3,5}$ and $M = N = 5$.

We select the initialization $(X, Y) = (a^{0,2}, \emptyset)$ and verify that it satisfies the requirement

$$a^{1,3,5} \subseteq \alpha(a^{0,2}, \emptyset) \subseteq a^{1,3} \cup a^5(a^3)^*.$$

Then, we carry out the "in-fill" operation in the first i-loop, $i = 0, \ldots, 2$, and determine that no new words of length at most 5 may be added to this initialization. We then proceed with the while-loop. Clearly, $\alpha(a^{0,2}, \emptyset) \neq a^{1,3} \cup a^5(a^3)^*$, and y is determined to be a^8. Executing the i-loop inside the while-loop, for $i = 6, \ldots, 8$, results in no words being added to X nor Y; consequently, the test whether y is contained in the approximate solution fails: No solution exists that contains the initialization $(a^{0,2}, \emptyset)$.

In order to determine whether this equation has any solution, it is necessary to exhaust systematically all possible initializations. This can be simplified here by observing that certain words cannot be in Y; these are a^0, a^1, and a^3 since in each case $Per((aY)^*)$ is incompatible with $Per(a^5(a^3)^*) = 3$. This argument suggests that a^2 is a possible word to be contained in Y. However, this is not valid since $a^2 \in Y$ implies $a(a^2)^* \subseteq a(aY)^* \subseteq a^{1,3} \cup a^5(a^3)^*$, which is impossible. Thus, we just have one possible initialization (consisting of words of length at most 5), namely $Y = \emptyset$, and in this case, it can be verified that the only possible initialization for X is $a^{0,2}$, which is clearly the case we dealt with above. Thus, there is no solution.

2. Consider the following single equation in the two variables X and Y:

$$a^2(a^2)^* = aX^3 \cup aX(aY)^*.$$

It follows that $L_0 = a^2$ and $M = N = 2$. Recall that this was the equation mentioned at the beginning of Section 9.3.

It can be verified that the only possible initializations (with words of length at most 2) are $(X, Y) = (a, a)$ and $(X, Y) = (a, \emptyset)$. Let us select the initialization $(X, Y) = (a, a)$; it clearly satisfies the requirement

$$a^2 \subseteq \alpha(a, a) \subseteq a^2(a^2)^*.$$

Then, we carry out the "in-fill" operation in the first i-loop, $i = 0, \ldots, 2$, and obtain $(X, Y) = (a(a^2)^*, a(a^2)^*)$. We note that for the other initialization, $(X, Y) = (a, \emptyset)$, the result after the in-fill operation (first i-loop in ILE) is the same at this point in the algorithm, namely $(X, Y) = (a(a^2)^*, a(a^2)^*)$. It follows that this is a solution; however, in order to determine whether other words can be added to these languages, we execute the while-loop with $K = 4$ and $J = \emptyset$. This results in no change; $(a(a^2)^*, a(a^2)^*)$ is the maximal solution containing (a, a). It follows that the resulting solution which is maximal with respect to containing (a, a) is, in fact, globally maximal.

Note that there are infinitely many solutions. For example, Y can be replaced by any subset of $a(a^2)^*$ as long as that subset contains a. A similar argument applies to X. Since there are uncountably many subsets of an infinite set, this equation has uncountably many solutions, including uncountably many nonregular ones.

3. Consider the following two equations in the three variables X, Y, and Z:

$$X^3 \cup Y^2 \cup Z* = \lambda \cup a^4 a^*,$$
$$aXY \cup YZ \cup a^4 = a^2 a^*.$$

It follows that $L_{1,0} = a^{0,4}$, $L_{2,0} = a^{2,3,4}$, and $M = N = 4$.

Let us select the initialization $(X, Y, Z) = (a^0, a^2, a^0)$. Then, the first in-fill operation (first i-loop) yields $(X, Y, Z) = (a^0, a^2 a^*, a^0)$. The while-loop results in adding $a^3 a^*$ to Y, and adding $a^4 a^*$ to X, Y, and Z. This results in the solution

$$(X, Y, Z) = (\lambda \cup a^4 a^*, a^2 a^*, \lambda \cup a^4 a^*).$$

Let us select another initialization, namely $(X, Y, Z) = (a^3, a^{2,3,4}, a^0)$. This produces (after some calculation) the following solution:

$$(X, Y, Z) = (a^2 a^*, a^2 a^*, \lambda \cup a^4 a^*).$$

Thus, we have constructed two different solutions. In fact, there are infinitely many, since in both cases, if we choose for Z any subset of $\lambda \cup a^4 a^*$ that contains the empty word λ, we obtain another solution.

4. Consider the following two equations in the single variable X:

$$aX^2 = a(a^2)^* \quad \text{and} \quad (aX)^* = a^*.$$

We first rewrite this so that the period of the two languages L_i is the same:

$$aX^2 = a(a^2)^* \quad \text{and} \quad (aX)^* = a^{0,1}(a^2)^*.$$

Now it follows that $L_{1,0} = a^1$, $L_{2,0} = a^{0,1}$, and $M = N = 1$. The only valid initialization is $X = a^0$. Adding the word a to X would violate the containment condition $[a \subseteq aX^2 \subseteq a(a^2)^*]$, but a^2 can be added, yielding $X = a^0 \cup a^2(a^2)^*$ or $X = (a^2)^*$. This solution is (globally) maximal. However, the solution is not unique, since for any $p \geq 2$, $(a^2)^* - \{a^{2p}\}$ is also a solution.

We conclude this section with two more examples which we do not work out in much detail. Example 5 illustrates a situation where $M \neq N$; Example 6 presents a system of equations with a unique solution which, moreover, consists of finite languages even though all languages L_i are infinite.

5. Consider the following equations in the variable X:

$$aX^3(a^2 X)^* \cup a^{4,7} = a^4(a^3)^*.$$

It follows that $L_0 = a^4(a^3)^* - a^{4,7} = a^{10}(a^3)^*$; therefore, $M = 4$ and $N = 10$. The resulting solution is $a(a^3)^*$. Since there is only one variable, this solution is maximal. It is clearly not unique since $X = a$ is also a solution—which happens to be minimal (i.e., contained in every other solution). In fact, any language T contained in the maximal solution $a(a^3)^*$ and containing the minimal solution a is also a solution.

6. Consider the following three equations in the single variable X:

$$(aX)^* = (a^2)^*, \quad (a^2 X)^* = (a^3)^*, \quad aX \cup a(aX)^* = a^{1,2} \cup a^3(a^2)^*.$$

We first rewrite this system as follows:

$$(aX)^* = a^{0,2,4}(a^6)^*,$$
$$(a^2 X)^* = a^{0,3}(a^6)^*,$$
$$aX \cup a(aX)^* = a^{1,2} \cup a^{3,5,7}(a^6)^*.$$

It turns out that $X = a$ is the only solution of this system of equations.

9.6   Conclusion

We have defined a class of implicit language equations in which unrestricted concatenation, union, and star occur as operators. Assuming the constant languages are regular and the equations are over a one-letter alphabet, we have given an effective method to determine whether a solution of a given system of such implicit language equations exists. We also have outlined an effective construction of a solution if one exists. In particular, it follows that any such system of equations with a solution must also have a regular solution. We have shown that single equations in a single variable have always a maximal solution if they have any. However, this does not hold for systems with more than one variable. Nevertheless, we managed to retain a restricted maximality property: Our construction yields a regular solution that is maximal in the sense that the solution contains a certain finite fixed set and any other solution that also contains that set must be contained in our solution. We raised the problem of determining whether a given solution is unique. Although we have indicated some approaches, the general question of determining uniqueness is still open.

9.7   Bibliographical Note

The material contained in this chapter is new and has not been published elsewhere.

9.8 Problems

1. For each of the following systems of implicit equations over the alphabet $A = \{a\}$, determine whether a solution exists; if so, construct a regular one, and finally determine whether it is unique.

   a. $\lambda \cup a^4 a^* = a(a^4)^* X^3 (aX)^* \cup \lambda$.

   b. $a \cup a^4 a^* = a(a^4)^* X^3 (aX)^* \cup a$.

   c. $\lambda \cup a^4 (a^2)^* = a(a^4)^* X^3 (aX)^* \cup \lambda$.

   d. $\lambda \cup a^{10} (a^4)^* = a(a^4)^* X^3 (aX)^* \cup \lambda$.

   e. $a^{7,11,13,17} (a^8)^* = (a^{0,4} \cup a^6 (a^4)^*) X^2 Y^3 (a^2 X^3)^*$,

   $\qquad a(a^4)^* = a(XYZ)^* (XY)^* (a^{1,2} YZ)^*$.

   f. $a^{7,11,13,17} (a^8)^* = (a^{0,4} \cup a^6 (a^4)^*) X^2 Y^3 (a^2 X^3)^*$,

   $\qquad aa^* = a(XYZ)^* (XY)^* (a^{1,2} YZ)^*$.

   g. $a^{7,11,13,17} (a^8)^* = (a^{0,4} \cup a^6 (a^4)^*) X^2 Y^3 (a^2 X^3)^*$,

   $\qquad a(a^2)^* = a(XYZ)^* (XY)^* (a^{1,2} YZ)^*$.

   h. $a^{11,16,17,18} \cup a^{21} a^* = a^3 X^4 (aX^3)^* (a^2 Y^2)^* (a^3 Z)^* (XYZ)^*$,

   $\qquad a^{17} (a^7)^* = a^5 X^2 Y^2 Z^2 (aX^3)^* (aY^3)^* (aZ^3)^*$.

10

Explicit Relations with Union and Left-Concatenation

About This Chapter: While systems of language *equations* have been studied in various contexts, the corresponding problems for general relations between languages have not received much attention. In this chapter, we examine relations where the operations involved are unrestricted union and left-concatenation; in other words, precisely the operations involved in classical equations. Note that for classical equations, each variable is equated to exactly one expression. In this chapter, relations also include the case of several equations for the same variable. First, we look at single explicit relations and resolve the question of whether there exists a solution, study how to find all solutions, and investigate adequate representations for the solutions. Then, we focus on systems of several explicit relations; the questions here are significantly more complicated since for a single variable X, there may be three types of relations, namely equality ($=$), superrelation ($\supseteq$), and subrelation ($\subseteq$). We consider, first, decoupled systems, where for each variable, at most one of the three relation types may occur. We study methods to answer the questions of whether there exists a solution, whether there is more than one solution, and how to represent these solutions.

10.1   Introduction

All previous chapters have dealt with equations. In this chapter and the next, we develop a theory of language relations that is an analogue to that of systems of classical equations outlined in Chapter 3. Thus, the operations involved in our expressions are unrestricted union and left-concatenation.

Specifically, in the present chapter, we study explicit relations; the next chapter deals with implicit relations.

For the remainder of this chapter, we assume that OP consists of unrestricted union and left-concatenation. Then the expressions considered in this chapter are elements of $EX_A(CONST; OP; X_1, \ldots, X_n)$, where CONST denotes the set of constant languages over the alphabet A. Let $\mathbb{R}$ stand for one of the following relations between languages:

Equality: $=$
Superrelation: $\supseteq$
Subrelation: $\subseteq$

[There may be other relations, such as inequality $(X \neq LX \cup M)$, but these three are the primarily ones we will consider in this chapter.] Then, our interest in this chapter is concentrated on systems of explicit language relations in the n variables $X_1, \ldots, X_n$ defined as follows:

$$X_i \mathbb{R}_{i,j} \alpha_{i,j} \quad \text{for } i = 1, \ldots, n, \ 1 \leq j \leq \sigma_i$$

where $\sigma_i \geq 0$ and for all i, j, $\mathbb{R}_{i,j} \in \{=, \supseteq, \subseteq\}$ and $\alpha_{i,j} \in EX_A(CONST; OP; X_1, \ldots, X_n)$. For each i, σ_i denotes the number of relations that the variable X_i has; note that σ_i may be 0 (i.e., there may not be any relation for a particular variable).

It should be clear that we have precisely a system of classical language equations if

$$\sigma_i = 1 \quad \text{and} \quad \mathbb{R}_{i,1} \ is \ =, \quad \text{for all } i.$$

Furthermore, if

$$\mathbb{R}_{i,1} = \mathbb{R}_{i,2} = \cdots = \mathbb{R}_{i,\sigma_i} \quad \text{for all } i,$$

the resulting system of explicit language relations will be called decoupled, and if

$$\sigma_i \leq 1 \quad \text{for all } i,$$

we have a so-called strictly decoupled system of explicit language relations.

We recall that any system of classical equations always has a solution and that all solutions can be written as regular expressions in terms of the constant languages $S_{i,j}$, regardless of whether the $S_{i,j}$ themselves are regular or not (Theorem 3.2). Furthermore, there exists an easily tested for condition for the uniqueness of a solution is unique (see Section 3.2). It turns out that the situation is more complicated when it comes to explicit language relations.

It is important to note that in systems of explicit language relations, more than one type may hold for the same variable; moreover, several relations of the same type may hold for the same variable. As an example, consider the following system of four explicit relations in the variables X, Y, and Z

over the alphabet $\{a, b\}$:

$$X = a^*X \cup bY \cup a^*,$$
$$X \supseteq bX \cup aY \cup abZ,$$
$$Y \supseteq aX \cup b^*Y \cup bZ,$$
$$Y \subseteq aX \cup bY \cup aZ.$$

Note that both X and Y have two relations (of two different types), whereas Z has none. It can be shown that this system has a solution (which is not unique) that is given by

$$(X, Y, Z) = ((a \cup b)^*, \quad b^*a(a \cup b)^*, \quad a(a \cup b)^*).$$

It can be easily verified by direct substitution that these three languages indeed constitute a solution.

We will concentrate primarily on decoupled systems; thus, for every variable X, relations of at most one of the three types $(=, \supseteq, \subseteq)$ hold. This restriction is motivated by the following example of a system of two relations in one variable X over the alphabet $\{a, b\}$:

$$X \subseteq bX \cup b,$$
$$X \supseteq aX \cup a.$$

It is easily seen that no solution can exist since, by the first relation (subrelation), all words in any solution would have to start with b, and by the second relation (superrelation), there must be at least one word in a solution that starts with a (namely a itself). This problem cannot occur in decoupled systems. Note that decoupled systems do not stipulate that each variable have only one relation; however, if there are two or more relations for the same variable, they must all be of the same type. Thus, the following is a decoupled system of explicit language relations in the three variables X, Y, and Z, with the constant languages $\{\lambda\}$, $\{a\}$, $\{b\}$, and $\{ab\}$:

$$X = aX \cup bY \cup \lambda,$$
$$X = b^*X \cup abZ,$$
$$Y \supseteq aX \cup bY \cup Z,$$
$$Y \supseteq bX \cup aY \cup aZ.$$

We will see that this decoupled system of relations has precisely the following solutions:

$$(X, Y, Z) = (A^*, A^*, T) \quad \text{with } T \text{ completely arbitrary.}$$

10.2 Properties of Single Explicit Relations in One Variable

First, we study single explicit language relations in a single variable X. Recall the classical result for equations where the normal form is

$$X = LX \cup M.$$

If $\lambda \notin L$, L^*M is the unique solution of this equation; if $\lambda \in L$, $L^*(M \cup T)$ gives a parameteric representation of all solutions with T ranging over all languages. Note that neither L nor M (nor T, in the second case) need be regular, even though the solution representation is a regular expression in L, M, and T.

Superrelation ($\supseteq$): Here, the normal form of a single relation in the variable X is

$$X \supseteq LX \cup M$$

with L and M arbitrary languages over the underlying alphabet A. We can formulate:

Proposition 10.1. *Consider a single explicit superrelation $X \supseteq LX \cup M$ in the single variable X.*

a. *L^*M is the minimal solution.*
b. *A^* is the maximal solution.*
c. *The set of all solutions is given by the expression $L^*(M \cup T)$, with T ranging over all languages in A^*.*

PROOF. It is trivial to verify that L^*M and A^* are indeed solutions and that A^* is the maximal solution. We show now that L^*M is the minimal solution. Suppose there exists a solution S that does not contain L^*M; thus, $L^*M - S \neq \emptyset$. Let w be a shortest word in $L^*M - S$. We know that $w \notin S$, and also $w \notin M$ since $S \supseteq M$ by assumption that S is a solution. Let $A^{<|w|}$ denote the set of all words in A^* strictly shorter than w. Because of the minimality of w,

$$S \cap A^{<|w|} = L^*M \cap A^{<|w|}.$$

Then, w must be in LS, $w \in LS$. If $\lambda \notin L$, we have

$$w \in LS \quad \text{iff} \ w \in L(S \cap A^{<|w|}) = L(L^*M \cap A^{<|w|}),$$

and since $w \in L^*M$ and $w \notin M$, we conclude that $w \in LL^*M$, thus, $w \in L(L^*M \cap A^{<|w|})$, and hence, $w \in LS$. However, this contradicts $S \supseteq LS$ since, by assumption, $w \notin S$. If $\lambda \in L$, then $LS = (L - \{\lambda\})S \cup S$. By assumption, $w \notin S$, and, therefore,

$$w \in LS \quad \text{iff} \ w \in (L - \{\lambda\})S$$

which means the argument above (stated for the case $\lambda \notin L$) carries over in its entirety.

Now consider (c). We first show that $L^*(M \cup T)$ is a solution:

$$L^*(M \cup T) \supseteq L[L^*(M \cup T)] \cup M = LL^*M \cup M \cup LL^*T$$
$$= L^*M \cup LL^*T.$$

Now, consider any word w contained in any solution S, $w \in S$. It follows that

$$L\{w\} \subseteq LS \subseteq S,$$

and, therefore, $L^*\{w\}$ must also be contained in S. Since this holds for any word w in S and since L^*M is minimal, any solution must be of the form $L^*(M \cup T)$ for some language T over A. □

One sees that in contrast to equations, no differentiation between $\lambda \in L$ and $\lambda \notin L$ is required. In fact, it follows from the form of the solution expression $L^*(M \cup T)$ that we can always remove the empty word from L in such a relation since $L^* = (L - \{\lambda\})^*$.

Subrelation ($\subseteq$): Here, the normal form of a single explicit relation in the variable X is

$$X \subseteq LX \cup M,$$

with L and M arbitrary languages over A. Let S/T denote the left quotient of S with respect to T : $S/T = \{w \in A^* \mid s = tw$ for words $s \in S$ and $t \in T\}$. For any language $S \subseteq L^*M$, define its closure $\mathrm{CL}_{L,M}(S)$ as follows:

$$\mathrm{CL}_{L,M}(S) = S \cup \bigcup_{x \in S-M} \{x\}/M.$$

Then we can formulate:

Proposition 10.2. *Consider a single explicit subrelation $X \subseteq LX \cup M$ in the single variable X.*

a. *$\emptyset$ is the minimal solution.*
b. *If $\lambda \notin L$, then L^*M is the maximal solution; if $\lambda \in L$, A^* is the maximal solution.*
c. *Assume $\lambda \notin L$. For any language $S \subseteq L^*M$, $\mathrm{CL}_{L,M}(S)$ is a solution. Conversely, if S is a solution, $S = \mathrm{CL}_{L,M}(S)$.*

PROOF. Parts (a) and (b) are straightforward. We first show that $C := \mathrm{CL}_{L,M}(S)$ is a solution for any $S \subseteq L^*M$. Let $u \in C$, then either $u \in M$ or $u \in C - M$. Since $S \subseteq L^*M$, by definition of $\mathrm{CL}_{L,M}(S)$, $u \in C - M$ can be written as $u = vu'$ with $v \in L$ and $u' \in C$. Thus, $u \in LC \cup M$. Now, if S is a solution of $X \subseteq LX \cup M$, then $u \in S$ implies $u \in M$, or $u \in LS$, in which case $u = vu'$ and $v \in L$, $u' \in S$; thus, $u' \in \mathrm{CL}_{L,M}(\{x\})$. Since this holds for all $x \in S - M$, $S - \mathrm{CL}_{L,M}(S)$. □

Note that this criterion allows for finite solutions; in fact, this is a major difference between superrelations and subrelations. While by Proposition 3.1, a solution of a superrelation is almost always infinite (L^*M is the minimal solution and this language is finite iff $M = \emptyset$ or M is finite and $L \in \{\emptyset, \{\lambda\}\}$), all subrelations $X \subseteq LX \cup M$ admit finite solutions.

We excluded the case $\lambda \in L$ in Part (c), for the following reason: If $\lambda \in L$, then we have

$$X \subseteq LX \cup M = X \cup (L - \{\lambda\})X \cup M$$

and this implies that every language over A is a solution in X. Consequently, subrelations $X \subseteq LX \cup M$ with $\lambda \in L$ are completely uninteresting. In particular, regardless of the value of M, they can always be removed from any system of relations, since they do not restrict the solution space at all.

The remainder of this chapter is organized as follows. In the Section 10.3 we discuss the question of how to solve a system of explicit *equations* where a variable X_i may have more than one defining equation. This problem turns out to be surprisingly difficult. In Section 10.4, we show how to solve any strictly decoupled system of explicit language relations. In Section 10.5, we discuss the reduction of arbitrary decoupled to strictly decoupled systems; we also comment on how to solve general systems and give examples.

10.3   Solving Systems with Several Explicit Equations for One Variable

Consider the situation where the same variable has several explicit equations of the same type. Recall that this is permitted in decoupled systems but not allowed in systems of classical equations. Thus, we are dealing with two (or more) equations for X:

$$X = LX \cup M,$$
$$X = PX \cup Q,$$

where, as always, M and Q represent expressions that may involve variables other than X.

One may be tempted to dismiss this problem as strange and even contradictory, since each equation will give rise to its solution and the resulting two solutions most likely will be incompatible. However, this argument requires closer scrutiny: If neither L nor P contain the empty word λ, and M and Q are constants, then the first equation has the unique solution L^*M, whereas the second has the unique solution P^*Q; an internal inconsistency of the system arises if and only if

$$L^*M \neq P^*Q.$$

Much more interesting is the situation where at least one of L and P contains λ. If both L and P contain λ, we get $L^*(M \cup T_1)$ as the parameterized representation of all solutions from the first equation and $P^*(Q \cup T_2)$ from the second. Thus, an internal inconsistency (and therefore proof that no solution can exist) arises only if there do not exist languages T_1 and T_2 such that

$$L^*(M \cup T_1) = P^*(Q \cup T_2).$$

However, in this example, there are obviously languages T_1 and T_2 that satisfy this, namely

$$T_1 = T_2 = A^*.$$

Interestingly, it is the case where only one of L and P contains the empty word that is more complicated and requires the use of implicit equation. Assume that L contains λ. Then, the first equation has the representation $L^*(M \cup T)$ of all its solutions, whereas the second has the unique solution P^*Q. Clearly, these two equation can be simultaneously satisfied if and only if there is a solution of the implicit equation in the variable T

$$L^*(M \cup T) = P^*Q.$$

Clearly, the main difficulty of the problem is related to the multiple solutions of a single equation. We first formulate a result assuming that X is the only variable occurring in the system of explicit equations:

Proposition 10.3. *Let* $X = L_i X \cup M_i$ *for* $i = 1, \ldots, n$ *be a system of* n *equations for the single variable* X. *Assume that the equations are numbered so that* $\lambda \in L_j$ *for all* $j = 1, \ldots, m$ *with* $0 \leq m \leq n$. *Then, the system has a solution in* X *iff*

a. $m = n$ *or*
b. $m < n$ *and*

$$(L_j)^* M_j = (L_n)^* M_n \quad \text{for all } j = m+1, \ldots, n-1$$

and there exists a solution in the variables T_s, $s = 1, \ldots, m$ *of the following system of implicit language equations:*

$$(L_s)^* T_s \cup (L_s)^* M_s = (L_n)^* M_n \quad \text{for } s = 1, \ldots, m.$$

PROOF. Let S be a solution; then, clearly, $S = L_i S \cup M_i$ for $i = 1, \ldots, n$. This implies the conditions of the proposition. Conversely, assume that the conditions hold. If (a) holds then $X = A^*$ is a solution. If (b) holds, then $X = (L_n)^* M_n$ is a solution of the system. □

It turns out that instead of solving the system of implicit equations in Case (b) of this proposition, we can equivalently substitute for the variable X the uniquely determined language $(L_n)^* M_n$ into the equations $X = L_i X \cup M_i$ for $i = 1, \ldots, n-1$. If this converts the equations into identities, $(L_n)^* M_n$ is a solution for X; otherwise, no solution exists.

Corollary 10.4. *Let $X = L_i X \cup M_i$ for $i = 1, \ldots, n$ be a system of n equations for the single variable X. Assume that the equations are numbered so that $\lambda \in L_j$ for all $j = 1, \ldots, m$ with $0 \le m \le n$. If $m < n$, then any solution is unique.*

Consider now the following two explicit equations over the alphabet $\{a, b\}$ for the single variable X:

$$X = a^* X \cup (ab)^*,$$
$$X = ab^* X \cup \lambda.$$

The first equation has the parametric solution representation $X = a^*((ab)^* \cup T)$, and the second equation has the uniquely determined solution $X = (ab^*)^*$. Thus, there exists a solution of this system if and only if

$$a^*(ab)^* \cup a^* T = (ab^*)^*.$$

This is a simple example of implicit language equations which were studied in Chapter 8. One can verify (by direct substitution) that this particular implicit language equation has the following solution in T:

$$T = a(a \cup b)^*.$$

[In fact, it has infinitely many regular solutions in the parameter T.] Alternatively, we can substitute $(ab^*)^*$ for X to the two equations and verify that this language is a solution.

Were we to change the second equation to

$$X = ab^* X \cup bb,$$

the resulting implicit language equation would be

$$a^*(ab)^* \cup a^* T = (ab^*)^* bb$$

for which no solution exists (see Chapter 8). Alternatively, we may again substitute $(ab^*)^* bb$ for X into the two equations and see in this way that this system of language equations has no solution.

These observations about systems in a single variable indicate the need for a more formal treatment of systems of explicit equations in which a variable may have more than one equation. Thus, for the remainder of this section, we assume that there exists at least one variable with more than one explicit equation.

[If for each variable there is exactly one equation, then obviously the results of Chapter 3 apply. If there are fewer equations than variables but no variable has more than one equation, the results of Chapter 3 still apply; those variables without defining equations then are simply treated as free parameters. This corresponds to augmenting the given system of equations with exactly one equation of the form $X_t = X_t$ for each variable X_t that did not have an equation in the original system.]

Let Σ_i be the set of all equations for the variable X_i,

$$\Sigma_i :: X_i = \bigcup_{j=1,\ldots,n} L_{i,j;t} X_j \cup M_{i;t} \quad \text{for } 1 \le t \le \sigma_i,$$

where σ_i is the number of equations of the variable X_i. Then, the system to be solved is

$$(\Sigma_1, \Sigma_2, \ldots, \Sigma_n).$$

The equation t for X_i is of type M iff at least one of the following conditions holds:

1. There exists a sequence $((i_0, t_0), (i_1, t_1), \ldots, (i_r, t_r))$ for some $r \ge 1$ such that

$$i_0 = i_r = i, t_0 = t, 1 \le t_j \le \tau_{i_j} \quad \text{for } j = 1, \ldots, r-1$$

and

$$\lambda \notin L_{i_{j-1}, i_j; t_{j-1}} \quad \text{for all } j = 1, \ldots, r.$$

2. For some variable X_k of type M, there exists a sequence $((i_0, t_0), (i_1, t_1), \ldots, (i_r, t_r))$ for some $r \ge 1$ such that

$$i_0 = i, i_r = k, t_0 = t, 1 \le t_j \le \tau_{i_j} \quad \text{for } j = 1, \ldots, r-1$$

and

$$L_{i_{j-1}, i_j; t_{j-1}} \ne \emptyset \quad \text{for all } j = 1, \ldots, r.$$

It is not difficult to verify that one can obtain a parameterized solution expression for X_i by using the results of Section 3.2 if and only if X_i is of type M. Loosely speaking, we will say that X_i has multiple solutions. Note that, ultimately, if there is to be any equation of type M for a variable, there has to be an equation of type M for at least one variable, according to Part 1 of the definition.

Note that this definition of having multiple solutions in a variable is based on syntactic properties of an equation. It should be pointed out that there are equations that meet our definition of multiplicity but that, in fact, do not have multiple solutions. An example is given by the equation in X over the alphabet $\{a, b\}$:

$$X = (a \cup b \cup \lambda) X \cup \lambda,$$

which has the parameterized representation of all its solutions

$$X = (a \cup b \cup \lambda)^* (\lambda \cup T) = (a \cup b)^* \cup (a \cup b)^* T,$$

but obviously this is equal to $(a \cup b)^*$ regardless of the choice of T; thus, there is exactly one solution even though X is of type M.

We first reduce a general system $(\Sigma_1, \Sigma_2, \ldots, \Sigma_n)$ to one where all variables have at least two equations.

Proposition 10.5. *Consider a general system of equations* $(\Sigma_1, \Sigma_2, \ldots,$ $\Sigma_n)$. *Any variable X_s with $\sigma_s = 1$ can be eliminated through syntactic substitution such that the resulting system* $(\Sigma'_1, \Sigma'_2, \ldots, \Sigma'_{s-1}, \Sigma'_{s+1}, \ldots, \Sigma'_n)$ *has a solution in the variables* $(X_1, \ldots, X_{s-1}, X_{s+1}, \ldots, X_n)$ *iff the original system* $(\Sigma_1, \Sigma_2, \ldots, \Sigma_n)$ *has a solution in* $(X_1, \ldots, X_n)$.

PROOF. If X_s has exactly one equation, we can solve it using the standard formula (Proposition 3.1) and substitute the resulting expression for any occurrence of X_s in the remaining equations. It is then trivial to verify that in the resulting system of explicit equations, the variable X_s does not occur any longer, and that the new system has a solution iff the original system has a solution. □

One must take care about situations where X_s is of type M. More specifically, if the single equation of X_s is of the form $X_s = LX_s \cup M$ with $\lambda \in L$, then a parameter T_{X_s} will occur in the expression. On the other hand, if X_s is of type M because of condition 2, the multiplicity of the solution will arise when the variable X_k that occurs in that condition yields a parametric representation.

Applying Proposition 10.5 repeatedly until all variables X_s with $\sigma_s = 1$ are eliminated and treating variables X_r with $\sigma_r = 0$ as free parameters yields the following.

Corollary 10.6. *Any given general system of explicit language equations can be equivalently replaced by a system* $(\Sigma_1, \Sigma_2, \ldots, \Sigma_n)$, *where for all* $i = 1, \ldots, n$, $\sigma_i \geq 2$.

Assume $n = 1$ (i.e., there is one variable X_1). By assumption, there are σ_1 equations for X_1, and $\sigma_1 \geq 2$. We solve each of the equations individually; this yields the following σ_1 equations:

$$X_i = (L_{1,1;t})^*(M_{1,1;t} \cup T_{1;t}) \qquad \text{if } \lambda \in L_{1,1;t}$$

$$X_i = (L_{1,1;t})^* M_{1,1;t} \qquad \text{if } \lambda \notin L_{1,1;t}.$$

Evidently, this is precisely the case of Proposition 10.3.

Now assume $n \geq 2$, i.e., there are at least two variables. Select one variable, say X_s; it has σ_s equations, $\sigma_s \geq 2$. We distinguish two cases:

A. If there exists one equation for X_s, say equation t, such that $\lambda \notin L_{s,s;t}$, then replace X_s by the expression

$$(L_{s,s;t})^* \left(\bigcup_{\substack{j=1,\ldots,n \\ j \neq s}} L_{s,j;t} X_j \cup L_{0;t} \right)$$

in all equations of the system $(\Sigma'_1, \Sigma'_2, \ldots, \Sigma'_{s-1}, \Sigma'_{s+1}, \ldots, \Sigma'_n)$ where Σ'_i is Σ_i with all X_s are replaced by the above formula. It follows that in the resulting system, only the $n - 1$ variables $X_1, \ldots, X_{s-1}$,

$X_{s+1}, \ldots, X_n$ occur. Assuming now inductively that we have a representation $(\gamma_1, \ldots, \gamma_{s-1}, \gamma_{s+1}, \ldots, \gamma_n)$ of all solutions of $(\Sigma'_1, \ldots, \Sigma'_{s-1}, \Sigma'_{s+1}, \ldots, \Sigma'_n)$ in the variables $X_1, \ldots, X_{s-1}, X_{s+1}, \ldots, X_n$, where the γ_i are expressions in which only parameters may occur in addition to constants (but no variables X_j), we then substitute these solution representations into the other equations of Σ_s (i.e., all the equations j for X_s with $j = 1, \ldots, t-1, t+1, \ldots, t_s$. Since all these must be equal to

$$(L_{s,s;t})^* \left(\bigcup_{\substack{j=1,\ldots,n \\ j \neq s}} L_{s,j;t} \gamma_j \cup L_{0;t} \right),$$

we obtain a system of two-sided language equations with the property that there is a solution of the original system $(\Sigma_1, \Sigma_2, \ldots, \Sigma_n)$ in the variables $(X_1, \ldots, X_n)$ if and only if this system of two-sided language equations has a solution in the parameters that occur in the γ_i.

B. If for every equation j for X_s, $\lambda \in L_{s,s;j}$, for $j = 1, \ldots, \tau_s$, then choose one of the equations, say equation t. This yields the expression

$$(L_{s,s;t})^* \left(\bigcup_{\substack{j=1,\ldots,n \\ j \neq s}} L_{s,j;t} X_j \cup L_{0;t} \cup T_{s;t} \right)$$

for X_s, with $T_{s;t}$ a parameter. Then, the remainder of the proof follows analogously, using this expression instead of

$$(L_{s,s;t})^* \left(\bigcup_{\substack{j=1,\ldots,n \\ j \neq s}} L_{s,j;t} \gamma_j \cup L_{0;t} \right),$$

In both cases, we reduce the original problem equivalently to one of solving a system of two-sided language equations.

Consider the following system of three equations in the two variables X and Y; we assume that none of the four constant languages L, M, N, and P contains the empty word λ:

$$X = LY,$$
$$X = MY,$$
$$Y = (\lambda \cup N)Y \cup P.$$

Therefore, it follows that

$$Y = N^*P \cup N^*T \quad \text{for an arbitrary parameter } T.$$

Clearly, Y is of type M according to Part 1 of the definition, while X is of type M according to Part 2. Substituting this expression for Y into the first two equations, we obtain

$$X = LN^*P \cup LN^*T,$$
$$X = MN^*P \cup MN^*T$$

and this system has a solution in X iff

$$LN^*P \cup LN^*T = MN^*P \cup MN^*T$$

has a solution in T.

Solving such two-sided language equations is, in general, an open problem (see Chapter 12). In specific cases, two-sided equations may turn out to be implicit (i.e., one side is a constant language) in which case, Chapter 8 provides a general solution method which allows us to determine all solutions.

Here are three examples. First, we consider the following system of four explicit equations in the variables X, Y, and Z, over the alphabet $\{a, b\}$:

i. $X = a^*X \cup b^*Y \cup aZ$
ii. $X = ab^*X \cup \lambda$
iii. $Y = (bbb)^*Y$
iv. $Z = (aa)^*Z.$

From (ii), we get

$$X = a(a \cup b)^* \cup \lambda \quad (= Q);$$

(iii) and (iv) yield

$$Y = (bbb)^*T_1,$$
$$Z = (aa)^*T_2.$$

Using this, we get from (i)

$$X = a^*(b^*Y \cup aZ \cup T_3)$$
$$= a^*b^*(bbb)^*T_1 \cup a^*a(aa)^*T_2 \cup a^*T_3$$
$$= a^*b^*T_1 \cup aa^*T_2 \cup a^*T_3.$$

Now the resulting implicit language equation is

$$a(a \cup b)^* \cup \lambda = a^*b^*T_1 \cup aa^*T_2 \cup a^*T_3$$

and the techniques of Chapter 8 allow us to determine solutions in (T_1, T_2, T_3), for example,

$$(\emptyset, (a \cup b)^*, \lambda).$$

This solution for (T_1, T_2, T_3) of the implicit language equation results in the following solution of the original system (i)–(iv):

$$Y = \emptyset,$$
$$Z = (a \cup b)^*,$$
$$X = a^*a(a \cup b)^* \cup a^* = a(a \cup b)^* \cup \lambda \quad (= Q)$$

and it is easy to verify that these three languages do, indeed, constitute a solution of the original system of equations.

Our second example is the following system of three explicit equations in the variables X and Y, over the alphabet $\{a, b\}$:

i. $X = aX \cup bY \cup \lambda$
ii. $X = ab^*X \cup \lambda$
iii. $Y = (bbb)^*Y$

We derive this implicit language equation

$$a(a \cup b)^* \cup \lambda = a^*b(bbb)^*T \cup a^*$$

and conclude that there is no solution of (i)–(iii) in (X, Y) since there is no solution of the implicit equation in T (see Chapter 8; alternatively, consider any $w \in T$, in which case $bw \notin a(a \cup b)^* \cup \lambda$ gives a contradiction).

The third example is the following system of three explicit equations in two variables:

i. $X = aY$
ii. $X = (aa \cup bb)^*X \cup \lambda$
iii. $Y = (ab)^*Y$

From (iii), we get $Y = (ab)^*T$, which when substituted into (i) yields

$$X = a(ab)^*T_X,$$

(ii) yields

$$X = (aa \cup bb)^* \cup (aa \cup bb)^*T_Y,$$

and this, in turn, yields the following two-sided language equation in the variables T_X and T_Y:

$$a(ab)^*T_X = (aa \cup bb)^* \cup (aa \cup bb)^*T_Y.$$

In this particular case, we find that no solution exists, since on the right of the equation we have the empty word, which can never be contained on the left for any choice of T_X (see Chapter 12).

One must realize that, at several points, choices can be made for parameters, but these choices may result in problems in subsequent steps. For example, in Proposition 10.3(a), A^* is always a solution. However, as this is not the only solution, choosing it will yield a system of equations with one variable less, but this new system may not have a solution even though the original system does (although for a different choice for that variable).

Here is an example to illustrate this observation: Consider the following four equations in two variables over the alphabet $A = \{a, b\}$:

$$X = (aa \cup b)X \cup aY \cup a,$$
$$X = (aab \cup b^*)X \cup bY \cup a(ab^*a)^*,$$
$$Y = a^*Y,$$

$$Y = b^*Y.$$

From the first equation for X, we obtain

$$X = (aa \cup b)^*a(\lambda \cup Y)$$

and from the two equations for Y, we get

$$Y = a^*T_{Y;1},$$
$$Y = b^*T_{Y;2}.$$

If we choose $T_{Y;1} = T_{Y;2} = A^*$, then

$$Y = A^* \quad \text{and} \quad X = b^*aA^* \quad \text{(from the first equation for } X\text{)}.$$

However, this yields the following implicit equation (from the second equation for X):

$$b^*aA^* = (aab \cup b^*)^*[a(ab^*a)^* \cup bA^* \cup T_{X;2}],$$

and according to the results in Chapter 8, this implicit equation does not have a solution. (This can also be seen directly by considering that b is always contained on the right-hand side, but is obviously not in the left-hand side.) Thus, if $Y = A^*$, the given system of four equations in two variables does not have a solution. However, if one chooses

$$T_{Y;1} = T_{Y;2} = \emptyset,$$

there is a solution of the original system of equations. This choice implies $Y = \emptyset$, and thus we obtain $X = (aa \cup b)^*a$ from the first equation and $X = (aab \cup b^*)^*[a(ab^*a)^* \cup T_{X;2}]$ from the second equation for X. Therefore, we must solve the following implicit equation in $T_{X;2}$:

$$(aa \cup b)^*a = (aab \cup b^*)^*[a(ab^*a)^* \cup T_{X;2}],$$

which has a solution, for example, for $T_{X;2} = \emptyset$. One can also verify directly, by substitution, that

$$(X, Y) = ((aa \cup b)^*a, \emptyset)$$

is a solution of the given system of four explicit equations in two variables.

10.4   Solving Strictly Decoupled Systems

We describe how to solve a system of explicit language relations involving union and left-concatenation in which each variable has at most one relation. Note that different variables may have relations of different types. For example, if we have three variables X, Y, and Z, and if we use L_i for the requisite constant languages, we may write

$$X \, \mathbb{R}_1 \, L_1X \cup L_2Y \cup L_3Z \cup L_4,$$

$$Y \; \mathbb{R}_2 \; L_5 X \cup L_6 Y \cup L_7 Z \cup L_8,$$
$$Z \; \mathbb{R}_3 \; L_9 X \cup L_{10} Y \cup L_{11} Z \cup L_{12},$$

where each of $\mathbb{R}_1$, $\mathbb{R}_2$, and $\mathbb{R}_3$ represents one of $=$, $\supseteq$, and $\subseteq$. Since it is not necessary that each variable have an equation, there are altogether 63 different (nonempty) strictly decoupled systems in three variables (with indeterminate constant languages).

Theorem 10.7. *Any strictly decoupled system of explicit language relations, involving union and left-concatenation as operators and arbitrary languages as constants, has a solution. If all constant languages in the system are regular, a regular solution can always be effectively determined.*

PROOF.   Given a strictly decoupled system of language relations

$$X_i \; \mathbb{R}_i \; L_{i,1} X_1 \cup \cdots \cup L_{i,n} X_n \cup L_{i,0}, \quad i = 1, \ldots, m \; (m \leq n),$$

with $\mathbb{R}_i \in \{=, \supseteq, \subseteq\}$, we can replace it equivalently with the following system of explicit equations

$$X_i = L_{i,1} X_1 \cup \cdots \cup L_{i,n} X_n \cup L_{i,0}, \quad i = 1, \ldots, m,$$

and solve this system of equations. By the classical theory outlined in Chapter 3, there is at least one solution $(S_1, \ldots, S_n)$ in $(X_1, \ldots, X_n)$ of this system of equations. This solution is regular if all the constant languages $L_{i,j}$ are. It should now be obvious that any solution of the new system of equations is also a solution of the original strictly decoupled system of explicit relations. This follows from the observation that for any $i \in \{1, \ldots, m\}$,

$$S_i = L_{i,1} S_1 \cup \cdots \cup L_{i,n} S_n \cup L_{i,0}$$

for languages $S_1, \ldots, S_n$ implies

$$S_i \supseteq L_{i,1} S_1 \cup \cdots \cup L_{i,n} S_n \cup L_{i,0}$$

and

$$S_i \subseteq L_{i,1} S_1 \cup \cdots \cup L_{i,n} S_n \cup L_{i,0}.$$

Consequently, $(S_1, \ldots, S_n)$ is a solution of the relations in $(X_1, \ldots, X_n)$ which is regular if all the constant languages $L_{i,j}$ are.   □

Whereas the existence of a solution of a strictly decoupled system is thus shown to be almost trivial, the question of a parameterized representation of all of its solutions is not. It should be noted that the solution given in Theorem 10.7 is neither minimal nor maximal in general: In replacing superrelations ($\supseteq$) by equations ($=$), we are effectively forcing the variable corresponding to the affected relation to be minimized according to Proposition 10.1, whereas in replacing subrelations ($\subseteq$) by equations ($=$), we are effectively forcing the variable corresponding to the affected relation to be maximized according to Proposition 10.2.

Corollary 10.8. *Given a strictly decoupled system of explicit language relations, it is possible to determine its minimal and its maximal solution in* $(X_1, \ldots, X_n)$. *If these are identical, the system has a unique solution.*

PROOF. Let $i_1, \ldots, i_a$ be all those indices for which X_{i_s} has a subrelation, $a \geq 0$:

$$X_{i_s} \subseteq L_{i_s,1} X_1 \cup \cdots \cup L_{i_s,n} X_n \cup L_{i_s,0}.$$

Let $i_{a+1}, \ldots, i_{a+b}$ be all those indices for which X_{i_s} has a superrelation, $b \geq 0$:

$$X_{i_s} \supseteq L_{i_s,1} X_1 \cup \cdots \cup L_{i_s,n} X_n \cup L_{i_s,0}.$$

Finally, let $i_{a+b+1}, \ldots, i_m$ be all those indices for which X_{i_s} has an equation, $m \leq n$:

$$X_{i_s} = L_{i_s,1} X_1 \cup \cdots \cup L_{i_s,n} X_n \cup L_{i_s,0}.$$

The maximal solution of the given system is obtained as follows: Replace all X_{i_s} with $s = 1, \ldots, a$ by

$$(L_{i_s,i_s})^* [L_{i_s,1} X_1 \cup \cdots \cup L_{i_s,i_s-1} X_{i_s-1}$$
$$\cup L_{i_s,i_s+1} X_{i_s+1} \cup \cdots \cup L_{i_s,n} X_n \cup L_{i_s,0}]$$

and all X_{i_s} with $s = a+1, \ldots, a+b$ by A^* in all the *equations* (and remove all relations that are not equations). This results in a system Σ of explicit language equations (without any other relations) in which each variable X_{i_s} with $s = a+b+1, \ldots, m$ has at most one equation. Thus, the system Σ has a parametric representation of all solutions in the variables X_{i_s}, $s = a+b+1, \ldots, m$. In these parametric solutions, set all parameters to A^*. This is the maximal solution of Σ. It is now trivial to see that the maximal solution of Σ together with the solutions for the variables X_{i_s} with $s = 1, \ldots, a$ and with $s = a+1, \ldots, a+b$ which were previously fixed (and may contain variables X_{i_s} with $s = a+b+1, \ldots, m$, which must be replaced by the languages from the solution of Σ and which were maximal according to Propositions 10.1 and 10.2) is the unique maximal solution of the given system of relations.

To determine the unique minimal solution, we proceed analogously, substituting the minimal solutions according to Propositions 10.1 and 10.2 for the variables with superrelations and subrelations and choosing the empty language for any parameters (including free variables) that occur in the parametric representations obtained by solving the resulting equations using Proposition 3.1.

It should be obvious that in the case where the minimal and the maximal solutions are identical, the solution must be unique.   □

All solutions must "lie between" the minimal and the maximal solutions. For superrelations, Proposition 10.1 indicates that we can choose an arbitrary language T and obtain a new solution (by adding to the minimal solution L^*M the term L^*T). For subrelations, this connection is not as clear since, according to Proposition 10.2, the required closure is more complicated. It is an open problem how to combine the two closure operations of Propositions 10.1 and 10.2 to obtain a representation of all solutions of a given strictly decoupled system of equations.

Consider the following strictly decoupled system of three explicit equations in the three variables X, Y, and Z, over the alphabet $\{a, b, c\}$:

$$X = a^*X \cup b^*Y \cup c^*Z,$$
$$Y \subseteq aaZ,$$
$$Z \supseteq c^*X \cup a^*b^*Z \cup \lambda.$$

According to the proof of Theorem 10.7, we obtain the following system of equations:

$$X = a^*X \cup b^*Y \cup c^*Z,$$
$$Y = aaZ,$$
$$Z = c^*X \cup a^*b^*Z \cup \lambda,$$

which has the following solution:

$$X = a^*(b^*aa \cup c^*)(a \cup b \cup c)^*[c^*a^*T_X \cup \lambda \cup T_Z] \cup a^*T_X,$$
$$Y = aa(a \cup b \cup c)^*[c^*a^*T_X \cup \lambda \cup T_Z],$$
$$Z = (a \cup b \cup c)^*[c^*a^*T_X \cup \lambda \cup T_Z],$$

where the T_X and T_Y are free parameters ranging over all languages. Consequently, each choice of T_X and T_Y yields a solution not only of the resulting system of equations but also of the original system of relations.

Here are the maximal and the minimal solutions according to Corollary 10.8:

Maximal: We start by setting $Z = A^*$; this implies $Y = aaA^*$ and, thus, X is the maximal solution of the equation

$$X = a^*X \cup b^*aaA^* \cup c^*A^*,$$

which is A^*. Thus, we obtain the following maximal solution:

$$(X, Y, Z) = (A^*, aaA^*, A^*).$$

Minimal: We start by setting $Z = (a \cup b)^*(c^*X \cup \lambda)$. It follows that the resulting minimal solution is

$$(X, Y, Z) = (A^*, \emptyset, A^*).$$

10.5 Solving General Decoupled Systems

Whereas strictly decoupled systems are very easily solved, general decoupled systems are differentiated from strictly decoupled by the possibility of having several relations (of the same type) for a single variable, and this has already been proven (in Section 10.2) to be a major problem for the best understood of our language relations, namely equations. It turns out that having several defining superrelations for the same variable is substantially easier to handle:

Proposition 10.9. *Assume the following two superrelations hold for the variable X_i:*

$$X_i \supseteq H_1 \cdot X_1 \cup \cdots \cup H_n \cdot X_n \cup H_0,$$
$$X_i \supseteq K_1 \cdot X_1 \cup \cdots \cup K_n \cdot X_n \cup K_0.$$

Then, these two relations have a solution in $X_1, \ldots, X_n$ if and only if the following relation has a solution in $X_1, \ldots, X_n$:

$$X_i \supseteq (H_1 \cup K_1) \cdot X_1 \cup \cdots \cup (H_n \cup K_n) \cdot X_n \cup (H_0 \cup K_0).$$

PROOF. First, assume that the two relations are solved by $X_1, \ldots, X_n$. It follows that

$$X_i \cup X_i \supseteq [H_1 \cdot X_1 \cup \cdots \cup H_n \cdot X_n \cup H_0]$$
$$\cup [K_1 \cdot X_1 \cup \cdots \cup K_n \cdot X_n \cup K_0]$$

and this implies

$$X_i \supseteq (H_1 \cup K_1) \cdot X_1 \cup \cdots \cup (H_n \cup K_n) \cdot X_n \cup (H_0 \cup K_0).$$

For the converse, we observe that

$$X_i \supseteq (H_1 \cup K_1) \cdot X_1 \cup \cdots \cup (H_n \cup K_n) \cdot X_n \cup (H_0 \cup K_0)$$
$$= [H_1 \cdot X_1 \cup \cdots \cup H_n \cdot X_n \cup H_0] \cup [K_1 \cdot X_1 \cup \cdots \cup K_n \cdot X_n \cup K_0]$$

and from this, it follows trivially that

$$X_i \supseteq H_1 \cdot X_1 \cup \cdots \cup H_n \cdot X_n \cup H_0$$

and

$$X_i \supseteq K_1 \cdot X_1 \cup \cdots \cup K_n \cdot X_n \cup K_0. \qquad \square$$

The significance of this proposition comes from the fact that it allows us to replace all explicit superrelations for the same variable by a single one in such a way that any solution of the original system is also a solution of the resulting system and vice versa. In other words, after applying Proposition 10.9 repeatedly to an arbitrary decoupled system, we obtain a decoupled system in which each variable has at most one superrelation. In fact, since this result was obtained without any reference to the specific type of system, decoupled or not, it follows that in any system of explicit language relations, all superrelations for the same variable can be replaced by a single superrelation.

We come now to subrelations—more specifically to systems where a single variable has more than one explicit subrelation. There is no direct analogue to Proposition 10.9 for these relations. However, we can state the following result:

Proposition 10.10. *Assume the following two subrelations hold for the variable X_i:*

$$X_i \subseteq H_1 \cdot X_1 \cup \cdots \cup H_n \cdot X_n \cup H_0,$$
$$X_i \subseteq K_1 \cdot X_1 \cup \cdots \cup K_n \cdot X_n \cup K_0.$$

Then, these two relations have a solution in $X_1, \ldots, X_n$ if and only if the following relation has a solution in $X_1, \ldots, X_n$:

$$X_i \subseteq [H_1 \cdot X_1 \cup \cdots \cup H_n \cdot X_n \cup H_0] \cap [K_1 \cdot X_1 \cup \cdots \cup K_n \cdot X_n \cup K_0].$$

PROOF.   First assume that the two relations are solved by $X_1, \ldots, X_n$. It follows that

$$X_i \cap X_i \subseteq [H_1 \cdot X_1 \cup \cdots \cup H_n \cdot X_n \cup H_0]$$
$$\cap [K_1 \cdot X_1 \cup \cdots \cup K_n \cdot X_n \cup K_0].$$

Conversely,

$$X_i \subseteq [H_1 \cdot X_1 \cup \cdots \cup H_n \cdot X_n \cup H_0] \cap [K_1 \cdot X_1 \cup \cdots \cup K_n \cdot X_n \cup K0]$$

implies

$$X_i \subseteq H_1 \cdot X_1 \cup \cdots \cup H_n \cdot X_n \cup H_0$$

and

$$X_i \subseteq K_1 \cdot X_1 \cup \cdots \cup K_n \cdot X_n \cup K_0. \qquad \square$$

Note that the "obvious" analogue of Proposition 10.9 is wrong: In general, the conclusion of Proposition 10.10 cannot be replaced by

$$X_i \subseteq (H_1 \cap K_1) \cdot X_1 \cup \cdots \cup (H_n \cap K_n) \cdot X_n \cup (H_0 \cap K_0).$$

This can be derived from the following example:

$$X \subseteq aaX \cup a \cup \lambda,$$
$$X \subseteq aX \cup \lambda.$$

Clearly, $X = a^*$ is a solution of this system of two subrelations. However, the subrelation

$$X \subseteq (aa \cap a)X \cup (a \cup \lambda) \cap \lambda,$$

which can be simplified to

$$X \subseteq \lambda,$$

clearly does not admit this solution.

This suggests that consolidating several explicit inclusions for the same variable into a single inclusion is unlikely to result in a single inclusion using only union and left-concatenation (note that the equivalent representation in Proposition 10.10 requires intersection as well).

Theorem 10.11. *Consider a decoupled system of explicit relations with union and left-concatenation, in which no variable may have more than one relation of type =. Then the system always has a solution. Furthermore, if all the constant languages involved in the relations are regular, the system always has a regular solution.*

PROOF. By Proposition 10.2, every subrelation has a universal solution, namely the empty language $\emptyset$. As a result, we can set any variable X defined by one or more inclusions to $\emptyset$, replacing every occurrence of X in the relations by $\emptyset$; by Proposition 10.9, we may assume that a variable has at most one superrelation. The resulting new system has the following property: Any solution of the new system is also a solution of the original system (with the variables defined by inclusions being $\emptyset$). Furthermore, by Theorem 10.7, the new system always has a solution, since it is strictly decoupled. The statement about the regularity of a solution is obvious.   □

The theorem excludes decoupled systems in which some variable has more than one equation, because we do not know, in general, how to handle this situation, as was discussed at length in Section 10.2. However, it should be clear that in many instances, Section 10.2 does provide methods that allow us to deal with variables with several defining equations, and in those cases, we can solve the general decoupled system.

The remainder of this section will deal with general systems of explicit language relations which differ from decoupled systems in that a particular variable may have defining relations of different types. It does not appear that there is a consolidation theorem that permits one to replace several relations for that variable by a single one. While this was possible for superrelations, no such results exist for subrelations nor for equations. Nevertheless, the techniques outlined below can be used to simplify a given general system and then attempt to solve that simpler system.

Consider the system of two explicit relations in one variable:

$$X \subseteq LX \cup M,$$
$$X \supseteq PX \cup Q.$$

Recall that for $\lambda \in L$, L^*M is the maximal solution for the inclusion, whereas P^*Q is the minimal solution for the containment, if we consider the relations separately. We have:

Proposition 10.12. *Consider the two relations $X \subseteq LX \cup M$ and $X \supseteq PX \cup Q$. Assume $\lambda \notin L$. If P^*Q is not contained in L^*M, then no solution of the system exists.*

PROOF. If P^*Q is not contained in L^*M, then consider a word $w \in P^*Q - L^*M$. By definition of P^*Q, w must be contained in any solution of the superrelation $X \supseteq PX \cup Q$. Since L^*M is the maximal solution of the subrelation $X \subseteq LX \cup M$ and $w \notin L^*M$, no solution of the system can exist.   □

Thus, $P^*Q \subseteq L^*M$ is a necessary condition for a solution to exist. It is an open question whether the condition $P^*Q \subseteq L^*M$ is also sufficient.

Consider the system in X over $\{a, b\}$:

$$X \subseteq ab^*X \cup \lambda,$$
$$X \supseteq aab^*X \cup a.$$

One can verify that the maximal solution of the first relation is

$$\lambda \cup a(a \cup b)^*$$

and that the second relation has the minimal solution

$$a(ab^*a)^*;$$

clearly, $a(ab^*a)^* \subseteq \lambda \cup a(a \cup b)^*$. One can verify that the maximal solution of the first relation is also a solution of the second. Whether this is always so is an open question.

Again, this suggests that, in general, there is no consolidation process available. However, while in the case of decoupled systems we could set all variables defined by subrelations to the empty language, this is no longer possible. One approach that can be tried is to view a general system as a decoupled system together with identifications of variables. This would lead to systems of implicit equations or to two-sided equations assuming we have parametric representations of all solutions.

We conclude this section with two examples. The first example is a system of six explicit relations in three variables over the alphabet $A = \{a\}$:

i. $X = (a^5)^*X \cup a^7Y \cup a^3Z \cup \lambda$
ii. $X \supseteq a^7X \cup a^5Z$
iii. $Y \subseteq aX \cup a^2Y \cup a^4Z$
iv. $Z \supseteq a^3X \cup a^5Y \cup a^7Z$
v. $Z \supseteq a^5X \cup a^7Y \cup a^3Z$
vi. $Z = a^7X \cup a^3Y \cup a^5Z \cup \lambda$

Consolidating (iv) and (v) yields

$$Z \supseteq (a^3 \cup a^5)X \cup (a^5 \cup a^7)Y \cup (a^3 \cup a^7)Z.$$

Equation (vi) has the following solution expression:

$$Z = (a^5)^*a^7X \cup (a^5)^*a^3Y \cup (a^5)^*.$$

Equation (i) has a parametrized representation of all its solutions:

$$X = (a^5)^*a^7Y \cup (a^5)^*a^3Z \cup (a^5)^*T_{X,1} \cup (a^5)^*.$$

Superrelation (ii) has a parameterized representation of all its solutions (by Proposition 10.1)

$$X = (a^7)^*a^5Z \cup (a^7)^*T_{X,2}.$$

Thus, we now have

$$X = (a^5)^*a^7Y \cup (a^5)^*a^3Z \cup (a^5)^*T_{X,1} \cup (a^5)^*,$$
$$X = (a^7)^*a^5Z \cup (a^7)^*T_{X'},$$
$$Y \subseteq aX \cup a^2Y \cup a^4Z,$$
$$Z = (a^3 \cup a^7)^*(a^3 \cup a^5)X \cup (a^3 \cup a^7)^*(a^5 \cup a^7)Y$$
$$\cup (a^3 \cup a^7)^*T_Z \quad \text{(Proposition 10.1),}$$
$$Z = (a^5)^*a^7X \cup (a^5)^*a^3Y \cup (a^5)^*.$$

By the last two equations, for a solution to exist, the following equation holds for some choice of T_Z:

$$(a^5)^*a^7X \cup (a^5)^*a^3Y \cup (a^5)^* = (a^3 \cup a^7)^*(a^3 \cup a^5)X$$
$$\cup (a^3 \cup a^7)^*(a^5 \cup a^7)Y \cup (a^3 \cup a^7)^*T_Z.$$

Now it follows that the left-hand side contains λ [since $\lambda \in (a^5)^*$] and cannot contain aaa [since $aaa \notin (a^5)^*a^7X$ for any language X, $aaa \notin (a^5)^*$, and $aaa \notin (a^5)^*a^3Y$ because $\lambda \notin Y$]. This, however, leads to a contradiction on the right-hand side: For λ to be contained there, we must have $\lambda \in T_Z$, but this implies that aaa must then also be contained in the right-hand side, in contradiction to the observation that aaa is not contained in the left-hand side. Therefore, the original system of language relations does not have a solution.

Our second example contains three explicit relations in two unknowns over the alphabet $A = \{a, b\}$:

i. $X \subseteq aX \cup bY \cup \lambda$
ii. $X \supseteq a^2X \cup b^3Y$
iii. $Y = a^*X \cup b^*Y$

From (iii), we get a parameterized representation of all solutions for Y:

$$Y = b^*a^*X \cup b^*T_Y.$$

Substituting this into (i) and (ii) gives

$$X \subseteq aX \cup bb^*a^*X \cup bb^*T_Y \cup \lambda,$$
$$X \supseteq a^2X \cup b^3b^*a^*X \cup b^3b^*T_Y,$$

and from the superrelation, we get the following parameterized representation of all solutions for X:

$$X = [a^2 \cup b^3b^*a^*]^*b^3b^*T_Y \cup [a^2 \cup b^3b^*a^*]^*T_X.$$

Substituting this into the equation for Y yields

$$Y = b^*a^*[a^2 \cup b^3b^*a^*]^*b^3b^*T_Y$$
$$\cup b^*a^*[a^2 \cup b^3b^*a^*]^*T_X \cup b^*T_Y.$$

We can now rewrite the subrelation (for X) as follows:

$$[a^2 \cup b^3 b^* a^*]^* b^3 b^* T_Y \cup [a^2 \cup b^3 b^* a^*]^* T_X$$
$$\subseteq (a \cup bb^* a^*)[a^2 \cup b^3 b^* a^*]^* b^3 b^* T_Y$$
$$\cup \ (a \cup bb^* a^*)[a^2 \cup b^3 b^* a^*]^* T_X \cup bb^* T_Y \cup \lambda.$$

It is quite obvious that

$$T_X = T_Y = \emptyset$$

is a solution of this relation in T_X and T_Y; this implies the following solution of the original system:

$$X = Y = \emptyset.$$

There are other solutions. For example, the choice

$$T_X = T_Y = (a \cup b)^*$$

also yields a solution, since on the left-hand side we have $[a^2 \cup b^3 b^* a^*]^* T_X$, which is equal to $(a \cup b)^*$; on the right-hand side, we have $bb^* T_Y = b(a \cup b)^*$, $(a \cup bb^* a^*)[a^2 \cup b^3 b^* a^*]^* T_X$ contains $a(a \cup b)^*$, and $(a \cup b)^* = a(a \cup b)^* \cup b(a \cup b)^* \cup \lambda$. This choice for T_X and T_Y yields the following solution of the original system:

$$X = Y = (a \cup b)^*.$$

Thus, these are the minimal and the maximal solutions of the original system of three relations in two variables.

10.6   Conclusion

This chapter introduced explicit language relations and derived methods for solving them under certain conditions. However, the general problem remains open. This is mainly due to an apparently innocent generalization of systems of classical language equations where several defining equations for the same variable may occur. Far from being classical, this generalization renders systems of equations not to have solutions in some cases, and in other cases, their solution is equivalent to the solution of two-sided language equations; it is the solution of those equations that is open. Intriguingly, there are major differences between superrelations and subrelations. For example, one permits consolidation of several defining explicit relations for the same variable into one, the other does not; one has a parameterized representation of all solutions, the other does not.

10.7   Bibliographical Note

The material presented in this chapter is adapted from [Leiss 97a].

10.8   Problems

1. For the following systems of equations, determine whether a solution exists, and if so, construct one:

   a. $X = (aa)^*Y \cup \lambda,$
   $X = (bb)^*Z,$
   $X = aY \cup bZ \cup \lambda.$
   Is the solution unique?

   b. $X = (aa \cup ba^*b)X \cup \lambda,$
   $X = (a^* \cup ba^*b)X.$

   c. $X = (a \cup ba^*b)b^*X \cup \lambda,$
   $X = (a^* \cup ba^*b)X.$

   d. $X = a^*X,$
   $X = b^*Y,$
   $Y = (ab \cup ba)^*Y \cup \lambda,$
   $Y = (ab \cup ba)(ab \cup ba)^*X.$

2. For the following strictly decoupled systems, determine the maximal and the minimal solutions, as well as the solution (or solutions, in the case of multiple ones) according to Theorem 10.7:

   a. $X = a^*X \cup (a \cup b)Z,$
   $Y \subseteq aa^*X \cup b^*Y,$
   $Z \supseteq a(a \cup bb)^*X \cup b(b \cup aa)^*Y \cup b^*a^*.$

   b. $X \subseteq aa^*Y \cup bZ \cup b,$
   $Y \supseteq ab^*X \cup aZ \cup a,$
   $Z \supseteq ab^*X \cup aY \cup \lambda.$

3. For the following general decoupled systems, construct a regular solution:

   a. $X = a^*X \cup (a \cup b)Z,$
   $Y \subseteq aa^*X \cup b^*Y,$
   $Y \subseteq aa^*Y \cup b^*Z,$
   $Y \subseteq aZ \cup b^*Y,$
   $Z \supseteq ab^*X \cup aY \cup \lambda,$
   $Z \supseteq b^*Z \cup a^*Y \cup \lambda,$
   $Z \supseteq b^*X \cup a^*Y.$

   b. $X \supseteq a^*X \cup (a \cup b)Z,$
   $X \supseteq aX \cup (a \cup b)Y \cup \lambda,$
   $Y \subseteq aa^*X \cup b^*Y,$
   $Y \subseteq aa^*Y \cup b^*Z,$
   $Y \subseteq aZ \cup b^*Y,$
   $Z \supseteq ab^*X \cup aY \cup \lambda,$
   $Z \supseteq b^*Z \cup a^*Y \cup \lambda,$
   $Z \supseteq b^*X \cup a^*Y.$

4. For the following general systems, determine whether a solution exists, and if so, construct a regular solution:

a. $X = a^*X \cup (a \cup b)Z,$ $X \subseteq aa^*X \cup b^*Y,$
   $Y \subseteq aa^*Y \cup b^*Z,$ $Y \subseteq aZ \cup b^*Y,$
   $Z \supseteq ab^*X \cup aY \cup \lambda,$ $Z \supseteq b^*Z \cup a^*Y \cup \lambda,$
   $Z \supseteq b^*X \cup a^*Y.$

b. $X = a^*X \cup (a \cup b)Z,$ $X \supseteq ab^*X \cup aY \cup \lambda,$
   $Y \subseteq aa^*X \cup b^*Y,$ $Y \subseteq aa^*Y \cup b^*Z,$
   $Y \subseteq aZ \cup b^*Y,$
   $Z \supseteq b^*Z \cup a^*Y \cup \lambda,$ $Z \supseteq b^*X \cup a^*Y.$

c. $X \supseteq a^*X \cup (a \cup b)Z,$ $X \subseteq aX \cup (a \cup b)Y \cup \lambda,$
   $Y \supseteq aa^*X \cup b^*Y,$ $Y \subseteq aa^*Y \cup b^*Z,$
   $Y \subseteq aZ \cup b^*Y,$
   $Z \supseteq ab^*X \cup aY \cup \lambda,$ $Z \subseteq b^*Z \cup a^*Y \cup \lambda,$
   $Z \supseteq b^*X \cup a^*Y.$

d. $X \subseteq a^*X \cup (a \cup b)Z,$ $X \supseteq aX \cup (a \cup b)Y \cup \lambda,$
   $Y \subseteq aa^*X \cup b^*Y,$ $Y \subseteq aa^*Y \cup b^*Z,$
   $Y \subseteq aZ \cup b^*Y,$
   $Z \subseteq ab^*X \cup aY \cup \lambda,$ $Z \supseteq b^*Z \cup a^*Y \cup \lambda,$
   $Z \supseteq b^*X \cup a^*Y.$

11

Implicit Relations with Union
and Left-Concatenation

About This Chapter: We describe how to solve systems of implicit language relations where the operations involved are union and concatenation from the left by a constant. This continues our study of language relations begun in the previous chapter. Implicit relations express a constant language in terms of an expression involving variables and require that the variables be determined so that the relation is satisfied. Primarily we consider systems of relations of the following three types: equality $[L = \alpha(X_1, \ldots, X_n)]$, superrelation $[L \supseteq \alpha(X_1, \ldots, X_n)]$, and subrelation $[L \subseteq \alpha(X_1, \ldots, X_n)]$. Building on results derived for implicit equations (in Chapter 8), we derive a complete characterization of the existence of a solution of a given system. This is in contrast to explicit language relations where no complete characterization of solutions is known. We also address the question of uniqueness and the effectiveness of our constructions.

In Chapter 8, we studied systems of implicit language equations. In Chapter 10, we studied explicit language relations. In the present chapter, we concentrate on solving implicit language relations.

Explicit language relations turned out to be rather difficult to solve; in fact, no general solution theory is known. This is in contrast to explicit language equations with at most one defining equation per variable, where a complete solution theory exists. The same is true for implicit equations: There is a complete characterization of solutions, including existence and uniqueness. Nevertheless, classical explicit equations are much easier to deal with than implicit equations. For this reason, one might expect that implicit language relations are more difficult than explicit relations. However, as we will see in this chapter, the reverse is true; although we do not have a complete theory for explicit relations, we will present a complete theory for implicit relations.

Throughout this chapter, we will consider the set of expressions

$$\mathrm{EX}_A(\mathrm{CONST}; \mathrm{OP}; X_1, \ldots, X_n),$$

where OP consists of union and left-concatenation [just as in Chapter 3 (classical, explicit equations), Chapter 8 (implicit equation), and Chapter 10 (explicit relations)]. We will concentrate our attention on CONST = REG, although the results apply generally to arbitrary sets of constant languages; however, if CONST $\neq$ REG, there is no guarantee that the languages specified can be obtained constructively.

A system of m implicit language relations in the variables $X_1, \ldots, X_n$ over the alphabet A is defined as:

$$L_i \, \mathbb{R}_i \, \alpha_i \quad \text{for } i = 1, \ldots, m,$$

where for all $i = 1, \ldots, m$, L_i is a language in CONST, $\mathbb{R}_i$ is a relation in $\{=, \supseteq, \subseteq\}$, and α_i is an expression in $\mathrm{EX}_A(\mathrm{CONST}; \mathrm{OP}; X_1, \ldots, X_n)$. We will call relations of the type $L \subseteq \alpha$ subrelations and relations of the type $L \supseteq \alpha$ superrelations.

In this chapter, we will develop a complete theory of implicit language relations. Closely following the development in Chapter 8, we can assume that each expression $\alpha_i \in \mathrm{EX}_A(\mathrm{CONST}; \mathrm{OP}; X_1, \ldots, X_n)$ involved in a system of implicit relations can be assumed to have the normal form

$$\alpha_i = M_{i,1} \cdot X_1 \cup M_{i,2} \cdot X_2 \cup \cdots \cup M_{i,n} \cdot X_n,$$

where the absence of a constant language is justified since one can introduce an additional implicit equation in a new variable $X_{i'}$ for each such constant C which can be stated as $X_{i'} = C$ and which must have the unique solution C in $X_{i'}$ if the system has any solution at all.

As an example of a system of implicit relations, consider the following system of three relations in two variables over the alphabet $\{a, b\}$:

$$a^*b(a \cup b)^* \supseteq a^*X \cup bY,$$
$$a(a \cup b)^* \subseteq aaX \cup b^*Y,$$
$$(ab \cup ba)(a \cup b)^* = aX \cup bY.$$

It can be verified that this system has a solution,

$$X = b(a \cup b)^* \quad \text{and} \quad Y = a(a \cup b)^*.$$

Indeed, as we will derive later, this solution is unique.

We first consider systems of the form

$$L_i \, \mathbb{R}_i \, \alpha_i \quad \text{for } i = 1, \ldots, m,$$

where for all $i = 1, \ldots, m$, L_i is a language in CONST, α_i is an expression in $\mathrm{EX}_A(\mathrm{CONST}; \mathrm{OP}; X_1, \ldots, X_n)$, and all $\mathbb{R}_i$ (in $\{=, \supseteq, \subseteq\}$) are identical.

We note that the results in Chapter 8 give a complete answer, if $\mathbb{R}_i$ is $=$ for all $i = 1, \ldots, m$.

Therefore, assume that $\mathbb{R}_i$ is $\subseteq$ for all $i = 1, \ldots, m$:

Proposition 11.1. *Consider a system of equations where all relations are of the form*

$$L_i \subseteq M_{i,1} \cdot X_1 \cup \cdots \cup M_{i,n} \cdot X_n, \quad i = 1, \ldots, m.$$

Then this system has a solution if and only if

$$X_1 = \cdots = X_n = A^* \text{ is a solution.}$$

PROOF.   Let us assume that no solution exists. This implies that for every choice of languages for $X_1, \ldots, X_n$, there exists a $t \in \{1, \ldots, m\}$ such that for some $w \in L_t$,

$$w \notin M_{t,1} \cdot X_1 \cup \cdots \cup M_{t,n} \cdot X_n.$$

But this implies that $X_1 = \cdots = X_n = A^*$ cannot be a solution either since

$$M_{t,1} \cdot X_1 \cup \cdots \cup M_{t,n} \cdot X_n \subseteq M_{t,1} \cdot A^* \cup \cdots \cup M_{t,n} \cdot A^*.$$

The converse of this claim is trivial. Thus, if all the $\mathbb{R}_i$ are $\subseteq$, determining whether a solution exists is equivalent to determining whether

$$L_i \subseteq M_{i,1} \cdot A^* \cup \cdots \cup M_{i,n} \cdot A^*, \quad i = 1, \ldots, m.$$

It follows that $X_1 = \cdots = X_n = A^*$ is the maximal solution if one exists.   □

How one may obtain solutions other than $(X_1, \ldots, X_n) = (A^*, \ldots, A^*)$ will be outlined when we treat the general case, in the next section.

Now assume that $\mathbb{R}_i$ is $\supseteq$ for all $i = 1, \ldots, m$:

Proposition 11.2. *Consider a system of equations where all relations are of the form*

$$L_i \supseteq M_{i,1} \cdot X_1 \cup \cdots \cup M_{i,n} \cdot X_n, \quad i = 1, \ldots, m.$$

Then, this system has a solution if and only if

$$X_1 = \cdots = X_n = \emptyset \text{ is a solution.}$$

PROOF.   It should be obvious that

$$X_1 = \cdots = X_n = \emptyset$$

is always a solution, which, moreover, is minimal.   □

Again, there may be other solutions; how to obtain them will be discussed later.

It follows that the cases where all $\mathbb{R}_i$ are identical are trivially solved. The next section deals with the general case, namely when the $\mathbb{R}_i$ are not all identical.

11.1   Existence of Solutions

In Chapter 8, the following necessary condition for the existence of a solution of a system of implicit language equations (i.e., $\mathbb{R}_i$ being $=$ for all $i = 1, \ldots, m$) was derived. Since it is the basis of our method for relations as well, we give a brief review.

Consider the ith equation of the system

$$L_i = M_{i,1} \cdot X_1 \cup \cdots \cup M_{i,n} \cdot X_n$$

(i.e., all $\mathbb{R}_i$ are equal to $=$). It follows that for any word w in L_i, if there is a solution in X, we must have

$$w \in M_{i,1} \cdot X_1 \cup \cdots \cup M_{i,n} \cdot X_n.$$

This, however, is true if and only if

$$\exists j \in \{1, \ldots, n\} \colon \exists u \in M_{i,j} \text{ and } u \text{ a prefix of } w, \ w/u \in X_j.$$

Similarly, for any word $w \notin L_i$, if there is a solution in X, w necessarily must not be in $M_{i,1} \cdot X_1 \cup \cdots \cup M_{i,n} \cdot X_n$. This is true if and only if

$$\forall j \in \{1, \ldots, n\} \colon \forall u \in M_{i,j} \text{ and } u \text{ a prefix of } w, \ w/u \notin X_j.$$

Here, x/y denotes the quotient of the word x with respect to its prefix y; if L and M are languages over the alphabet A, L/M is the quotient of L with respect to M, and $\mathrm{PREF}(L)$ for any language L denotes the set of all prefixes (not necessarily proper) of L. Thus, we have

$$\bigcup_{i=1,\ldots,m} \ \bigcup_{j=1,\ldots,n} \left[\overline{L_i}/M_{i,j} \cap X_j \right] = \emptyset.$$

If we define

$$X_j = \overline{\overline{L_1}/M_{1,j} \cup \overline{L_2}/M_{2,j} \cup \cdots \cup \overline{L_m}/M_{m,j}} \quad \text{for } j = 1, \ldots, n, \quad (11.1)$$

then the X_j defined in that way satisfy the preceding requirement and, furthermore, they are maximal.

Recall that the existence of a solution of the given system of implicit language equations is equivalent to "$\exists j \in \{1, \ldots, n\} \colon \exists u \in M_{i,j}$ and u a prefix of w, $w/u \in X_j$" holding for all $w \in L_i$ and "$\forall j \in \{1, \ldots, n\} \colon \forall u \in M_{i,j}$ and u a prefix of w, $w/u \notin X_j$" holding for all $w \notin L_i$, for $i = 1, \ldots, m$. From the first condition, we derive

$$\mathop{\forall}_{i=1,\ldots,m} \ \mathop{\forall}_{w \in L_i} \left[\bigcup_{j=1,\ldots,n} (w/M_{i,j} \cap X_j) \right] \neq \emptyset. \quad (11.2)$$

The main result of Chapter 8 can then be stated as follows:

The system $L_i = M_{i,1} \cdot X_1 \cup \cdots \cup M_{i,n} \cdot X_n$ for $i = 1, \ldots, m$ of implicit language *equations* has a solution iff the languages X_j defined in (11.1) satisfy (11.2).

Note that determining whether the condition (11.2) is satisfied is not effective in general. However, we can substitute the languages defined by (11.1) directly into the given system of implicit language equations. Then, a solution exists if and only if (11.2) is a solution of the system of implicit language equations. Furthermore, this solution is guaranteed to be maximal and regular.

We now return to our original systems of language relations

$$L_i \ \mathbb{R}_i \ \alpha_i \quad \text{for } i = 1, \dots, m,$$

where for all $i = 1, \dots, m$, L_i is a language in CONST, α_i is an expression in $\text{EX}_A(\text{CONST}; \text{OP}; X_1, \dots, X_n)$, and $\mathbb{R}_i \in \{=, \supseteq, \subseteq\}$. We observe that (11.1) deals precisely with those words that are *not* in the L_i's. Let us determine how this applies to relations.

Assume that the m equations are grouped into those with $\mathbb{R}_i = $ "$=$," followed by those with $\mathbb{R}_i = $ "$\supseteq$," followed by those with $\mathbb{R}_i = $ "$\subseteq$." More specifically, we define two integers m_1 and m_2 with

$$0 \leq m_1 \leq m_2 \leq m$$

such that the original system of language relations can be restated as

$$L_i = M_{i,1} \cdot X_1 \cup \dots \cup M_{i,n} \cdot X_n \quad \text{for all } i = 1, \dots, m_1,$$
$$L_i \supseteq M_{i,1} \cdot X_1 \cup \dots \cup M_{i,n} \cdot X_n \quad \text{for all } i = m_1 + 1, \dots, m_2,$$
$$L_i \subseteq M_{i,1} \cdot X_1 \cup \dots \cup M_{i,n} \cdot X_n \quad \text{for all } i = m_2 + 1, \dots, m.$$

Note that any group can be empty (if $m_1 = 0$, or $m_1 = m_2$, or $m_2 = m$); but if any two groups are empty, the introductory observations resolve the problem of determining solutions.

It follows now that words that are *not* contained in L_i *must not* be contained in the corresponding right-hand side α_i, for all $i = 1, \dots, m_1$ and for all $i = m_1 + 1, \dots, m_2$. Note that because the right-hand side may contain additional words for $i = m_2 + 1, \dots, m$ (the third group), an analogous statement does not hold for the third group.

Based on this observation, we define languages X_j for all $j = 1, \dots, n$ as follows:

$$X_j = \overline{\overline{L_1}/M_{1,j} \cup \dots \cup \overline{L_{m_1}}/M_{m_1,j} \cup \overline{L_{m_1+1}}/M_{m_1+1,j} \cup \dots \cup \overline{L_{m_2}}/M_{m_2,j}}.$$
$$(11.3)$$

It follows that with this definition, the X_j have the property that all words that *must not* be in L_i are not in $M_{i,1} \cdot X_1 \cup \dots \cup M_{i,n} \cdot X_n$ for all $i = 1, \dots, m_2$. This holds by construction and follows in exactly the same way as in Chapter 8. By construction of (11.3), it follows now, in the same way as before, that the languages (11.3) are maximal; i.e., there do not exist languages other than the X_j that contain these X_j and satisfy the same property.

In order to determine whether the languages defined by (11.3) are indeed a solution of the given system of language relations, we must perform an additional test, namely we must determine whether the maximal X_j defined by (11.3) do, in fact, satisfy

$$L_i = M_{i,1} \cdot X_1 \cup \cdots \cup M_{i,n} \cdot X_n \quad \text{for all } i = 1, \ldots, m_1,$$
$$L_i \subseteq M_{i,1} \cdot X_1 \cup \cdots \cup M_{i,n} \cdot X_n \quad \text{for all } i = m_2 + 1, \ldots, m.$$

If the answer to this question is yes, the languages defined by (11.3) constitute the maximal solution of the given system of language relations; if the answer is no, the system does not have a solution. The first part of this assertion is obvious. The second part follows from the maximality of the X_j; if there were a solution of the system, it would have to be contained in (11.3) which is not possible since (11.3) excludes no more than all words *not* permitted. Thus we can summarize:

Theorem 11.3. *Consider the system*

$$L_i \; \mathbb{R}_i \; \alpha_i \quad \text{for } i = 1, \ldots, m,$$

where for all $i = 1, \ldots, m$, L_i is a language in CONST, α_i is an expression in $\text{EX}_A(\text{CONST}; \text{OP}; X_1, \ldots, Xn)$,

$$\alpha_i = M_{i,1} \cdot X_1 \cup \cdots \cup M_{i,n} \cdot X_n$$

and $\mathbb{R}_i \in \{=, \supseteq, \subseteq\}$.

a. *If all constant languages in all α_i and all L_i are regular, there exists an algorithm to determine whether a solution exists.*

b. *If a solution exists, the maximal solution is given by (11.3) for arbitrary* CONST.

c. *If* CONST = REG, *the solution defined by (11.3) consists exclusively of regular languages.*

Several observations are in order:

1. If the constant languages of the given system are not all regular, the languages defined by (11.3) still constitute a maximal solution if they satisfy the first group (equations) and the third group (superrelations) of the given system of language relations, but the methods of determining (11.3) need not be effective any longer. Thus, whether our method for determining the existence of solutions is an algorithm or not depends on the languages involved in the system.

2. Theorem 11.3 is applicable even if only one group of the given system is nonempty.

   a. If $m_2 = 0$, (11.3) yields precisely the maximal solution derived in the previous section:

   $$X_1 = \cdots = X_n = A^*.$$

   b. If $m_1 = 0$ and $m_2 = m$, the minimal solution was derived as

   $$X_1 = \cdots = X_n = \emptyset.$$

Clearly, if (3.7) yields these languages, the minimal solution equals the maximal one, which is therefore unique. However, in general, Theorem 11.3 will yield a different solution.

11.2   Uniqueness of Solutions

Theorem 11.3 establishes a necessary and sufficient condition for the existence of a solution. We now come to the question of uniqueness of a solution; related to this is the problem of how to determine more than one solution if the maximal solution is not unique.

In Chapter 8, we derived the following criterion for implicit *equations*: The maximal solution $X = (X_1, \ldots, X_n)$ of a system of implicit language equations

$$L_i = M_{i,1} \cdot X_1 \cup \cdots \cup M_{i,n} \cdot X_n \quad \text{for all } i = 1, \ldots, m_1$$

is unique iff

for all $j = 1, \ldots, n$, there does not exist a word $w \in X_j$ such that $M_{i,j}w$ is contained in $M_{i,1}X_1 \cup \cdots \cup M_{i,j-1}X_{j-1} \cup M_{i,j+1}X_{j+1} \cup \cdots \cup M_{i,n}X_n$, for all $i = 1, \ldots, m_1$.

We will adapt this criterion to our systems of implicit relations. More specifically, assume that there is a solution and that $X = (X_1, \ldots, X_n)$ defined by (11.3) is the maximal solution. We observe that in our given system of language relations, for the second group of relations where the languages L_i contain the right-hand side, omitting any word or words from our maximal solution will never create a problem since the superrelation will continue to hold. However, for the first and the third group, this is not necessarily true. This reasoning leads to the following result:

Theorem 11.4. *Consider the system of language relations*

$$L_i \, \mathbb{R}_i \, \alpha_i \quad \text{for } i = 1, \ldots, m,$$

where for all $i = 1, \ldots, m$, L_i is a language in CONST, α_i *is an expression in* $\mathrm{EX}_A(\mathrm{CONST}; \mathrm{OP}; X_1, \ldots, X_n)$,

$$\alpha_i = M_{i,1} \cdot X_1 \cup \cdots \cup M_{i,n} \cdot X_n$$

and $\mathbb{R}_i \in \{=, \supseteq, \subseteq\}$. Assume that $\mathbb{R}_i =$ "$=$" for all $i = 1, \ldots, m_1$, $\mathbb{R}_i =$ "$\supseteq$" for all $i = m_1 + 1, \ldots, m_2$, and $\mathbb{R}_i =$ "$\subseteq$" for all $i = m_2 + 1, \ldots, m$. Assume that a solution exists. The maximal solution $X = (X_1, \ldots, X_n)$ of this system defined by (11.3) is unique iff for all $j = 1, \ldots, n$, there does not exist a word $w \in X_j$ such that for all $i = 1, \ldots, m_1$ and all $i = m_2 + 1, \ldots, m$,

$$M_{i,j}\{w\} \cap L_i \subseteq M_{i,1}X_1 \cup \cdots \cup M_{i,j-1}X_{j-1} \cup M_{i,j+1}X_{j+1} \cup \cdots \cup M_{i,n}X_n,$$

Furthermore, if all constant languages $M_{i,j}$ and L_i are regular, this test for uniqueness is effective.

PROOF.

A. Assume there exists a word $w \in X_j$ violating the condition of the theorem. We claim that $Y = (Y_1, \ldots, Y_n)$ with $Y_s = X_s$ for $s \in \{1, \ldots, n\} - \{j\}$ and $Y_j = X_j - \{w\}$ is a solution (which is clearly different from X). Now, Y is a solution if for all i in the first and third groups of our system such that $M_{i,j} \neq \emptyset$, the language $M_{i,j}\{w\} \cap L_i$ is contained in $M_{i,1}X_1 \cup \cdots \cup M_{i,j-1}X_{j-1} \cup M_{i,j+1}X_{j+1} \cup \cdots \cup M_{i,n}X_n$. This, however, is precisely the condition of the theorem since for $M_{i,j} = \emptyset$, $M_{i,j}\{w\} = \emptyset$, which is trivially contained in any set. Thus, we have constructed another solution different from X which shows that X is not unique.

B. For the converse, we observe that X is the maximal solution; therefore, if there exists a different solution $Y = (Y_1, \ldots, Y_n)$, there exists an $s \in \{1, \ldots, n\}$ such that $X_s - Y_s \neq \emptyset$. Let $w \in X_s - Y_s$. We claim that for this s and this w, the language $M_{i,s}\{w\} \cap L_i$ is contained in

$$M_{i,1}Y_1 \cup \cdots \cup M_{i,s-1}Y_{s-1} \cup M_{i,s+1}Y_{s+1} \cup \cdots \cup M_{i,n}Y_n$$

for all $i = 1, \ldots, m_1$ and for all $i = m_2 + 1, \ldots, m$. Now for the first group, we obviously have $M_{i,s}\{w\} \cap L_i = M_{i,s}\{w\}$ since we are dealing with equations; thus, since $M_{i,s}\{w\}$ is contained in L_i, it must also be contained in the right-hand side of the equation. For the third group, we use a similar argument, except it now applies only to words in $M_{i,s}\{w\} \cap L_i$. Since by assumption, Y is a solution, the claim of the theorem follows.

We now show that the condition of the theorem can be tested for effectively if all constant languages are regular. To do this, consider the following construction. For each $j = 1, \ldots, n$ and for each $i = 1, \ldots, m_1, m_2 + 1, \ldots, m$, we determine the largest subset $Z_{i,j}$ of X_j such that

$$M_{i,j}Z_{i,j} \cap L_i \subseteq M_{i,1}X_1 \cup \cdots \cup M_{i,j-1}X_{j-1} \cup M_{i,j+1}X_{j+1} \cup \cdots \cup M_{i,n}X_n.$$

Let us denote the (regular) union on the right by $N_{i,j}$. Then, for all $i = 1, \ldots, m_1$,

$$Z_{i,j} = N_{i,j}/M_{i,j}$$

since $M_{i,j}Z_{i,j} \cap L_i = M_{i,j}Z_{i,j}$ for these values of i. For all $i = m_2 + 1, \ldots, m$,

$$Z_{i,j} = (N_{i,j}/M_{i,j} \cup \overline{L}_i/M_{i,j}) \cap X_j.$$

All these operations on regular languages are effective. Therefore, if we define

$$Z_j = \bigcap_{\substack{i \in \{1, \ldots, m\} \\ \text{such that } M_{i,j} \neq \emptyset}} Z_{i,j},$$

it follows that Z_j is regular, can be effectively constructed, and has the property that it contains precisely all those words w for which the language $M_{i,j}\{w\} \cap L_i$ is contained in $M_{i,1}X_1 \cup \cdots \cup M_{i,j-1}X_{j-1} \cup M_{i,j+1}X_{j+1} \cup \cdots \cup M_{i,n}X_n$ for all $i = 1, \ldots, m$. Thus, the test for uniqueness is equivalent to the effective test of whether

$$Z_j \neq \emptyset.$$

This concludes the proof of Theorem 11.4.   □

Let us refer to this test as the Z-test in the following; it is analogous to the test (with the same name) defined in Chapter 8 for implicit equations only. As for implicit equations, the maximality of the X_i's does not come into play in this test. Therefore, the Z-test can be applied to any given solution; if it succeeds (i.e., if there exists a j such that $Z_j \neq \emptyset$), then this solution contains at least one subset that is also a solution. This brings us to the question of how to construct additional solutions; more specifically, if there are finitely many solutions, we want to construct all of them, and if there are infinitely many solutions, we want to determine a construction that yields an arbitrarily large number of solutions. First, however, we give a test of whether there are infinitely many solutions.

It is clear from the proof of Theorem 11.4 that removal from the maximal solution X_j of any word in Z_j yields another solution. Let us construct Z_j for all $j = 1, \ldots, n$; then, there are infinitely many solutions if and only if any one of them is infinite because there are infinitely many words that can be removed if any Z_s is infinite and there are only finitely many subsets of the Z_j if all Z_j are finite. Again, this is an effective test if CONST = REG.

Corollary 11.5. *Assume we are given a system of implicit language relations with union and left-concatenation where all constant languages are regular. There exists an effective test of whether this system has finitely many solutions.*

It follows that every solution can be constructed if there are only finitely many solutions since, in this case, all solutions must be regular (every subset of any of the Z_j's is finite and therefore regular). Care must be taken with the iterative selection of subsets of Z_j since choosing a specific subset for one j may restrict the possible choices of subsets for other indices (see Chapter 8). In the case of infinitely many solutions, we can construct an arbitrarily large number of them by using the above method of removing a single word in arbitrarily many ways.

11.3 Examples

We illustrate these constructions with three examples.

1. Assume the alphabet $A = \{a, b\}$ and consider the following three relations in the two variables X and Y:

$$aA^*A \supseteq ab^*X \cup aa^*Y,$$
$$A(aa \cup bb)^* \supseteq aX \cup aY,$$
$$aaa(aa)^* \cup bbb(bb)^* \subseteq bX \cup aY.$$

Thus, $m_1 = 0$, $m_2 = 2$, and $m = 3$. Using (11.3), we obtain from the first two relations (after a good deal of work)

$$X = (aa \cup bb)(aa \cup bb)^*,$$
$$Y = (aa \cup bb)(aa \cup bb)^*,$$

and it is now quite easy to verify that with these two maximal solutions of the first two relations, the third is also satisfied. [Note that none of the first two relations is an equation; therefore, whatever (11.3) yields is a solution. If there were one equation, we would still have to verify that the languages obtained from (11.3) are a solution of the equation before we proceed to testing the subrelation.] Thus, writing L^+ for $L \cdot L^*$, we have that

$$X = Y = (aa \cup bb)^+$$

is a solution of the given system of three relations. Furthermore, it is the maximal solution.

2. Assume the alphabet $A = \{a, b\}$ and consider the following two relations in the two variables X and Y:

$$(a^*b)^+ = aX \cup bY,$$
$$(b^*a)^+ \supseteq aX \cup aY.$$

Thus, $m_1 = 1$, $m_2 = 2$, and $m = m_2 = 2$. We obtain from these two relation

$$X = \emptyset,$$
$$Y = \{\lambda\}.$$

Since the first relation is an equation, it is necessary to test whether $(X, Y) = (\emptyset, \{\lambda\})$ satisfies the equation; the answer is negative, and therefore no solution exists [even though $(X, Y) = (\emptyset, \{\lambda\})$ satisfies the second relation].

3. Assume the alphabet $A = \{a, b\}$ and consider the following two relations in the three variables X, Y, and Z:

$$A^*aa = aX \cup bbY \cup baZ,$$
$$AA^*aa \subseteq bX \cup aY.$$

Thus, $m_1 = 1$, $m_2 = m_1 = 1$, and $m = 2$. We obtain from the first relation

$$X = aa^* \cup a^*bA^*aa,$$

$$Y = A^*aa,$$
$$Z = aa^* \cup a^*bA^*aa \quad (= X).$$

Since the first relation is an equation, it is necessary to test whether these languages for X, Y, and Z satisfy the equation; the answer is positive. Therefore, we must verify whether this choice of X, Y, and Z also satisfies the second relation. This turns out to be true as well. Consequently, the two relations in the three unknowns have the (maximal) solution

$$X = Z = aa^* \cup a^*bA^*aa, \qquad Y = A^*aa.$$

To conclude this section, let us determine for the solutions of Examples 1 and 3 whether other solutions exist in addition to the maximal ones we determined. (Since in Example 2, there is no solution, applying the Z-test makes no sense in this case.)

For Example 1, we get from the Z-test (numbering X and Y as X_1 and X_2, respectively),

$$Z_{3,1} = (bb)^*aa(aa \cup bb)^* \quad (= Z_1),$$
$$Z_{3,2} = (aa)^*bb(aa \cup bb)^* \quad (= Z_2).$$

Since Z_1 and Z_2 are infinite, there are infinitely many solutions of this system of relations; for example, any pair (S, T) of languages that satisfy

$$bb(bb)^* \subseteq S \subseteq (aa \cup bb)(aa \cup bb)^*$$

and

$$(aa)^* \subseteq T \subseteq (aa \cup bb)(aa \cup bb)^*$$

is a solution of the relations in (X, Y).

For Example 3, we get, from the Z-test (numbering X, Y and Z as X_1, X_2, and X_3):

$$Z_{1,1} = [bbA^*aa \cup ba(aa^* \cup a^*bA^*aa]/a = \emptyset,$$
$$Z_{1,2} = [(a \cup ba)(aa^* \cup a^*bA^*aa]/bb = \emptyset,$$
$$Z_{1,3} = [aaa^* \cup aa^*bA^*aa \cup bbA^*aa]/ba = \emptyset.$$

Consequently, regardless of the values of $Z_{2,1}$, $Z_{2,2}$, and $Z_{2,3}$, which ordinarily would have to be determined as well, $Z_1 = Z_2 = Z_3 = \emptyset$ and the maximal solution in X, Y, and Z is unique.

11.4   Conclusion

We have defined implicit language relations and have given algorithms for determining whether systems of such language relations have solutions. We have also outlined how to determine the unique maximal solution (if one exists) and how to use it to determine other solutions, and all of them if there finitely many. The approach taken here is closely patterned after that for implicit language equations (see Chapter 8). Whereas *implicit* equations are more difficult to deal with than *explicit* equations, the situation is reversed for relations: Implicit language relations are easier to resolve than explicit language relations.

11.5 Bibliographical Note

The material presented in this chapter is new and has not been published (see [Leiss 97b]).

11.6 Problems

1. For each of the following systems of implicit language relations

    i. Determine whether it has a solution.
    ii. If a solution exists, determine the maximal one.
    iii. Determine how many solutions exist; if there are finitely many, construct all of them.

    a.

$$a^*b^* \subseteq aX \cup bY \cup \lambda$$
$$a^*b^* \supseteq aaX \cup bb^*Y \cup \lambda.$$

    b.

$$(a^*b)^* = aX \cup Y \cup bZ,$$
$$b(a^*b)^* \subseteq X \cup aY \cup bZ,$$
$$(a^*b)^* \supseteq Z \cup aX \cup bY.$$

    c.

$$a^*b^* \cup b^*a^* \subseteq aa^*X \cup b^*Y,$$
$$(a \cup b)(a \cup b)^* \supseteq a(a \cup bb)^*X \cup b(b \cup aa)^*Y,$$
$$a^*b^*a^* \supseteq aX \cup bY.$$

    d.

$$(aa)^*(bb)^* \cup (bb)^*(aa)^* \subseteq aa^*X \cup b^*Y,$$
$$[(a \cup b)(a \cup b)]^* \supseteq a(a \cup bb)^*X \cup b(b \cup aa)^*Y,$$
$$a^*b^*a^* \supseteq aX \cup bY.$$

2. Show that the process of solving relations by replacing superset and subset relations by equality (which works well for explicit relations, provided the resulting system contains at most one equation per variable) does not work for implicit relations. Specifically, there exist systems of implicit relations that have solutions whereby the corresponding system of equations (obtained by replacing $\subseteq$ and $\supseteq$ by $=$) does not have a solution.

Hint: Consider the single relation $a^*X \supseteq a$, or $aX \subseteq a^*b^*$.

12

Two-Sided Language Equations

About This Chapter: Two-sided language equations are the most general types of language equations. We discuss several approaches to determining whether a solution exists and of determining such a solution. The question of uniqueness is also of interest. However, in general, none of these approaches is guaranteed to work; in fact, it is not known how to determine whether a given system of m two-sided equations in n variables has a solution, even in the case where $m = n = 1$.

Let $\alpha_i, \beta_i \in \mathrm{EX}_A(\mathrm{REG}; \mathrm{OP}; X_1, \ldots, X_n)$, $i = 1, \ldots, m$, where OP consists of union and left-concatenation. A system of m two-sided language equations with union and left-concatenation in n variables is given by

$$\alpha_i = \beta_i \quad \text{for } i = 1, \ldots, m.$$

Thus, the expressions α_i and β_i are of the same type as those studied in Chapters 3 (explicit equations) and 8 (implicit equations). We know from these chapters that any equation $\alpha \in \mathrm{EX}_A(\mathrm{REG}; \mathrm{OP}; X_1, \ldots, X_n)$ with OP consisting of union and left-concatenation has the following normal form:

$$\alpha = L_1 \cdot X_1 \cup \cdots \cup L_n \cdot X_n \cup L_0.$$

Thus, if for all $i = 1, \ldots, m$,

$$\alpha_i = L_{i,1} \cdot X_1 \cup \cdots \cup L_{i,n} \cdot X_n \cup L_{i,0}$$

and

$$\beta_i = M_{i,1} \cdot X_1 \cup \cdots \cup M_{i,n} \cdot X_n \cup M_{i,0},$$

the given system to be considered can be written as

$$L_{i,1} \cdot X_1 \cup \cdots \cup L_{i,n} \cdot X_n \cup L_{i,0}$$
$$= M_{i,1} \cdot X_1 \cup \cdots \cup M_{i,n} \cdot X_n \cup M_{i,0} \quad \text{for } i = 1, \ldots, m.$$

We would like to determine whether this system has a solution. Unfortunately, no algorithm is known to do this, even though all constants ($L_{i,j}$, $M_{i,j}$ for $i = 1, \ldots, m$ and $j = 0, 1, \ldots, n$) are assumed to be regular. In fact, even for a single equation in a single variable, no general method is known for determining whether a solution exists or for determining a solution!

Let us consider first the situation where

$$m = n = 1;$$

in other words, we are considering the equation

$$L \cdot X \cup M = N \cdot X \cup P,$$

where L, M, N, and P are regular languages and X is the variable. It is clear that for any solution S to exist, we must have

$$L \cdot S \cup M \supseteq P \quad \text{and} \quad N \cdot S \cup P \supseteq M.$$

This implies the following:

Lemma 12.1. *If $L \cdot A^* \cup M \not\supseteq P$, then no solution exists of $L \cdot X \cup M = N \cdot X \cup P$. If $N \cdot A^* \cup P \not\supseteq M$, then no solution exists of $L \cdot X \cup M = N \cdot X \cup P$.*

Unfortunately, the converse of Lemma 12.1 does not hold; that is, it is not true that

$$L \cdot A^* \cup M \supseteq P \quad \text{and} \quad N \cdot A^* \cup P \supseteq M$$

imply the existence of a solution. To see this, consider the equation

$$aa^* X \cup b^* = bb^* X \cup \lambda$$

over the alphabet $A = \{a, b\}$. Clearly, $aa^* A^* \cup b^* \supseteq \lambda$ and $bb^* A^* \cup \lambda \supseteq b^*$, so the conditions of Lemma 12.1 are satisfied. However, no solution exists; this can be seen as follows. Clearly, $X = \emptyset$ is not a solution; thus any solutions must be nonempty. However, in this case, $aa^* S$ is nonempty and any word in this language starts with a, but no word on the right-hand side of the supposed equation starts with a.

Let $\alpha = L \cdot X \cup M$, $\beta = N \cdot X \cup P$. Consider the generalized derivatives α/w and β/w for $w \in A^*$, as defined in Chapter 5. We can use these derivatives to obtain an approach to determining whether a solution exists. Before we formulate this technique, let us look at a few examples.

The first example is the already mentioned equation over the alphabet $A = \{a, b\}$:

$$aa^* X \cup b^* = bb^* X \cup \lambda.$$

Clearly, $\lambda \in$ RHS (right-hand side), thus λ must also be in the LHS (left-hand side), which is true since $\lambda \in b^*$. Also $b^* \subseteq$ LHS, thus b^* must also be in the RHS (i.e., $b^* \subseteq bb^*X \cup \lambda$). This necessarily requires

$$\lambda \in X.$$

Now consider

$$(aa^*X \cup b^*)/a = a^*X \quad \text{and} \quad (bb^*X \cup \lambda)/a = \emptyset,$$

thus, $a^*X = \emptyset$, or

$$X = \emptyset,$$

since clearly the derivative of the LHS with respect to any word w must be identical to the derivative of the RHS with respect to the same word w. However, this is a contradiction since $\lambda \in X$ and $X = \emptyset$ cannot hold at the same time. Hence, no solution exists.

The second example is a system of two equations in three variables, over $A = \{a, b\}$:

$$aX \cup bY = aa^*Z \cup a,$$
$$ab^*Y \cup ba^*Z \cup a^* \cup b^* = a^*X \cup b^*Z.$$

Let us denote by LHS_i (RHS_i) the left-hand (right-hand) side of equation i, $i = 1, 2$. Clearly, since $a \in \text{RHS}_1$, we must have

$$\lambda \in X.$$

Also, since $a^* \cup b^* \subseteq \text{LHS}_2$, $a^* \cup b^* \subseteq \text{RHS}_2$, and this implies

$$(\lambda \in X \text{ and } (\lambda \in Z \text{ or } b \in Z)) \quad \text{or} \quad (a \in X \text{ and } \lambda \in Z).$$

Combining these two conclusions yields

$$\lambda \in X \quad \text{and} \quad (\lambda \in Z \text{ or } b \in Z).$$

If there is a solution, then we must have

$$(\text{LHS}_i)/w = (\text{RHS}_i)/w \quad \text{for } i = 1, 2 \text{ and for all } w \in A^*.$$

Therefore, consider

$$(\text{LHS}_1)/a = X, \qquad (\text{RHS}_1)/a = a^*Z \cup \lambda;$$

thus,

$$X = a^*Z \cup \lambda.$$

Consider

$$(\text{LHS}_1)/b = Y, \qquad (\text{RHS}_1)/b = \emptyset;$$

thus,

$$Y = \emptyset.$$

Substituting $X = a^* Z \cup \lambda$ and $Y = \emptyset$ into the two equations yields

$$aa^* Z \cup a = aa^* Z \cup a \text{ (an obvious identity)},$$
$$ba^* Z \cup a^* \cup b^* = a^* Z \cup a^* \cup b^* Z.$$

Let LHS (RHS) refer to this last equation. Clearly,

$$\text{LHS}/a = a^* \quad \text{and} \quad \text{RHS}/a = a^* Z \cup Z_a \cup a^*.$$

This implies

$$Z \subseteq a^*.$$

Also, $\text{LHS}/b = a^* Z \cup b^*$ and $\text{RHS}/b = Z_b \cup b^* Z$. Since $Z \subseteq a^*$, Z_b must be empty; thus,

$$a^* Z \cup b^* = b^* Z.$$

Now, $(a^* Z \cup b^*)/b = Z_b \cup b^* = b^*$ (since $Z_b = \emptyset$) and $(b^* Z)/b = b^* Z \cup Z_b = b^* Z$. Thus, $b^* = b^* Z$, which implies

$$Z \subseteq b^*.$$

Since $Z \subseteq a^*$ and $Z \subseteq b^*$,

$$Z \subseteq a^* \cap b^* = \lambda$$

and, therefore, there are exactly two possibilities for Z:

$$Z = \emptyset \quad \text{and} \quad Z = \lambda.$$

Substituting this into $X = a^* Z \cup \lambda$ yields the following two candidates for solutions:

$$(X, Y, Z) = (a^*, \emptyset, \lambda) \quad \text{and} \quad (X, Y, Z) = (\lambda, \emptyset, \emptyset).$$

However, neither of these possibilities constitutes a solution of the original system of equations:

$(a^*, \emptyset, \lambda):$ 　　　　　　　$aa^* \cup \emptyset = aa^* \cup a$　　(which is valid)

　　　　　　$\emptyset \cup ba^* \cup a^* \cup b^* = a^* \cup b^*$　　(which is invalid);

$(\lambda, \emptyset, \emptyset):$ 　　　　　　　$a \cup \emptyset = a \cup \emptyset$　　(which is valid)

　　　　　　$\emptyset \cup \emptyset \cup a^* \cup b^* = a^* \cup \emptyset$　　(which is invalid).

Consequently, no solution exists.

For any language L over the alphabet A, let $\text{PF}(L)$ be the set of all words in L that are not proper prefixes of any word in L nor have a proper prefix in L,

$$\text{PF}(L) = \{w \in L \mid w \notin LAA^* \text{ and } L \cap \{w\}AA^* = \emptyset\}.$$

Again, consider the single equation in the single variable X,

$$L \cdot X \cup M = N \cdot X \cup P.$$

Then, we can state:

Lemma 12.2. *Let S be a solution of the equation $L \cdot X \cup M = N \cdot X \cup P$. For any word w in $\mathrm{PF}(L)$ that does not have a prefix in N,*

$$S \cup M/w = N/w \cdot S \cup P/w.$$

Similarly, for any word w in $\mathrm{PF}(N)$ that does not have a prefix in L,

$$S \cup P/w = L/w \cdot S \cup M/w.$$

The proof is obvious.

Thus, we may focus on equations of the following form:

$$X \cup B = C \cdot X \cup D,$$

where B, C, and D are arbitrary languages. We have:

Lemma 12.3. *Consider the equation $X \cup B = C \cdot X \cup D$.*

If $B \subseteq C^* \cdot D$, then $C^* \cdot D$ is a solution of the equation.
If $B \not\subseteq C^* \cdot D$ and $\lambda \notin C$, then no solution can exist.

PROOF.   We first recall from Chapter 11 that the subrelation $X \subseteq C \cdot X \cup D$ has the maximal solution $X = C^* \cdot D$ if $\lambda \notin C$, which is also the unique solution of the equation $X = C \cdot X \cup D$. Thus, if $B \subseteq C^* \cdot D$, then $C^* \cdot D$ is a solution of the equation. Moreover, if this condition is not satisfied (with $\lambda \notin C$), then, clearly, no solution can exist.   □

Consider now the case $\lambda \in C$; obviously, $X = A^*$ is always a solution. However, in general, there are multiple solutions: The solutions of the equation $X = C \cdot X \cup D$ have the representation $C^* \cdot (D \cup T)$ for arbitrary T over A; thus, any T such that

$$B \subseteq C^* \cdot (D \cup T)$$

yields a solution of the equation $X \cup B = C \cdot X \cup D$ if $\lambda \in C$.

Although $C^* \cdot D$ is the unique solution of the equation $X = C \cdot X \cup D$ if $\lambda \notin C$, we want to raise the question of whether the solution $C^* \cdot D$ of the equation $X \cup B = C \cdot X \cup D$ (for $\lambda \notin C$) is unique as well. The answer is negative, as the following example demonstrates. Consider

$$X \cup a^* b = aX \cup (b \cup ab).$$

We obtain $a^* b$ as a solution by Lemma 12.3, but one can verify that $aa^* b$ is also a solution. Since, in general, we do not know how to represent all solutions contained in the solution $C^* \cdot D$, we do not know a parametric representation of all solutions. This result has negative implications for our ability to find solutions, as will become clear later.

Returning to the question of determining whether a given equation $L \cdot X \cup M = N \cdot X \cup P$ has a solution, we can apply Lemma 12.2 for all words that satisfy its conditions. Specifically, let S_w be the solution that we obtain according to Lemma 12.3 for the equations $X \cup M/w = N/w \cdot X \cup P/w$

or $X \cup P/w = L/w \cdot X \cup M/w$. (Note that for any word w, the two conditions of Lemma 12.2 are mutually exclusive; thus, at most one of the two cases will apply.) The following observation concerning these "partial" solutions should now be clear: If all the S_w, for all applicable words w, are equal, say to S, then S is a solution of the original equation. However, since there may be multiple solutions S_w and since we do not have a representation of all solutions of the equations $X \cup M/w = N/w \cdot X \cup P/w$ or $X \cup P/w = L/w \cdot X \cup M/w$, this process can be rather complicated, as the following examples will illustrate.

Consider the equation over the alphabet $A = \{a, b\}$:

$$(a \cup b)X \cup (a \cup b)b = (aa \cup ba \cup baa)X \cup (a \cup b)b.$$

Clearly, the necessary conditions of Lemma 12.1 are satisfied. Now, consider the generalized derivatives:

$$a: \quad ((a \cup b)X \cup (a \cup b)b)/a = X \cup b$$

and

$$((aa \cup ba \cup baa)X \cup (a \cup b)b)/a = aX \cup b.$$

Consequently, we obtain the equation

$$X \cup b = aX \cup b,$$

which has the maximal solution

$$S_a = a^*b.$$

From the derivatives with respect to b, we obtain the equation

$$X \cup b = (\lambda \cup aa)X \cup b;$$

for this equation, we can specify all its solutions S_b by the following parametric representation, since $B (= b)$ and $D (= b)$ are identical:

$$S_b = (aa)^*(b \cup T) \quad \text{for } T \text{ an arbitrary language over } A.$$

Now, if there is to be any solution S of this equation, it must be contained in

$$S_a \cap S_b = a^*b,$$

using $T = ab$, for example. Thus, we obtain in $S = S_a \cap S_b$ a possible candidate for a solution of the given equation; that S is indeed a solution must be verified directly.

Consider now the equation

$$(a \cup b)X \cup ab^* \cup b = aaX \cup ab^* \cup b.$$

a: $X \cup b^* = aX \cup b^*$, which yields the maximal solution $S_a = a^*b^*$
b: $X \cup \lambda = \lambda$, which yields the maximal solution $S_b = \lambda$

Now, $S_a \cap S_b = \lambda$, but one can verify that $S = \lambda$ is not a solution. However, the requirement for a solution S is $S \subseteq S_a \cap S_b$, not $S = S_a \cap S_b$, and $S = \emptyset$ satisfies this requirement and is also a solution (which, moreover, must then also be unique).

It should be obvious that the approach suggested by Lemmas 12.2 and 12.3 may not be applicable; for example, if every word in $L(N)$ is a proper prefix of another word in $L(N)$. Consider, for example, the following equation over $A = \{a, b\}$:

$$(aa^* \cup bb(bbb)^*)X \cup b(bb)^* = (aa(aa)^* \cup bb^*)X \cup a(aaa)^*.$$

Obviously, no word in $aa^* \cup bb(bbb)^*$ and no word in $aa(aa)^* \cup bb^*$ satisfy the condition of Lemma 12.2. Consequently, this lemma cannot be applied. Nevertheless, we can proceed by taking generalized derivatives:

$a:$ $\quad a^*X = a(aa)^*X \cup (aaa)^*$, which necessarily implies that $\lambda \in X$,
$b:$ $\quad b(bbb)^*X \cup (bb)^* = b^*X$, which also implies that $\lambda \in X$
$aa:$ $\quad a^*X \cup X_a = (aa)^*X \cup aa(aaa)^*$
$ab:$ $\quad X_b = \emptyset$
$ba:$ $\quad \emptyset = X_a$
$bb:$ $\quad (bbb)^*X \cup b(bb)^* = b^*X \cup X_b$

At this point, we can stop, since $\lambda \in X$ and $X_a = \emptyset$ and $X_b = \emptyset$ necessarily imply that

$$X = \{\lambda\}.$$

However, one can easily verify that this is not a solution of the given equation:

LHS: $(aa^* \cup bb(bbb)^*)\{\lambda\} \cup b(bb)^* = aa^* \cup b^{1,2,3,5}(b^6)^*$
RHS: $(aa(aa)^* \cup bb^*)\{\lambda\} \cup a(aaa)^* = a^{1,2,4,6}(a^6)^* \cup bb^*$

and it is clear that LHS $\neq$ RHS. Thus, no solution exists.

Consider the single equation in the variables X and Y, over the alphabet $A = \{a, b\}$:

$$(a \cup b^*)X \cup b = aaX \cup bY \cup \lambda \cup a.$$

Since λ is in the RHS, we conclude that $\lambda \in X$. Then, we take generalized derivatives:

$a:$ $\quad X \cup X_a = aX \cup \lambda$
$b:$ $\quad b^*X \cup X_b \cup \lambda = Y, \quad \lambda \in Y$
$aa:$ $\quad X_a \cup X_{aa} = X, \quad \lambda \in X_a$ or $\lambda \in X_{aa}$
$ab:$ $\quad X_b \cup X_{ab} = \emptyset, \quad X_b = \emptyset$ and $X_{ab} = \emptyset$

From this, it follows that $Y = b^*X \cup \lambda$, and since $\lambda \in X$, we conclude

$$Y = b^*X.$$

ba: $X_a \cup X_{ba} = Y_a$
bb: $b^*X \cup X_b \cup X_{bb} = Y_b$ or $b^*X \cup X_{bb} = Y_b,\ \lambda \in Y_b$
aaa: $X_{aa} \cup X_{aaa} = X_a$
aab: $X_{ab} \cup X_{aab} = X_b,\ X_{aab} = \emptyset$
baa: $X_{aa} \cup X_{baa} = Y_{aa}$
bab: $X_{ab} \cup X_{bab} = Y_{ab}$ or $X_{bab} = Y_{ab}$
$aaaa$: $X_{aaa} \cup X_{aaaa} = X_{aa}$

In studying the derivatives for X, we can see that X must be contained in a^* and, furthermore,

$$X_{a^i} \cup X_{a^{i+1}} = X_{a^{i-1}} \quad \text{for all } i \geq 1.$$

This, combined with $\lambda \in X$, implies however that $\lambda \in X_{a^i}$ for all $i \geq 0$, which, in turn, implies that

$$X = a^*.$$

Since we already determined that $Y = b^*X$, it follows that

$$Y = b^*a^*.$$

Since all conclusions in this derivation are forced, this implies that

$$(X, Y) = (a^*, b^*a^*)$$

is the only possible candidate for a solution of the given equation. That $(X, Y) = (a^*, b^*a^*)$ is, in fact, a solution can be verified directly:

LHS: $(a \cup b^*)a^* \cup b = aa^* \cup b^*a^* \cup b = b^*a^*$
RHS: $aaa^* \cup bb^*a^* \cup \lambda \cup a = a^* \cup bb^*a^* = b^*a^*$

The following example indicates that, in general, it is not possible to obtain a forced conclusion (i.e., we may not have enough information to conclude necessarily what languages constitute a solution). In such cases, it may be required to make an arbitrary assignment of the empty word λ to the generalized derivatives that arise in order to obtain a solution language. That there may be problems associated with this process is also illustrated with examples.

Consider the following equation over $A = \{a, b\}$:

$$a(a^* \cup b^*)X \cup \lambda = aX \cup (ab)^*.$$

a: $(a^* \cup b^*)X = X \cup b(ab)^*$
b: $\emptyset = \emptyset$
aa: $a^*X \cup X_a = X_a$, thus $X_a \supseteq a^*X$
ab: $b^*X \cup X_b = X_b \cup (ab)^*$, thus $\lambda \in X$ or $\lambda \in X_b$
aaa: $a^*X \cup X_a \cup X_{aa} = X_{aa}$, thus $X_{aa} \supseteq X_a \supseteq a^*X$
aab: $X_b \cup X_{ab} = X_{ab}$, thus $X_{ab} \supseteq X_b$
aba: $X_a \cup X_{ba} = X_{ba} \cup b(ab)^*$, thus $(\lambda \notin X_{ba} \Rightarrow \lambda \notin X_a)$

abb: $b^*X \cup X_b \cup X_{bb} = X_{bb}$, thus $X_{bb} \supseteq b^*X \cup X_b$

abab: $X_{ab} \cup X_{bab} = X_{bab} \cup (ab)^*$, thus $\lambda \in X_{ab}$ or $\lambda \in X_{bab}$

It becomes now rather obvious that there is not enough information to allow us definitive conclusions about whether X_v contains the empty word or not (which is, of course, equivalent to saying that the state—in some automaton—corresponding to the derivative X_v is accepting or not). Thus, we must make an assignment of λ to the derivatives X_v, which is consistent with the partial information that has been derived. For example, we may make the following assumptions:

$X_{a^i} = a^*X$ for all $i \geq 0$ (consistent with $X_{a^i} \supseteq a^*X$ for all $i \geq 1$)
$X_{ab} = X_b$ (consistent with $X_{ab} \supseteq X_b$)
$X_{bb} = b^*X$ (consistent with $X_{bb} \supseteq b^*X \cup X_b$)
$\lambda \in X$ $\lambda \in X_{ba}$ and $\lambda \in X_a$ and $\lambda \notin X_b$

This gives rise to the following finite automaton A $= (\{a, b\}, \{1, 2\}, \tau, 1, \{2\})$ with the transition function given by

	a	b
1	1	2
2	1	1, 2

In this nondeterministic finite automaton, state 1 corresponds to X and state 2 to X_b. Thus, we effectively have captured the following relationships:

$$X = aX \cup bX_b,$$
$$X_b = aX \cup b(X \cup X_b) \cup \{\lambda\}.$$

One can show with little effort that these relationships are consistent with the partial information about a possible solution that we obtained above. It can be verified (with some work) that $X = L(A)$ is, indeed, a solution of the given equation:

$$L(A) = a^*b(a^*b)^*.$$

LHS: $a(a^* \cup b^*)X \cup \lambda = a(a^* \cup b^*)a^*b(a^*b)^* \cup \lambda = \lambda \cup aa^*b(a^*b)^*$
RHS: $aX \cup (ab)^* = aa^*b(a^*b)^* \cup (ab)^* = \lambda \cup aa^*b(a^*b)^*$

To summarize what we have learned from these examples, let us formulate precisely the notion of taking generalized derivatives in order to solve two-sided language equations. Recall the notation $[\alpha(X)/w]_L$ that we used in Proposition 5.1.

Theorem 12.4. *Let $\alpha_i = \beta_i$ for $i = 1, \ldots, m$ be a system of m two-sided language equations in n variables, with $\alpha_i, \beta_i \in \mathrm{EX}_A(\mathrm{REG}; \mathrm{OP}; X_1, \ldots, X_n)$ for $i = 1, \ldots, m$, where OP consists of union and left-concatenation. There exists a solution $(S_1, \ldots, S_n)$ of this system iff for all $i = 1, \ldots, n$ and for all $w \in A^*$,*

$$\lambda \in [\alpha_i(X_1, \ldots, X_n)/w]_{(S_1, \ldots, S_n)}(S_1, \ldots, S_n)$$

iff

$$\lambda \in [\beta_i(X_1, \ldots, X_n)/w]_{(S_1, \ldots, S_n)}(S_1, \ldots, S_n).$$

The proof is a consequence of Proposition 5.1.

This leads to the requirement for a globally consistent λ-assignment to all corresponding generalized derivatives. Specifically, consider again the most general form of the two-sided language equations studied in this chapter:

$$\alpha_i = \beta_i \quad \text{for } i = 1, \ldots, m$$

with $\alpha_i, \beta_i \in \mathrm{EX}_A(\mathrm{REG}; \mathrm{OP}; X_1, \ldots, X_n)$, $i = 1, \ldots, m$, where OP consists of union and left-concatenation. Then, consider the generalized derivatives

$$\alpha_i/w \quad \text{and} \quad \beta_i/w \quad \text{for } i = 1, \ldots, m.$$

A λ-assignment Λ to the X_i/v for $i = 1, \ldots, n$ and $v \in A^*$ is a (syntactic) mapping that replaces each X_i/v by either $\emptyset$ or $\{\lambda\}$:

$$\Lambda \colon \{X_i/v \mid i = 1, \ldots, n \text{ and } v \in A^*\} \to \{\emptyset, \{\lambda\}\}.$$

Given any generalized derivative γ/w for $\gamma \in \mathrm{EX}_A(\mathrm{REG}; \mathrm{OP}; X_1, \ldots, X_n)$, $\Lambda(\gamma/w)$ is an expression in $\mathrm{EX}_A(\mathrm{REG}; \mathrm{OP}; \emptyset)$ obtained by replacing every occurrence of X_i/v, for any $i = 1, \ldots, n$ and $v \in A^*$, by $\Lambda(X_i/v)$. It should be obvious that $\Lambda(\gamma/w)$ is indeed an expression in $\mathrm{EX}_A(\mathrm{REG}; \mathrm{OP}; \emptyset)$ since $X_i = X_i/\lambda$. A globally consistent λ-assignment Λ is then a λ-assignment with the property that for all $i = 1, \ldots, n$ and all $w \in A^*$,

$$\lambda \in \Lambda(\alpha_i/w) \quad \text{iff} \quad \lambda \in \Lambda(\beta_i/w).$$

Using this formalism, we now can formulate

Theorem 12.5. *Let $\alpha_i = \beta_i$ for $i = 1, \ldots, m$ be a system of m two-sided language equations in n variables, with $\alpha_i, \beta_i \in \mathrm{EX}_A(\mathrm{REG}; \mathrm{OP}; X_1, \ldots, X_n)$ for $i = 1, \ldots, m$, where OP consists of union and left-concatenation. Let*

$$\Lambda \colon \{X_i/v \mid i = 1, \ldots, n \text{ and } v \in A^*\} \to \{\emptyset, \{\lambda\}$$

be a globally consistent λ-assignment to the X_i/v for $i = 1, \ldots, n$ and $v \in A^*$. Then, there exists a solution in $X_1, \ldots, X_n$ of the given system of equation, defined by

$$S_i = \{w \in A^* \mid \lambda \in \Lambda(X_i/w)\}, \quad i = 1, \ldots, n.$$

The proof of this theorem is a direct consequence of the definitions of generalized derivatives and globally consistent λ-assignments and will be left to the reader.

Unfortunately, in general it is not possible to determine whether a λ-assignment is globally consistent since it involves knowing all generalized derivatives. This leaves us again with the open problem of how to determine whether a solution exists of the given system of two-sided language equations!

We conclude this chapter with a few more examples.

Consider the following equation in the variables X and Y over the alphabet $A = \{a, b\}$:

$$ab^*X \cup ba^*Y \cup b = (ab^*a \cup ab^*)Y \cup ba^*b^*X \cup a^*b.$$

Here are the first few generalized derivatives:

a: $b^*X = (b^*a \cup b^*)Y \cup a^*b$
b: $a^*Y \cup \lambda = a^*b^*X \cup \lambda$
aa: $X_a = Y \cup Y_a \cup a^*b$
ab: $b^*X \cup X_b = (b^*a \cup b^*)Y \cup Y_b \cup \lambda$, thus $\lambda \in X$ or $\lambda \in X_b$
ba: $a^*Y \cup Y_a = a^*b^*X \cup X_a$
bb: $Y_b = b^*X \cup X_b$, thus $\lambda \in Y_b$
aaa: $X_{aa} = Y_a \cup Y_{aa} \cup a^*b$
aab: $X_{ab} = Y_b \cup Y_{ab} \cup \lambda$, thus $\lambda \in X_{ab}$
aba: $X_a \cup X_{ba} = Y \cup Y_a \cup Y_{ba}$
abb: $b^*X \cup X_b \cup X_{bb} = (b^*a \cup b^*)Y \cup Y_b \cup Y_{bb}$
baa: $a^*Y \cup Y_a \cup Y_{aa} = a^*b^*X \cup X_a \cup X_{aa}$
bab: $Y_b \cup Y_{ab} = b^*X \cup X_b \cup X_{ab}$, thus $\lambda \in Y_{bb}$
bba: $Y_{ba} = X_a \cup X_{ba}$
bbb: $Y_{bb} = b^*X \cup X_b \cup X_{bb}$, thus $\lambda \in Y_{bb}$
$\vdots$

One can see that any conclusion that can be reached on the basis of these generalized derivatives is one to the effect that the empty word must be contained in some X_v or Y_v, but never that λ cannot be in X_v or Y_v. Thus, it follows that the following λ-assignment is globally consistent:

$$\lambda \in X_v \quad \text{and} \quad \lambda \in Y_v \quad \text{for all } v \in A^*.$$

One can of course verify directly that the choice

$$(X, Y) = (A^*, A^*),$$

which corresponds precisely to this globally consistent λ-assignment is, indeed, a solution.

To see how a globally consistent λ-assignment can fail to exist, consider the following equation over $\{a, b\}$:

$$abX \cup (b \cup ba)Y \cup a^*bb^* = (ab^*a \cup ab)Y \cup ba^*bX \cup a^*b.$$

We obtain:

a: $bX \cup a^*bb^* = (b^*a \cup b)Y \cup a^*b$
b: $Y \cup aY \cup b^* = a^*bX \cup \lambda$
aa: $a^*bb^* = Y \cup a^*b$, thus $\lambda \notin Y$

ab: $X \cup b^* = b^* aY \cup Y \cup \lambda$
ba: $Y_a \cup Y = a^* bX$, thus $\lambda \notin Y_a$
bb: $Y_b \cup b^* = X$, thus $\lambda \in X$
aaa: $a^* bb^* = Y_a \cup a^* b$, thus $\lambda \notin Y_a$
aab: $b^* = Y_b \cup \lambda$
aba: $X_a = Y \cup Y_a$, thus $\lambda \notin X_a$
abb: $X_b \cup b^* = b^* aY \cup Y_b$, thus $\lambda \in Y_b$

Combining $\lambda \in Y_b$ with the equation for *aab* yields

$$Y_b = b^*.$$

Consequently, the equation for *bb* yields

$$X = b^*.$$

However, now the equation for *ab* becomes

$$b^* = b^* aY \cup Y \cup \lambda$$

and this yields a contradiction (if Y is nonempty, the RHS contains words containing the letter a while the LHS does not; $Y = \emptyset$ obviously is no solution). Thus, no globally consistent λ-assignment can exist.

Corollary 12.6. *Let $\alpha_i = \beta_i$ for $i = 1, \ldots, m$ be a system of m two-sided language equations in n variables, with $\alpha_i, \beta_i \in \mathrm{EX}_A(\mathrm{REG};$ OP; $X_1, \ldots, X_n)$ for $i = 1, \ldots, m$, where OP consists of union and left-concatenation. Then, there exists a procedure to determine whether this system has no solution.*

PROOF.   The process used in Theorem 12.5 will terminate if at any point, a contradiction is encountered [i.e., for some $i \in \{1, \ldots, n\}$ and some $v \in A^*$, both $\lambda \in (X_i)/v$ and $\lambda \notin (X_i)/v$ have been concluded]. This, however, obviously precludes the existence of a globally consistent λ-assignment. It should be clear that such a conclusion must always be reached if no globally consistent λ-assignment exists.   □

Thus, we are in the following curious situation: Although we do not have a procedure to determine that a solution exists, we have a procedure that determines if no solution exists. Thus, in order to make existence of a solution of a system of two-sided language equations with union and left-concatenation a decidable problem, it is necessary (and sufficient) to obtain a procedure that terminates with a solution if one exists. Note that such a procedure exists trivially if we knew that any such system must have a regular solution if it has any solution, for, in this case, we could effectively enumerate all (n-tuples of) regular languages and test whether they constitute a solution. Although it appears eminently reasonable to assume that any system of two-sided language equations with regular constants and union and left-concatenation as operators must have a regular solution if it has any solution, we do not know how to prove this conjecture. Thus, it is not known whether the question of existence of solutions is decidable (since languages in general are not enumerable, although regular languages are).

We observe that one can easily formulate an analogue of Theorem 12.5 for the most general type of expressions considered in this book, namely for α_i and β_i being expressions in $\mathrm{EX}_A(\mathrm{CONST};\ \mathrm{OP};\ X_1,\ldots,X_n)$ for $i = 1,\ldots,m$, where OP consists of union, concatenation, complementation, and star. However, since it is unknown even for the drastically restricted case of CONST = REG and OP consisting only of union and left-concatenation how to test whether a solution exists, it is unlikely that this major generalization will yield significant results. This is even more so the case if we are interested in two-sided language relations (instead of equations). Language relations are significantly more difficult to handle than language equations (of any type), and there is no reason to assume that generalizing the problem makes it easier to solve.

12.1 Bibliographical Note

Most of the material in this chapter is new. The notion of a globally consistent λ-assignment is adapted from [Leiss 81d].

12.2 Problems

1. Show that the following equation does not have a globally consistent λ-assignment:
$$abX \cup ba^*Y \cup a^*bb^* = (ab^*a \cup ab)Y \cup ba^*bX \cup a^*b \text{ over } \{a,b\}.$$

2. Show that the following equation has a globally consistent λ-assignment:
$$a^*X \cup b^*Y = aa^*Y \cup bb^*X \cup a \text{ over } \{a,b\}.$$

3. Show that the following equation over $\{a,b\}$ has exactly two globally consistent λ-assignments:
$$A^*X = aY \cup bX \cup a \cup b.$$

4. Determine for each the following systems whether it has a solution, and if so, construct (at least) one:

   a. $A = \{a,b\}$:
   $$abX \cup ba^*Y \cup b = a^*V \cup bZ,$$
   $$aX \cup bY = ab^*V \cup ba^*Z \cup a.$$

b. $A = \{a, b\}$:

$$abX \cup ba^*Y \cup b = a^*V \cup bZ,$$
$$aX \cup bY = ab^*V \cup ba^*Z \cup a,$$
$$aY \cup ba^* = (a \cup b)Z.$$

c. $A = \{a, b\}$:

$$abX \cup ba^*Y \cup b = a^*V \cup bZ,$$
$$aX \cup bb^*Y = ab^*V \cup ba^*Z \cup a.$$

d. $A = \{a, b\}$:

$$abX \cup ba^*Y \cup b = a^*V \cup bZ,$$
$$aX \cup bb^*Y = ab^*V \cup ba^*Z \cup a,$$
$$a^*Y \cup b^*A^* = (a \cup b)Z \cup \lambda.$$

13

Mixed Systems

About This Chapter: We address the question of combining explicit and implicit equations. It turns out that the existence of a parametric representation of all solutions of the explicit equations contained in the mixed system, together with a solution method for implicit systems, yields a general method for determining whether such a system has a solution, and if so, how to find it. Consequently, provided there is at most one explicit equation for each variable, we can solve such systems in the case where the operations are union and left-concatenation, as well as in the case where the alphabet contains one letter, the constants are regular, and the operations are union, concatenation, and star.

Consider a system of language equations

$$X_i = \alpha_i \quad \text{for } i = 1, \dots, k,$$
$$L_j = \beta_j \quad \text{for } j = k + 1, \dots, m,$$

where the α_i and β_j are expressions in $\mathrm{EX}_A(\mathrm{CONST}; \mathrm{OP}; X_1, \dots, X_n)$ and the L_j constants in CONST, $i = 1, \dots, k$, $j = k + 1, \dots, m$, with $k \leq m$. In other words, the first k equations are explicit and the subsequent $m - k$ equations are implicit. We are interested in solving this types of mixed systems of equations.

Note that this formulation already requires that there be at most one defining explicit equation for each variable. While it is, of course, possible to formulate the problem more generally (and we do this in the next sections), the results below only hold if this condition is satisfied. Furthermore, the results of Section 10.3 strongly indicate that dropping this assumption only creates difficulties.

In this chapter, we outline methods that produce solutions of such mixed systems, if any exist, in the following two cases:

A. A and CONST are arbitrary, and OP consists of union and left-concatenation.

B. $A = \{a\}$, CONST = REG, and OP consists of union, concatenation, and star.

Both methods make heavy use of the corresponding separate results for implicit and explicit equations and then combine them. Crucial in both cases is that we have a complete parametric representation of a solutions of the explicit portion of the system. This knowledge then enables us to obtain a solution of the mixed system.

13.1   Mixed Systems of Equations with Union and Left-Concatenation

Throughout this section, let A be arbitrary, CONST be arbitrary, and OP consist of union and left-concatenation. We are interested in mixed systems of equations:

$$X_{h_i} = \alpha_i \quad \text{for } i = 1, \ldots, k,$$
$$L_j = \beta_j \quad \text{for } j = k + 1, \ldots, m$$

with α_i and β_j expressions in $\mathrm{EX}_A(\mathrm{CONST}; \mathrm{OP}; X_1, \ldots, X_n)$ and L_j constants in CONST, $h_i \in \{1, \ldots, n\}$, $i = 1, \ldots, k$, $j = k + 1, \ldots, m$, with $k \leq m$. We can formulate the following.

Theorem 13.1. *Let $X_{h_i} = \alpha_i$ for $i = 1, \ldots, k$, $L_j = \beta_j$ for $j = k + 1, \ldots, m$ be a mixed system of language equations, with $\alpha_i, \beta_j \in \mathrm{EX}_A(\mathrm{CONST}; \mathrm{OP}; X_1, \ldots, X_n)$, $L_j \in \mathrm{CONST}$, $i = 1, \ldots, k$, $j = k + 1, \ldots, m$, with $k \leq m$, where OP consists of union and left-concatenation. Assume that $s \neq t$ implies $h_s \neq h_t$.*

a. *We can determine whether a solution exists of this system.*

b. *If a solution exists, we can determine whether a single, a finite number, or infinitely many solutions exist.*

c. *The tests in (a) and (b) are effective if CONST = REG.*

PROOF.   Since the condition "$s \neq t$ implies $h_s \neq h_t$" means that each variable X_i has at most one explicit equation, we can apply the results of Chapter 3 for classical equations to the explicit portion of our system. This results in expressions for the variables X_{h_i} for $i = 1, \ldots, k$ that are in $\mathrm{EX}_A(\mathrm{CONST}; \mathrm{OP}; (\{X_1, \ldots, X_n\} - \{X_{h_i} \mid i = 1, \ldots, k\}) \cup \{T_{X_{h_i}} \mid$

$i = 1, \ldots, k\}$), where the $T_{X_{h_i}}$ are the parameters corresponding to the equation $X_{h_i} = \alpha_i$ which are required only if there is a parametric representation of all solutions of that equation. Thus, this yields a parametric representation of all solutions in the variables X_{h_i}:

$$X_{h_i} = \gamma_i \quad \text{for } i = 1, \ldots, k$$

with

$$\gamma_i \in \text{EX}_A(\text{CONST}; \text{OP}; (\{X_1, \ldots, X_n\} - \{X_{h_i} \mid i = 1, \ldots, k\})$$
$$\cup \{T_{X_{h_i}} \mid i = 1, \ldots, k\}).$$

We then substitute γ_i for each X_{h_i} occurring in β_j for all $i = 1, \ldots, k$, $j = k+1, \ldots, m$. This results in the following system of implicit equations:

$$L_j = \delta_j \quad \text{for } j = k+1, \ldots, m,$$

where δ_j is the result of this substitution process. Clearly, for all $j = k+1, \ldots, m$,

$$\delta_j \in \text{EX}_A(\text{CONST}; \text{OP}; (\{X_1, \ldots, X\} - \{X_{h_i} \mid i = 1, \ldots, k\})$$
$$\cup \{T_{X_{h_i}} \mid i = 1, \ldots, k\}).$$

Furthermore, it follows that $(X_1, \ldots, X_n) = (S_1, \ldots, S_n)$ is a solution of the original mixed system of equations iff $(X_1, \ldots, X_n) = (S_1, \ldots, S_n)$ is a solution of the implicit system $L_j = \delta_j$ for $j = k+1, \ldots, m$. However, since the latter system is an implicit system of equations, we can apply the results of Chapter 8. This allows us to determine whether there is a solution, what the maximal solution is if one exists, and testing whether this solution is unique, or whether there are finitely or infinitely many solutions. Furthermore, if there are finitely many solutions, we can determine all of them, if there are infinitely many solutions, we can determine an arbitrary number of them. Finally, according to Chapter 8, all these tests and constructions are effective if $\text{CONST} = \text{REG}$.   □

Let us look at an example. Consider the following mixed system of equations:

$$X = bba^*X \cup a^*Y \cup \lambda,$$
$$Y = (bb)^*X \cup (aa)^*Y \cup aZ,$$
$$(a \cup bb)^* = aX \cup bbY \cup \lambda.$$

We first apply the theory developed in Chapter 3 and obtain (after a good deal of work) the following representation of all solutions of the first two (explicit) equations:

$$X = (a \cup bb)^*[aZ \cup T_X \cup T_Y \cup \lambda],$$
$$Y = (a \cup bb)^*[aZ \cup T_X \cup T_Y \cup \lambda].$$

Substituting this into the single implicit equation then yields

$$(a \cup bb)^* = a(a \cup bb)^*[aZ \cup T_X \cup T_Y \cup \lambda]$$
$$\cup \, bb(a \cup bb)^*[aZ \cup T_X \cup T_Y \cup \lambda] \cup \lambda$$

or, after simplification,

$$(a \cup bb)^* = (a \cup bb)(a \cup bb)^*[aZ \cup T_X \cup T_Y \cup \lambda] \cup \lambda$$

and applying the results of Chapter 8 to this implicit equation in the three variables Z, T_X, and T_Y results (again after some effort) in the following maximal solution in X, Y, and Z:

$$(X, Y, Z) = ((a \cup bb)^*, (a \cup bb)^*, (a \cup bb)^*).$$

Finally, applying the Z-test yields that there are infinitely many solutions; for example, any subset of $(a \cup bb)^*$ is a solution for Z, with $X = Y = (a \cup bb)^*$.

Suppose now we were to replace in this mixed system the single implicit equation by the following one:

$$(a \cup bb)^* = aX \cup bY \cup \lambda.$$

Substituting the parametric representation of all solutions obtained from the explicit equations into it, we obtain the following two implicit equations in the three variables Z, T, and W (where, for simplicity, we replaced $T_X \cup T_Y$ by T):

$$(a \cup bb)^* = (a \cup b)(a \cup bb)^* aZ \cup (a \cup b)(a \cup bb)^* T \cup W,$$
$$(a \cup b)(a \cup bb)^* \cup \lambda = W,$$

and from this, (8.2) yields

$$(Z, T, W) = (\emptyset, \emptyset, a(a \cup bb)^*),$$

which clearly is not a solution, as one can verify by direct substitution. Therefore, this second mixed system of equations does not have a solution.

We note that the requirement "$s \neq t$ implies $h_s \neq h_t$" in Theorem 13.1 cannot be dropped. This follows from the discussion in Section 10.3, where we demonstrated the difficulties of dealing with the situation where the same variable has two (or more) defining explicit equations. Specifically, the approach taken in Theorem 13.1 requires us to have a parametric representation of all solutions of the explicit portion of the mixed system. This, however, is not available if the requirement "$s \neq t$ implies $h_s \neq h_t$" is not satisfied. Therefore, we are not able to apply the theory on implicit equations developed in Chapter 8. If one were to derive a parametric representation of all solutions of the explicit portion of the mixed system without imposing the condition "$s \neq t$ implies $h_s \neq h_t$", the approach of Theorem 13.1 would be fully applicable. Note that even though the theory on implicit equations developed in Chapter 8 allows us to determine an arbitrarily large number of solutions, it does not yield a parametric representation of all solutions. This has the consequence that we must not interchange the order in which we solve the two portions of the mixed system; that is, we may not first deal with the implicit portion, and then solve the resulting explicit equations, even though the techniques developed in Chapter 8 are guaranteed to encounter eventually any specific solution of the system of implicit equations. To see this, consider again the second mixed system for which we have determined that no solutions exists:

$$X = bba^*X \cup a^*Y \cup \lambda,$$
$$Y = (bb)^*X \cup (aa)^*Y \cup aZ,$$
$$(a \cup bb)^* = aX \cup bY \cup \lambda.$$

If we were to solve first the implicit equation, we would obtain the following maximal solution in the variables X and Y:

$$(X, Y) = ((a \cup bb)^*, b(a \cup bb)^*).$$

However, if one were to solve now the explicit portion of this mixed system of equations, one would obtain (as before)

$$X = Y = (a \cup bb)^*[aZ \cup T \cup \lambda];$$

from this one would then derive the following system of implicit equations:

$$(a \cup bb)^* = (a \cup bb)^*[aZ \cup T \cup \lambda],$$
$$b(a \cup bb)^* = (a \cup bb)^*[aZ \cup T \cup \lambda],$$

and one would then conclude that no solution of this system exists. However, since the solution $(X, Y) = ((a \cup bb)^*, b(a \cup bb)^*)$ of the implicit portion was maximal, one would have to repeat this process for every valid solution (S_X, S_Y) (which is, of course, contained in the maximal solution $(X, Y) = ((a \cup bb)^*, b(a \cup bb)^*))$. While in the present example, one can make the case (using ad hoc considerations) that no such solution (S_X, S_Y) can exist, in general this is not possible. Thus, although one would eventually find a solution if one exists, this process would never terminate if no solution existed.

13.2   Mixed Systems of Equations over a One-Letter Alphabet with Regular Constants and Union, Concatenation, and Star

Throughout this section, let the alphabet A be $\{a\}$, let CONST be the set of all regular languages over $\{a\}$, and let OP consist of union, concatenation, and star. We are interested in mixed systems of equations:

$$X_{h_i} = \alpha_i \quad \text{for } i = 1, \ldots, k,$$

$$L_j = \beta_j \quad \text{for } j = k+1, \ldots, m$$

with α_i and β_j expressions in $\text{EX}_{\{a\}}(\text{REG}; \text{OP}; X_1, \ldots, X_n)$ and L_j constants in CONST, $h_i \in \{1, \ldots, n\}$, $i = 1, \ldots, k$, $j = k+1, \ldots, m$, with $k \leq m$. We can formulate the following:

Theorem 13.2. *Let $X_{h_i} = \alpha_i$ for $i = 1, \ldots, k$, $L_j = \beta_j$ for $j = k+1, \ldots, m$ be a mixed system of language equations, with $\alpha_i, \beta_j \in \text{EX}_{\{a\}}(\text{REG}; \text{OP}; X_1, \ldots, X_n)$, $L_j \in \text{REG}$, $i = 1, \ldots, k$, $j = k+1, \ldots, m$, with $k \leq m$, where OP consists of union, concatenation, and star. Assume that $s \neq t$ implies $h_s \neq h_t$.*

a. *We can determine whether a solution exists of this system.*
b. *If a solution exists, we can determine whether a single, a finite number, or infinitely many solutions exist.*
c. *The tests in (a) and (b) are effective.*

PROOF. Since the condition "$s \neq t$ implies $h_s \neq h_t$" means that each variable X_i has at most one explicit equation, we can apply the results of Chapter 7 (specifically Sections 7.5 and 7.6) to the explicit portion of our system. This results in expressions for the variables X_{h_i} for $i = 1, \ldots, k$ that are in

$$\text{EX}_{\{a\}}(\text{REG}; \text{OP}; (\{X_1, \ldots, X_n\} - \{X_{h_i} \mid i = 1, \ldots, k\})$$
$$\cup \{T_{X_{h_i}} \mid i = 1, \ldots, k\}),$$

where the $T_{X_{h_i}}$ are the parameters corresponding to the equation $X_{h_i} = \alpha_i$ which are required only if there is a parametric representation of all solutions of that equation [according to Theorems 7.9(c) and 7.13]. Thus, this yields a parametric representation of all solutions in the variables X_{h_i}:

$$X_{h_i} = \gamma_i \quad \text{for } i = 1, \ldots, k$$

with

$$\gamma_i \in \text{EX}_{\{a\}}(\text{CONST}; \text{OP}; (\{X_1, \ldots, X_n\} - \{X_{h_i} \mid i = 1, \ldots, k\})$$
$$\cup \{T_{X_{h_i}} \mid i = 1, \ldots, k\}).$$

We then substitute γ_i for each X_{h_i} occurring in β_j for all $i = 1, \ldots, k$, $j = k+1, \ldots, m$. This results in the following system of implicit equations:

$$L_j = \delta_j \quad \text{for } j = k+1, \ldots, m,$$

where δ_j is the result of this substitution process. Clearly, for all $j = k+1, \ldots, m$,

$$\delta_j \in \text{EX}_{\{a\}}(\text{REG}; \text{OP}; (\{X_1, \ldots, X_n\} - \{X_{h_i} \mid i = 1, \ldots, k\})$$
$$\cup \{T_{X_{h_i}} \mid i = 1, \ldots, k\}).$$

Furthermore, it follows that $(X_1, \ldots, X_n) = (S_1, \ldots, S_n)$ is a solution of the original mixed system of equations iff $(X_1, \ldots, X_n) = (S_1, \ldots, S_n)$ is a solution of the implicit system $L_j = \delta_j$ for $j = k+1,\ldots,m$. However, since the latter system is an implicit system of equations, we can apply the results of Chapter 9. This allows us to determine whether there is a solution, what the maximal solution is if one exists, and testing whether this solution is unique or whether there are finitely or infinitely many solutions. Furthermore, if there are finitely many solutions, we can determine all of them; if there are infinitely many solutions, we can determine an arbitrary number of them. Finally, according to Chapter 9, all these tests and constructions are effective. □

Again, the assumption "$s \neq t$ implies $h_s \neq h_t$" is important, for exactly the same reasons as in the previous section. Note also that, again, we must first solve the explicit portion and only then deal with the implicit portion of the given mixed system; interchanging these two processes generally will not result in a satisfactory answer.

Consider the following mixed system of equations:

$$X = (a^2)^*(a^2 X^2 Y)^* X^3 \cup a^2,$$
$$a^{0,2,4} \cup a^6 a^* = a^2 X \cup Y \cup a^7.$$

We must begin by solving the explicit equation. Following the approach in Section 7.5, we first apply Theorem 7.9(c) and obtain

$$X = [(a^2)^*(a^2 X^2 Y)^*(a^2 \cup T \cup \lambda)^2]^*(a^2 \cup T \cup \lambda)$$
$$= T^*(a^2)^*(a^2 Y X^2)^* \quad \text{with } T \text{ completely arbitrary.}$$

Then, we apply Theorem 7.10 and obtain

$$X = T^*(a^2)^*[a^2 Y(T^*(a^2)^*)^2]^*$$
$$= T^*(a^2)^*(a^2 Y)^*.$$

Substituting this parametric representation of all solutions into the implicit equation, we now must solve the following implicit equation for the two variables Y and T:

$$a^{0,2,4} \cup a^6 a^* = a^2 T^*(a^2)^*(a^2 Y)^* \cup Y \cup a^7.$$

Applying the results of Chapter 9, we obtain the following solution in Y and T:

$$Y = a^{0,2,4} \cup a^6 a^*, \qquad T = a^{0,2} \cup a^4 a^*.$$

Substituting these languages, we obtain the following solution of the original mixed system in its two variables X and Y:

$$X = a^{0,2} \cup a^4 a^*, \qquad Y = a^{0,2,4} \cup a^6 a^*$$

and one can verify directly that this is, indeed, a solution.

Note, however, that the solution $(Y,T) = (a^{0,2,4} \cup a^6 a^*, a^{0,2} \cup a^4 a^*)$ is not the only one for the implicit equation in Y and T. There is also

$$Y = a^7, \qquad T = a^7.$$

With this choice of solutions, we obtain the following solution of the mixed system:

$$X = a^{0,2,4} \cup a^6 a^*, \qquad Y = a^7.$$

In fact, it is easily verified that there are infinitely many solutions of the implicit equation $a^{0,2,4} \cup a^6 a^* = a^2 T^*(a^2)^*(a^2 Y)^* \cup Y \cup a^7$, each of which will give rise to different solutions for Y and T, which, in turn, result in different solutions for X and Y.

13.3 Bibliographical Note

The material in this chapter is new and has never been published before.

13.4 Problems

1. For the following mixed systems over the alphabet $A = \{a, b\}$ with OP consisting of the operations union and left-concatenation:

   i. Determine whether a solution exists.
   ii. If there exists a solution, determine a regular solution.
   iii. Determine how many solutions exist. If there are finitely many, determine all of them.

   a.

   $$X = (ab)^* X \cup (ba)^* Y \cup \lambda,$$
   $$Y = (aa)^* X \cup (bb)^* Y \cup \lambda,$$
   $$(AA)^* a^* = (abab)^* X \cup (baba)^* Y \cup aa \cup bb.$$

   b.

   $$X = (ab)^* X,$$
   $$Y = (ba)^* Y,$$
   $$a^3 (ba)^* = aaX \cup bbY,$$
   $$ba(a \cup ba)^* = ba^* X \cup ab^* Y.$$

   c.

   $$X = aX \cup bY,$$
   $$Y = bX \cup aY \cup \lambda,$$
   $$aa^* b(a \cup ba^* b) \cup bA^* = ba^* X \cup bY.$$

d.

$$X = aX \cup bY,$$
$$Y = b^*X \cup aY \cup \lambda,$$
$$a^*bA^* = b^*Y \cup a^*X.$$

e.

$$X = aX \cup b^*Y,$$
$$Y = b^*X \cup aaY \cup a,$$
$$A^*aa = aX \cup bY.$$

2. For the following mixed systems over the alphabet $A = \{a\}$ with OP consisting of the operations union, concatenation, and star:

i. Determine whether a solution exists.

ii. If there exists a solution, determine a regular solution.

iii. Determine how many solutions exist. If there are finitely many, determine all of them.

a.

$$X = (a^2)^*[(a^4)^*X^3]^* \cup a,$$
$$a^6a^* = a^8X^5 \cup a^3(a^3X^4)^*.$$

b.

$$X = (a^2)^*[(a^4)^*X^3]^* \cup a^4,$$
$$a^6a^* = a^8X^5 \cup a^3(a^3X^4)^*.$$

c.

$$X = a^6X^2 \cup a^4X^3 \cup a^2X^4 \cup a^2,$$
$$a^7(a^4)^* = a^3(a^4)^*X^2,$$
$$a^{2,9,11} \cup a^{16}a^* = a^2(a^{1,3}X^3)^* \cup a^{21,22}.$$

d.

$$X = a^2(X^2Y^2)^*,$$
$$Y = a^3(X^3Y^3)^*,$$
$$a^4 \cup a^6a^* = (a^3)^*X^3 \cup (a^3)^*Y^2 \cup (a^4)^*Y.$$

e.

$$X = a(aX^4)^*Y \cup a^2Y^3 \cup \lambda,$$
$$a^* = X \cup aaY.$$

14
Open Problems

We will give a list of problems that have not yet been resolved. This list complements the open problems (mainly directly related to material covered there) that have already been mentioned in the appropriate chapters. The difficulty of the problems ranges from fairly simple to (most likely) impossible to solve. The nature of a book such as this is that it provides a snapshot of what we know about the general theory, at a certain point in time. It should be clear that one might well find solutions to some of the (easier) problems listed here were one to work on them just another six months or a year.

14.1 Classification

In general, we have several "dimensions" (independent variables or aspects) to the problem of language relations:

- The choice of alphabet A
- The choice of constant languages CONST
  [One could, in fact, distinguish two different sets: the set of constants that occur in the expressions and the set of languages from which solutions may be drawn; throughout this book, we have assumed that the two are identical. Consequently, we have also assumed (mostly implicitly) that CONST be closed under the operations occurring in OP, as well as some others that the solution approach requires (e.g., taking quotients) for the implicit equations studied in Chapter 8.]
- The choice of operations OP

- The distinction between explicit, implicit, and two-sided equations or relations
- The kind of relations that are involved

  Throughout, we have concentrated only on the relations subset and superset (in addition to equality). Others that could be considered are inequality ($\neq$), strict subset, and strict superset. We expect that the techniques given in the book can be extended to these relations as well. Substantially different relations, such as those that involve the length of words involved, most likely require fundamentally different approaches.

- The distinction, relevant in this book only for explicit equations, whether a variable may have at most one or more than one defining equation

14.2   The Cardinality of the Alphabet

Let us start our discussion with open questions related to one-letter alphabets. In general, one might expect things to be easier if the alphabet contains just one letter. Clearly, the results in Sections 7.1 through 7.6 bear this out. Nevertheless, as Section 7.7 very graphically demonstrates, unrestricted complementation in conjunction with unrestricted concatenation creates major problems, even if the alphabet contains only one letter. Since the results of Chapter 5 on generalized derivatives apply, one of the few open questions in this area relates to language relations; namely, we are posing the problem of developing a theory of language relations. Specifically, a system of explicit language relations in the n variables $X_1, \ldots, X_n$ is defined as

$$X_i \, \mathbb{R}_{i,j} \, \alpha_{i,j} \quad \text{for } i = 1, \ldots, n, \ 1 \leq j \leq \sigma_i$$

where $\sigma_i \geq 0$ and for all i, j, $\mathbb{R}_{i,j} \in \{=, \supseteq, \subseteq\}$ and $\alpha_{i,j} \in \mathrm{EX}_{\{a\}}(\mathrm{CONST};$ OP; $X_1, \ldots, X_n)$; OP consists of union, concatenation, and star. A system of implicit language relations in the n variables $X_1, \ldots, X_n$ is given by

$$L_i \, \mathbb{R}_i \, \alpha_i \quad \text{for } i = 1, \ldots, m,$$

where for all i, $\mathbb{R}_i \in \{=, \supseteq, \subseteq\}$, $\alpha_i \in \mathrm{EX}_{\{a\}}(\mathrm{CONST};$ OP; $X_1, \ldots, X_n)$, and OP consists of union, concatenation, and star. Finally, a system of two-sided language relations in the n variables $X_1, \ldots, X_n$ is given by

$$\alpha_i \, \mathbb{R}_i \, \beta_i \quad \text{for } i = 1, \ldots, m,$$

where for all i, $\mathbb{R}_i \in \{=, \supseteq, \subseteq\}$, $\alpha_i, \beta_i \in \mathrm{EX}_{\{a\}}(\mathrm{CONST};$ OP; $X_1, \ldots, X_n)$, and OP consists of union, concatenation, and star. We would expect that of these three problems, explicit relations are relatively easy, implicit relations are harder, and two-sided relations are virtually impossible to solve.

Another problem that might be substantially easier with a one-letter alphabet than with a multiletter one is solving two-sided equations over

$\{a\}$. It is possible that there exists an analogue to the results of Chapter 9, especially Proposition 9.2 and the algorithm ILE.

Whereas there are questions in formal language theory where a problem with an underlying two-letter alphabet behaves differently from the same problem for an alphabet with three or more letters, for language equations the major distinction appears to be between alphabets with one letter and those with two or more letters. Specifically, we are not aware of a problem in language relations where the results for a two-letter alphabet are qualitatively different from those for alphabets with three or more letters.

In the remaining sections, everything addresses multiletter alphabets (i.e., two or more letters).

14.3 The Class of Constant Languages

By and large, any question one can raise can be substantially affected by varying CONST. However, in most cases, we are interested in closure properties. For example, the class REG of regular languages is closed under equations of almost any type. (This is shorthand for saying that the solutions of systems whose constant languages are all from CONST are also in CONST. Although one has to be careful in the case of systems with multiple solutions, it should be clear what is meant by this statement, even though it is, of course, true that some of the multiple solutions need not be in CONST. In this case, we imply that there is at least one solution in CONST.) The only exception for CONST = REG is provided by the result in Section 7.7. For other classes in CONST the situation may change dramatically; thus, CFL is not closed under implicit equations with union and left-concatenation. Various open questions can be formulated by varying CONST.

14.4 The Set of Operations Involved

The major classification device employed in this book was the set OP of operations involved in our expressions. In general, we had considered four operations: union, concatenation (in two versions, unrestricted concatenation and left-concatenation), complementation, and star. We have used the following choices for OP at some point in the book:

OP consists of *union*: Chapter 8 (restricted implicit equations)

OP consists of *union* and *left-concatenation*: Chapters 3 and 8 for equations, and Chapters 10 and 11 for relations

OP consists of *union*, *left-concatenation*, and *complementation*: Chapter 4

OP consists of *union* and *concatenation*: Section 3.5

OP consists of *union, left-concatenation,* and *star*: Chapter 6

OP consists of *union, concatenation,* and *star*: Chapter 7

OP consists of (*union, star,*) *concatenation* and *complementation*: Section 7.7

There are, of course, other subsets of these four operations that could be considered. For example, consider the case OP consisting of *union* and *complementation.* For both equations and for relations, we may consider explicit, implicit, or two-sided systems. At least for equations, these problems are likely to be quite easy. In fact, this may be the only easy case for two-sided equations. The reason is that we can most likely replace complemented variables by new, uncomplemented ones (in somewhat modified equations). Solving for the new variables yields then a solution for the old variables by complementing the results.

Ordinarily, we think it unlikely that a set OP that does not contain union will yield interesting questions. A possible exception might be systems of equations involving unrestricted concatenation. This is related to the fact that we are concerned with systems of equations, not just single equations. Complementation and star are unary operators, and restricted concatenation is rather similar to a unary operator in that no two variables can be combined using this operation.

Finally, it is, of course, natural to introduce additional operations. An obvious one that we did not consider is intersection; although intersection can always be expressed in terms of union and complementation, one might consider expressions with union and intersection, but without complementation. Intersection would also occur in the approach to solving the case where OP consists of union and complementation, which we touched upon two paragraphs earlier, since

$$\overline{L \cup \overline{X}} = \overline{L} \cap X,$$

and while $\overline{L}$ is again a constant, we now have introduced intersections.

Also, completely different operations, such as shuffles, pattern matching, or others, can be contemplated. It is likely that the solution approaches required for these operations will differ radically from those used here for the classical language operations.

14.5   Two-Sided, Implicit, and Explicit Equations

The major open problem, for any set OP, relates to two-sided language equations and relations. This is not just of interest on its own but also since two-sided equations may occur within the context of other problems. An example of this is provided by Section 10.3, in the form of systems where a variable may have several defining explicit equations. Additionally, one approach to solving mixed systems (Chapter 13) requires a parametric representation of all solutions of a system of equations, and again this is related to two-sided equations.

Explicit equations are the most widely studied and best known of the systems. In fact, the major open problem here relates to explicit equations with more than one defining equation for a variable. This was discussed in Section 10.3 for OP consisting of union and left-concatenation. Also of interest would be the case of $A = \{a\}$ and OP consisting of union, concatenation, and star where we also have parameterized representations of all solutions of an explicit equation; consequently, we are likely to encounter the same problem as in Section 10.3, namely a reduction to the solution of a system of two-sided language equations in the parameters.

Implicit equations have numerous open problems. Most important is the case where OP consists of union, left-concatenation, and complementation; this would be the implicit analogue to the boolean (explicit) equations studied (and virtually completely solved) in Chapter 4. Also, one could pose the implicit analogue to the (explicit) star equations (Chapter 6).

Both explicit and implicit relations have only been studied for OP consisting of union and left-concatenation. Clearly, for different sets OP, different problems arise. Explicit relations with union, left-concatenation, and complementation would correspond to Chapter 4 (for equations). Explicit relations over $A = \{a\}$ with OP consisting of union, concatenation, and star would correspond to Sections 7.1 through 7.6. The corresponding implicit versions of these problems are likely to be harder.

Finally as pointed out above, additional relational operators can be considered. In addition to the relations $\{=, \supseteq, \subseteq\}$, one might use $\neq$, $\supset$, and $\subset$. Other operators can also be contemplated. It should be clear that within the context of this book, for explicit relations, solving the single relation

$$X_i \subset \alpha_{i,j}$$

is equivalent to solving the two relations

$$X_j \subseteq \alpha_{i,j},$$
$$X_i \neq \alpha_{i,j}.$$

(Although a similar statement holds for implicit relations, it is ordinarily only for explicit equations that having more than one equation for the same variable is of major concern.)

14.6   Effectiveness of Constructions

The question of constructiveness (effectiveness of the constructions and tests involved in the derivation of the results) has been an important issue throughout this book. This was the major reason why our focus was usually on regular languages (for CONST and, consequently, also for the solutions).

However, the effective construction of solutions may be possible for more general classes of constant languages, as well. These questions have not really been adequately addressed in the previous chapters.

References

[Brzoz 63] J.A. Brzozowski, Canonical regular expressions and minimal state graphs for definite events, *Mathematical Theory of Automata*, Symposia Series 12, Polytechnical Institute of Brooklyn, Brooklyn, NY, 1963.

[Brzoz/Leiss 80] J.A. Brzozowski and E.L. Leiss, On equations for regular languages, finite automata, and sequential networks, *Theoretical Computer Science* **10**(1) (1980).

[Ginzb/Rice 62] S. Ginzburg and H.G. Rice, Two families of languages related to ALGOL, *Journal of the ACM* **93**, 350–371 (1962).

[Hopcr/Ullma 79] J.E. Hopcroft and J.D. Ullman, *Introduction to Automata Theory, Languages, and Computation*, Addison-Wesley, Reading, MA, 1979.

[Kari 94] L. Kari, On language equations with invertible operations, *Theoretical Computer Science* **132**, 129–150 (1994).

[Leiss 81a] E.L. Leiss, On generalized language equations, *Theoretical Computer Science* **13**(1) (1981).

[Leiss 81b] E.L. Leiss, Concise representation of regular languages by boolean automata, *Theoretical Computer Science* **13** (1981).

[Leiss 81c] E.L. Leiss, The complexity of restricted regular expressions and the synthesis problem for finite automata, *Journal of Computer and System Sciences* **23**(3) (1981).

[Leiss 81d] E.L. Leiss, Solving arbitrary language equations, Proceedings of the 1981 Conference on Information Sciences and Systems, Baltimore, March 25–27, 1981.

[Leiss 85a] E.L. Leiss, On classes of tractable unrestricted regular expressions, *Theoretical Computer Science* **35**, 313–327 (February 1985).

[Leiss 85b] E.L. Leiss, Succinct representation of regular languages by boolean automata II, *Theoretical Computer Science* **38**, 133–136 (August 1985).

[Leiss 85c] E.L. Leiss, On solving star equations, *Theoretical Computer Science* **39**, 327–332 (1985).

[Leiss 86] E.L. Leiss, Generalized language equations with multiple solutions, *Theoretical Computer Science* **44**, 155–174 (1986).

[Leiss 94a] E.L. Leiss, Language equations over a one-letter alphabet with union, concatenation, and star: A complete solution, *Theoretical Computer Science A*, **131**, 311–330 (1994).

[Leiss 94b] E.L. Leiss, Unrestricted complementation in language equations over a one-letter alphabet, *Theoretical Computer Science A*, **132**, 71–84 (1994).

[Leiss 95] E.L. Leiss, Implicit language equations: Existence and uniqueness of solutions, *Theoretical Computer Science A*, **145**, 71–93 (1995).

[Leiss 97a] E.L. Leiss, Solving systems of explicit language relations, *Theoretical Computer Science A*, **186**, 83–105 (1997).

[Leiss 97b] E.L. Leiss, Solving implicit language relations with union and left-concatenation: A complete characterization, unpublished.

[Leiss 97c] E.L. Leiss, Solving implicit language equations with arbitrary concatenation over a one-letter alphabet when all constants are regular, unpublished.

[Leiss 97d] E.L. Leiss, Explicit language equations over {a} with union, concatenation, and star: Multiple equations for the same variable, unpublished.

[Meyer/Stock 73] A.R. Meyer and L. Stockmeyer, Nonelementary word problems in automata and logic, Proceedings AMS Symposium on Complexity of Computation, April 1973.

[Mirki 66] B.G. Mirkin, An algorithm for constructing a base in a language of regular expressions, *Iz. Akad. Nauk SSSR, Techn. Kibernet* 113–119 (1966) (in Russian). English Transl. *Engineering Cybernetics* **5**, 110–116 (1966).

[Salom 69] A. Salomaa, *Theory of Automata*, Pergamon Press, Oxford, 1969.

[Stear 67] R.E. Stearns, A regularity test for pushdown machines, *Information and Control* **11**(3) (1967).

Index